Every[illegible]
Wa [illegible] ce
Wi [illegible] me

Stepping into love
with my daughter with
Down's syndrome

Liz Arriens-Troy

Published by Big Ideas Library 2025

First published in the United Kingdom in 2025
by Big Ideas Library.
ISBN: 978-1-7384604-8-9
A CIP catalogue record for this book is available from the British Library

Printed in the UK by Bell and Bain Ltd, Glasgow

Big Ideas Library
20 Fountayne Street, York YO31 8HL
Design by Ned Hoste
Big Ideas Library is the publishing division of The Big Ideas Collective Ltd.

FSC www.fsc.org MIX Paper | Supporting responsible forestry FSC® C007785

Dedication

For Coraline and Kevin.

For all new parents, guardians or carers of a child with Down's syndrome and their families, friends and professionals working with their child.

For every one of our family and friends, and Coraline's godmother Payne, who have loved Coraline from the moment she was born.

For Coraline's cousins Collette, James and Jowan.

For our old neighbour Margaret, for showing me what unconditional love is, and Dave for his love and kindness to Coraline, and us.

For all the professionals who have touched our lives, who have worked with us and Coraline, thank you. You make a difference with every word you say.

For Sophia for starting me on my journey of speaking to myself differently.

For my coaches Declan, Christa and Jo who helped me to set the goal of writing this book, to believe in myself and it, and to do it.

For you, for the very reason you are reading this book, whatever that reason may be.

Contents

Reactions from readers of Liz's writing:

"Well I'm only on chapter three and my eyes have welled about four times already. What an art you have to writing. I am not a reader and whizzed through these first few chapters." Laura

"This brought tears to my eyes (on a packed train). I think you're so brave to share this." Minda

"Such moving writing Liz – very honest and also upbeat." Hazel

"Your honesty is refreshing. Your strength and good humour shine through." Suzi

"I love the way you write, I love what you write and how you see life. Thank you. You really move me." Reema

"Your writing is beautiful Liz and you seem to be cutting through so much of what we are fed about childbirth and the aftermath. Thank you." Emily

Reactions from readers of Liz's writing:

"At this time of pregnancy (with four weeks to go) you can't help but worry that everything will go well with the birth, but your updates really make me feel much more like I will find the strength to deal with whatever may lie ahead, and embrace it all with an open heart as you have done." Roz

"These insights are making me smile on a daily basis." Tamsin

"You can't imagine how touching, life affirming and inspirational your words are." Ian

Preface:

May you find these

When I learned Coraline had Down's syndrome shortly after she was born in 2017, I was searching the Internet continually for stories from families to give me hope.

Some years later, a friend put me in touch with a lady who was expecting a child with Down's syndrome so she could ask me questions that she had. When I spoke to this lady she told me:

> *I have been scouring the Internet for photographs of families with a child with Down's syndrome. I've been studying the photos to see if they are smiling.*

She was looking for happiness.

I believe we were looking for the same thing. In looking for hope, I saw happiness; in looking for happiness, she saw hope.

May this book share both hope and happiness.

Before sitting down in earnest to write this book, I tentatively asked a group of people with whom I was doing coaching towards achieving my personal and professional goals: "Would you read a book if I wrote one based on the life lessons I have learned from Coraline?"

"Absolutely," was the collective answer.

"There are people waiting to read your book. I am waiting to read it," was one individual answer which has stuck in my mind ever since.

So, I had better begin because I know you are waiting.

Chapter 1:

Coraline's birth, and the unexpected news

"Firstly, just to let you know our baby is doing well and Liz is OK and recovering well from the caesarean. We have named her Coraline. Secondly, we've just been told there's a very strong possibility our baby has Trisomy 21, Down's syndrome. There will be genetic tests to confirm this and there is a potential for her having a congenital heart defect."

Kevin followed up during each of his calls with a quick chaser: "All we want to hear is 'Congratulations on the birth of your baby!' We're going to be very positive about this. She's our beautiful little girl and we love her."

It was up to Kevin to ring all of our family, and my best friend Payne who was to be Coraline's godmother, in those first hours after her birth to let them know she had been born. It was not something I was capable of doing at the time. Coraline was the firstborn in our antenatal group and Kevin also texted our friends in this group with the news of her arrival.

My dad said a week later, after he came to visit us at home to meet Coraline, "My respect for Kevin has always been high but now it's stratospheric. He has set the tone for us all. You've got a treasure there. He's just the right mix of quick-witted and immensely practical."

Kevin and I had been together for almost three years when Coraline arrived on Monday 7th August 2017, the day after Kevin's 40th birthday. I had a relaxed pregnancy. She was born at our local hospital in Surrey just outside London, England.

People often exclaimed about the quaint little pale green

cottage in which Kevin and I first lived together, "It's like a fairy-tale cottage". Our visitors would walk down its path under a bridge of plants intertwined, to our front door with white roses blooming above it and a horseshoe peeping out from under them.

The previous night, I had been tucked up in bed watching the tree outside the window moving in the breeze. I was about to turn the bedside light out to go to sleep when I noticed a ladybird climbing up it. It was the night before our baby was due to be born by planned caesarean section. I followed the ladybird's climb with my eyes. "I never see ladybirds," I thought to myself.

I looked up the symbolism of the ladybird who had arrived on my lamp: luck, protection, blessings (particularly for babies), intuition, being open to receiving gifts if you get out of your own way, and wishes being fulfilled.

I woke up the next morning all set for Kevin to drive us to our local hospital 20 minutes away for my planned caesarean. We knew what was ahead. There was a stillness and a neatness to our house. My caesarean had been arranged for the Monday as the consultant obstetrician at the hospital had spotted something to do with our baby's growth rate on the Friday, but they did not do elective caesareans over the weekend. She suggested our baby come out straight away on the next available day, though we were a couple of weeks off my due date. She didn't seem worried though. We weren't worried either.

I sat on our immaculate sofa before we set off clutching a page of affirmations I had written down from the day-long active birthing workshop that had been led by Rhian, a midwife with 30 years' experience, and one of my two pregnancy yoga teachers. I repeated out loud, "I fully relax and turn my birthing over to nature."

We arrived at the hospital early and walked around the temporary worksite cabins off to the side across patches of grass next to the road we knew so well. Cars drove along with people going about their daily journeys while we chatted with anticipatory wonder that our baby was going to arrive that day.

As the early morning hour at which we had been told to arrive approached, we went into the hospital and were taken to a little waiting room all of our own, with a bed in it. I reread my page of affirmations. Kevin makes me feel surrounded by love. He has been at once extraordinarily thoughtful towards me, and a whole ton of fun ever since we met, making me laugh throughout the day each day. Of course we have our moments where, more often than not, I get snippy about something but then it's over and forgotten about within the hour, mostly because of his not rising to it. We have interchangeably hilarious and deep conversations each day, and this depth and ease of relationship is one I constantly value and am grateful for. He drives me mad, too, as he operates at speed and jumps from one thing to the next whereas I want things pinned down, ordered.

Kevin had brought my favourite books and magazines along for me, so that I could feel at ease before the caesarean. We waited for a couple of hours. The hospital had warned us that emergencies might arrive before they could call us in. Then it was time, and we were taken from our waiting room into the operating theatre. A team of half a dozen people were in the room; all warm, efficient and friendly. Kevin sat by my side, holding my hand. We smiled at each other, aware of the enormity of the moment. We had a carefully chosen playlist ready for the hospital theatre room, including my favourites Bruce Springsteen and Enrique Iglesias, which we asked them if we could put on. My friend Rachel had told me you could have a playlist during a caesarean as that's what she had had when her first son was born, and I am so glad she let me know that was something I could do. I listen to that playlist to this day on special occasions, such as Coraline's birthday each year.

Coraline was born at 12.15pm that Monday 7th August 2017. She arrived into the world to Lionel Ritchie's *Penny Lover.*

"Oh, that's too much!" one of the medical team in the room exclaimed with delight when she heard the song. Lionel Ritchie is actually one of Kevin's favourite singers. Kevin lights up and starts singing when a song of his comes on the radio when he's driving. After our baby was born, the team whisked her off to a table at the side of the room. They weighed her; she was 6.45lb. We knew in advance that we were expecting a girl as we had chosen to find out during my pregnancy. I felt so in awe of the fact our baby had just been born and asked intently if she could come over to me for skin-to-skin as this is what I had read was so important straight after our baby was born. "Yes, we will bring her to you shortly," they said, yet still took a few minutes checking her over.

I nudged Kevin and said in an aside to him, "Can you ask them again?"

He stood up, about to do so, but then they brought her over to him. He laid our baby on me, which was the most beautiful moment. They said, "We will ask a paediatrician to come and check her over too." We were first-time parents, so we thought nothing of it.

They then wheeled my hospital bed out of the room, with me and Coraline together in it, and Kevin walking by our side. We were transferred across the corridor into a small windowless room, with another couple next to us with their new baby. We were separated only by a paper curtain. I have a photo of Coraline and me maybe half an hour after she was born taken by Kevin in this windowless room. This was the half hour where the beauty really sank in that I was a mother, and I had a baby. I lay on the hospital bed absorbed in this feeling, admiring Coraline. A nurse was with me initially trying to see if she could help Coraline to latch on to breastfeed, but we couldn't quite manage it. Somewhere along the line the nurse left. Then it was Kevin and me and our daughter who we had not yet named.

"This is amazing, isn't it? She's here," I said to Kevin. He echoed my thoughts and feelings.

Sometime after that the paediatrician came to see us, accompanied by a colleague.

"I need to examine your baby." There was something impersonal and official about her tone.

Kevin asked, "Is there anything particular you are worried about?"

"Let us look and then we will tell you."

This is like a moment on TV (which I watch a lot and is one of my great loves of an evening), as you know they have spotted something. I thought perhaps it was a detail to do with our baby's kidneys as they had mentioned there was fluid on one of them during my pregnancy.

They looked her over and the paediatrician said, "You remember those tests you had at 12 weeks for Down's syndrome which you thought were low probability? They are just a guide. It looks like your baby is exhibiting characteristics of Down's syndrome. There are worse conditions she could have."

I lay on the hospital bed in shock. I stared at the paediatrician and her colleague. I stared at Kevin. A long, long stare. I have no idea what we said to them. I have no idea what happened next in that little space of a separated room. I was supremely aware of the paediatrician telling us this news with another couple and their baby so close by behind the curtain and feeling conscious of their presence.

Our hospital bed, with Coraline and me on it, was then wheeled to a different, far bigger room at the front of the hospital for me to recover after the caesarean. Kevin said it was only around the corner. I felt like we had gone down miles of corridors. There were no others in this next cavernous room, only Kevin, me, our baby and two nurses who had come to be with us. To set the backdrop – which I probably hadn't accounted for at the time – I could not feel my legs from the ribs down after my caesarean, had not eaten in 15 hours or so, and had post-birth hormones and post-surgery medication coursing through my body. Ordinarily I believe all this would be transcended when you quietly spend time with your new baby. However, spending this time with my new baby was complicated by my thoughts, my preconceptions and my runaway mind about what her having Down's syndrome meant.

For many years afterwards I found it heartbreaking when I thought of myself and our tiny, innocent, loving baby in that bed and how I was. But now I have come to a place of self-compassion, of not judging the emotions that I had and of being kind to myself about how I was after she was born. I know now that my body needed time to process the news and the emotions which had engulfed me. Of course I would love to have been different for Coraline herself, but I was doing the best I could at the time.

"Baby", as she was still called, was taken at that point to the Neonatal Intensive Care Unit (NICU) for tests. Kevin immediately said he was going with her, and I said, "Of course, of course."

He later told me that when they were in the NICU, he held her hand and even said "Ommmm" to her, which he said calmed her, just like in a video which was going around at the time of a father who did that. I couldn't do that as I could not yet move from my hospital bed, since the effects of the caesarean had not yet worn off. Maybe I could have somehow, I don't know, but nobody suggested it as an option.

They checked her sucking reflex (which can be poor in babies with Down's syndrome). They checked her hips as she had been in the breech position before she was born, and they checked her breathing. Her bloods came back with a very high haemoglobin level. The haematocrit (volume percentage of red blood cells in the blood) was very high, which could possibly have increased the risk of a clot or blockage. So, she had treatment for these and at the same time a glucose IV drip for 48 hours. Quite a bit for age zero. She remained calm, so Kevin tells me.

The medical staff at the hospital also checked to see if Coraline had a heart condition as approximately 50% of babies with Down's syndrome are born with one. I didn't know that fact at the time.

Meanwhile I was in the middle of this large, bare, functional room glazed, at sea and unable to move from the waist down. The two nurses were with me, on and off. The window was open, and the driving rain was in rivulets down the windows, on a summer's day.

The icy paediatrician from earlier came in. She chose this moment to say, "You realise your baby will be in and out of hospital for the rest of her life, and she could have problems with her ears, her eyes, her heart and her thyroid?" The two nurses were stood one either side of my bed. Again, I stared at the paediatrician. The more I stared the more I began to hyperventilate, unable to catch my breath. I began to get distressed after she told me these things. Each of the nurses held one of my hands and continued to do so as my breathing ramped up.

This kind of breathing had only happened to me once some years before when I had altitude sickness on a holiday hike with Payne and another friend Matt heading towards the summit of Jebel Toubkal in Morocco, the highest mountain in North Africa. I wasn't much of a hiker. But Payne, a former trekking leader, knew her stuff inside out. I think at one stage Payne may have been carrying both my and Matt's bags and I have vague recollections of Matt haring down the mountain at the end of our hike headed for fast food. I had sat down heavily on a rock at one point on our ascent and Payne took over from our guide in helping me to catch my breath, telling me exactly, and encouragingly, how to breathe. Payne is as commanding of a room as Kevin; she is as bright and ebullient as he is. She has a gift for making me, and everyone around her, dissolve into laughter simply through being herself. But this time there was no Payne to talk me through my breaths. And no Kevin as he was away with Coraline.

Kevin reappeared sometime after this – I have no idea how long afterwards – and saw how I was breathing. The two nurses were both still there holding my trembling hands, talking to me as I gasped for air. He immediately led me in the "in for four and out for eight" breaths to stimulate my parasympathetic nervous system but I was beyond calming! He looked around him and asked the nurses in his characteristically assertive yet calm way, "What on earth is happening here? She was fine when I left."

I was emitting rasping sounds I have never made before. They gave me a drug called Oramorph to calm me which Kev told me is morphine; we think it sounds like something from *The Lord of the Rings*. It worked. I mean it absolutely worked as after a time I politely enquired if it might be possible to have a room off the main road. And that's very me. I do like quiet. They did then kindly move us to a quieter room.

Kevin asked to see the paediatrician privately to discuss the way she had listed all the possible health issues for our daughter to me so bluntly and without him present, and said, "Please don't say anything to Liz without me in future, I need to be there with her." Kevin's manner is never angry, nor accusatory, just polite in stating his opinion. As the morphine did its best to calm my system which felt as if it had gone haywire, all I could think about were the tests they were running, the fact I was not with our baby and the enormity of all the news we'd been given.

Chapter 2:

Trying to be the surgeon

After I had eventually found some rather stunned composure in our new room, I could ask Kevin how our baby was.

"She's doing well in the NICU. They are running the tests but she's fine and I've been with her. I really think we need to give her a name as they keep calling her 'baby'."

"I want to see her again so I can be sure what her name is Kev."

During my pregnancy we had bought a names book and we had adored poring over it and making lists of possible names. We had shared our ideas for her name with family and a few friends. We had thought of names like Brooke and Inesa. By the time she was born we had narrowed it down to those two names and one other.

Dazed, I reiterated my wish to Kevin: "I need time, I want to see her, I just want to be sure."

We kept talking and we knew we wanted a name for her whilst she was in her little incubator and, because I could not get there to see her, we said together there and then, "OK, yes, let's go with Coraline." This was a name that had come to us over the past week. We pronounce it "Coraleen".

I had read Oprah Winfrey's magazine *O* when I was pregnant and there was a story in it where the protagonist was called Cora. My list of possible names for our baby near me whilst I was reading, I wrote it down. Reading the article in the magazine reminded me I had always loved names like "Corey". We looked the name Cora up in our names book and saw there was an extrapolation of it: Coraline. We immediately loved that and, in our names book, it said it meant "of the sea". By the sea is my favourite place. Much later on, a friend told us it also has another meaning, that is "heart".

We love her name.

It's funny, we haven't known (or met) anyone else yet called Coraline in her whole eight years so far. We found out about the book and movie *Coraline* after we had named our daughter. A friend gave Coraline a copy of the book as a present after we got home from the hospital. We have yet to sit down and read it. Or to watch the movie. I have no idea why on earth not. Perhaps we will manage this before she is nine! My niece Collette and nephew James came to stay one weekend when Coraline was about four years old and Collette read it in one sitting.

After we had named our daughter, Kevin went back to the NICU to see her. On his return to me he said, "I've made a little sign on orange card for her bed in the NICU with her name on it and stickers that they have there. 'Coraline,' it says, I know you love stickers."

We have that sign up on her bedroom door now. I imagine it will be up somewhere in her room for evermore.

The staff in the NICU had given Coraline a little square of blanket and they had given me a matching one to hold in my room. Each little square was the same and they were hand knitted in peach and white stripes. I didn't realise it then, but volunteers make these knitted squares, smaller than a face flannel, for parents whose babies are in the NICU. These were swapped between Coraline and me so she had my scent with her. Kevin and the nurses came to tell me that Coraline was very calm in the NICU. In the remainder of the afternoon and the night to come that little scrap of material felt so poignant. She had this; but she should have had me. Yet she wasn't on her own as she had an amazing, committed dad by her side every step of the way, as well as all the skilled nurses.

I could not yet try to get out of my hospital bed as my legs were still numb, and I had a catheter in. I found it extremely challenging to turn over without pain.

One of the lovely, dedicated nurses in the NICU took photos of our daughter. She printed them for me to have in our hospital room so that I could look at the photos and get my oxytocin going and then hand-express colostrum for Coraline (milk of the first three days before breast milk comes in) which could be given to her with a syringe. I remember these photos as clear as day: how they were a glossy finish and how Kevin proudly rushed back to our room with them from the NICU to show me our little baby. We have kept the photos for Coraline when she is older, along with the pieces of knitted blanket.

The nurse who had taken the photos came to visit me in my room all the way from the NICU and tried to help me to hand-express the colostrum, but none of it would come. She told me all about Coraline and how she was doing.

"It's vital for you to at least try to express it for her," she encouraged me, though I was not really responding to her. "Colostrum is high in antibodies and immunoglobulins and is like liquid gold for babies!" she told me.

Another nurse who was in the room and had also been trying to help me produce colostrum said to the NICU nurse about me, "She's in distress so she won't be producing any oxytocin, this won't work."

I felt addled and I didn't have the wherewithal to apply myself to do this. It was like all the energy had drained from my body and all the will to do anything. I couldn't make the colostrum come through massage like the nurses were showing me. And I wasn't sharp enough to realise how vital it was that our baby receive this in addition to the glucose drip she was on, even though they had told me it was important. However, there was someone who did realise, and he took it upon himself to hand-express for me and ferry the syringe to Coraline in the NICU.

I credit Kevin with getting my milk supply going and for getting our daughter this "best-we-can-offer" start against infection. I honestly don't think I would have done it had it not been for him, as I was so utterly lost to myself and to my thoughts. It is of course everyone's individual choice as to whether to breastfeed. Kevin got my milk going by reassuring me with his presence, his chat and his confidence that it was good for Coraline for me to do this. As I trusted Kevin, I wanted to do what he was encouraging me to do.

I remained numb from the anaesthetic of the operation the afternoon and night of the day Coraline was born. I had to sleep face up as I couldn't turn and my catheter remained in. Kevin scampered off in his slippers from our hospital room to read Coraline a story at the end of that first night. The book he read to her was a gift from our Australian relatives called *Bilby Moon* about an Australian animal I wasn't familiar with – a bilby.

I found it hard to speak and catch my breath the day Coraline was born. Every midwife who entered our room – and there were many – conversed with me whilst my face was strewn with rolling tears. This river of tears was to last several days.

After Kevin had read Coraline her story that night, he came back to our room, turned off the light and settled down to sleep on the floor as there was only one bed in the room – my hospital bed.

From the darkness I declared grandly to Kevin, "I will never look at life in the same way again." I thought the profound, deadening shock I felt would be a backdrop to anything I ever experienced from that moment onwards. I felt it was in me to stay. I was still feeling the effects of the operation, and my hormones and tears were a veil through which I saw everything.

Little did I know that I would be living this phrase of "never looking at life in the same way again" in quite the opposite way in our future life together.

Little did I know that we would read Khalil Gibran's passage *On Joy and Sorrow* from *The Prophet* in that same hospital room days later and that it would ring so true:

> *Your joy is your sorrow unmasked. And the selfsame well from which your laughter rises was oftentimes filled with your tears.*

At 5am the day after she was born, Kevin leapt up and said, "I'm going to see Coraline."

Early on that day he messaged our friends Chris and Debs who lived in Australia. They had a very sweet one-year-old daughter called Elsden with Down's syndrome and we had seen photos of their lives over the past year on social media.

We had sat on Debs and Chris's table at a wedding a few years previously. We loved them as they were friendly and hilarious, and we had stayed in touch after the wedding.

Kevin sent them a messagc as he felt that I needed to hear some words from them. Chris, Debs and their daughter were our point of reference and the speed and loving tone with which they replied to us is something I will always remember and be deeply grateful for.

They recommended two books to us about Down's syndrome. One was *Babies with Down Syndrome: A New Parents' Guide* edited by Susan J. Skallerup, as they said it explained what we needed to know about Down's syndrome in a broad sense. The other was *Down's Upside: A Positive View of Down's Syndrome* by Eva Snoijink, which is a beautiful book of photographs of children with Down's syndrome and a short paragraph to accompany each picture written by their parents. They recommended it "as you can get information overload and this is just lovely photos of gorgeous kids".

Kevin was convinced that once I visited Coraline in the NICU the tide would turn for me. My catheter was removed that morning so he got me there in a wheelchair as I couldn't walk more than a few steps. I had begun to feel my legs again so we could do this. Coraline looked so peaceful lying in her incubator, as though she had an immense steadfastness about her. I realised when they lifted her out to me, with such trust and smallness, doing skin-to-skin, that she was ours and we were hers and we would live this new reality together, and we would be there to love her. It was a turnaround for me when I held her in my lap as Kevin knew it would be. She was so sweet looking, and light, with the tiniest of hands and such soft hair, making little snuffling sounds.

My older brother Julian visited that night, and he held Coraline in the NICU, smiling down at her as she looked up at him. I had warned him I wouldn't be in any fit state for his visit, and he assured me that was exactly why he wanted to come, and that he wanted to meet his niece. His wife, Chris, and Coraline's two young cousins, Collette and James, were at home, eager to hear about her. As we both sat there in the NICU, him holding little Coraline, he said, "She will be the making of you." My brothers Ed and Julian are dependable through and through for me. Ed was still in Los Angeles (where he lived for three years); he wished he could have come in and visited us that week, but he was in another country. I marvelled at his life as a TV Producer working on big TV shows and had loved his invites to different filmings across the years when he was based in the UK.

Ed flew over a couple of weeks after Coraline was born and appeared at our house with a silver Tiffany hairbrush for her. My mum, my dad and his partner Elisabeth, Kevin's mum and Julian's family travelled to our house and met her early on after we were home from hospital. Kevin's older brother Mick also came to the hospital that week, as Julian had done. Mick's partner Roxy met Coraline soon after and wider family on Kevin's side met her in the months to come. Kevin's dad was unable to make it over from Ireland to meet Coraline as he had dementia and Kevin's mother cared for him at home.

In the evening after Julian's visit, Kevin messaged my old life coach Sophia, to let her know Coraline had been born and most likely had Down's syndrome. He also felt it would be good for me to hear some words from her.

I sat up a little in bed and her words began to penetrate my haze and to take on a hint of meaning and a glimmer through my fog. I knew I loved Coraline, but I also had so many thought loops and tears about how everything was going to be. Sophia used to say when she introduced a new concept to me, "Can you be open to a different possibility? All you need to do is to be open to the possibility."

Kevin read out Sophia's prescient reply to his text:

> *You will soon see what a gift children with Down's syndrome are to their parents and to this world. It's a huge, huge gift to you both once the shock has passed.*

Pure love. Unfiltered. Unconditional. True.

Life's biggest gifts are often most unexpected happenings. Life is never how we think it's going to be. Your baby will teach you unconditional love. Unfiltered, simple beingness.

And if you let her, she will also teach you how to love and accept yourself even more. That's her gift to you.

Coraline is so lucky that you are her parents. Already, you are just accepting what is, and allowing the gifts of that to flow to you. Opening your heart to unconditional love is really the only true purpose of life, and the reason we are all here.

"Wow, Kev," I said. "Well, I'm not really accepting what is, but what amazing words. Read them to me again."

Coraline spent her first 48 hours or so in the Neonatal ICU. The nurses from the NICU, so taken with Kev's energy and devotion to visiting and being with her there, found a bed and wheeled it to our room for him to sleep in at night (dads normally sleep in a chair, or on the floor as Kevin had chosen readily without protest, so we were really touched by this gesture).

Kevin said to me in our hospital room: "Just feel the feelings, let them be, I know it sounds like a trivial analogy but I know you will be fine as it's just like the mirror in our house; you're not good with change at first, and then you're fine after a couple of days, so I know you just need time to get used to this."

A big thing Kevin has taught me is to feel my feelings fully and not to try to stop them. If I feel them, I can process them and then they pass through. If I resist and enter into a dialogue with them in my mind, they persist.

As regards the mirror, one night I had been to pregnancy yoga on the bus and Kevin had spent the whole evening sorting and tidying for our baby's arrival. He had proudly hung a large square mirror on the wall by our front door after finding it in a cupboard. I came home and the first thing I said when I came through the door was, "That looks awful, it looks ridiculous, it sticks out over the window," as he had hung it so it did indeed jut out in front of the window in that wall.

However, what happened was that I got used to the mirror in a day or two. Kevin told me regarding the mirror, there was no hook on the back of it to hang it up vertically and thereby not partly cover the window, so that was the way it had to be. The initial change to our house – or to my "just so" way of things – was too disruptive and I thought I'd never get used to it, but then I came to rather enjoy that it was like that as I passed by it each day. I suppose this is linked to expectations. I find that whenever I cling to an expectation of how something is meant to be, or the perfect vision I had for it, then I get into trouble as it is exhausting. I am also not entering into life's flow if I keep wanting things to adhere to some vision I had. And who is to define what is perfect?

Similarly, Sophia used to say, "What if whatever is happening right now is already perfect for you, it's just your thinking getting in the way?" So, I find that once I let go of my rigid expectations of how something must turn out and go with what is, things begin to fall into place.

Sophia also said to me in our coaching, long before Coraline arrived, "Life is the surgeon and you're the assistant. You're trying to be the surgeon."

All my life I found change scary, in any form that it came in, and Kevin knew this. Since then, and in the years that have followed, I have thought about what is behind my fear of change and I think it is about: "The unknown is not safe. What if I can't do this? What if it doesn't turn out how I want it to?" And that again comes from a place of judgement about myself and also judgement that my expectation about what should happen after I make a decision is right or the only way something is supposed to be. That is rather a rigid way to live. Yet, it had pretty much worked for me so far in my life, though it was a tiring way of being.

What if the path to freedom is to let go of judgement? To be open to a different outcome which might be bringing me something important that I hadn't even dreamed of? To accept every aspect of myself and all my emotions? And to instead think about the words in Susan Jeffers' book *Feel The Fear And Do It Anyway* where she says that true security doesn't come from knowing how things will turn out, but from trusting that you'll be equipped for whatever life brings. That simple shift in thinking stayed with me.

A poem, which has become my favourite, for me encapsulates experiencing our feelings and emotions and the true benefit of this. I first heard it at pregnancy yoga one Saturday morning a few weeks before Coraline's birth. I loved Rumi anyway. We had a book of his poems in our spare room at home; our very own guest house. But I had not heard this poem before.

It was a coincidence that I was at that Saturday class, and not my regular Thursday one. Rhian had a different theme for each class, so the poem was particular for those in the group that Saturday. And so it was that I heard the poem.

The Guest House

This being human is a guest house.
Every morning a new arrival.
A joy, a depression, a meanness,
some momentary awareness comes
as an unexpected visitor.
Welcome and entertain them all!
Even if they're a crowd of sorrows,
who violently sweep your house
empty of its furniture,
still, treat each guest honourably.
He may be clearing you out
for some new delight.
The dark thought, the shame, the malice,
meet them at the door laughing,
and invite them in.
Be grateful for whoever comes,
because each has been sent
as a guide from beyond.

Jalaluddin Rumi. *The Guest House*. Translated by © Coleman Barks with John Moyne, *The Essential Rumi*, HarperOne, 1995

From our hospital room, when Coraline was two days old, I

created an Instagram account called *Coraline and Us* and began writing little pieces from my heart for family and friends. I cross-posted them to my personal Facebook account as well. I just began to write, and the words came. I wrote about my feelings.

I was wholly uninformed about Down's syndrome. As a result, I felt out of kilter. I wanted to write because we had our beautiful baby, she was brand new to the world, and we were going to learn. My instinct was to share what we learned with our friends and family as I felt they would be interested. I also knew their wisdom would come back to us in response to what I wrote. My instinct to write was so strong, I think, because it is something I have always deeply loved. It is my "go to". So, it felt comfortable and natural that this was what I would do.

Feeling everything, and allowing it, is liberating. When I enter that space, I have the chance to pay attention to what my emotions are telling me and to give myself love and care around what I am feeling.

On the other occasions, which are many, when I repeatedly say to myself, "You should not be feeling this, you should be feeling differently," then I am creating an internal struggle and a sensation of "lack" towards myself. I am denying my instinctual emotions.

I saw a wonderful coach, Jo, when Coraline was six and a half years old. She has children with additional needs herself, including a son with Down's syndrome. I had a revelation when I worked with her. She asked me to see all emotions just as emotions; not "good" or "bad" emotions as I had been seeing them. As emotions. And she asked me to include in my daily gratitude journal thanks for all the emotions of life.

I wrote in my journal that day I spoke to her:

> *What if all my emotions are OK and I'm not doing them "wrong"? I have this sense that I can't do "bad" emotions, that when I have them I not only label them as "bad" but feel "bad" for having them. What if they're just emotions? That's very freeing and very validating of what I feel – as trying to not have certain emotions or criticising myself for having them is rather exhausting and I didn't realise it.*

Chapter 3:

Life as we know it

The trajectory of my life, before Coraline arrived, was all just as I had planned it. I had worked hard to keep it that way.

My mother was Australian and was from a large family in Melbourne who I love. My father is of Dutch descent and grew up in Perth, Australia, after his family moved there. The relatives on my dad's side, who are also very dear to me, lived in Australia as well as in Holland. One of Mum's two sisters moved to Long Island, New York, and so we also have another lovely branch of our family there.

My mum and dad decided to settle in an English village just outside Cambridge. This is where I grew up with them, my two brothers and lots of pets.

My mother and father separated when I was in my twenties which had been a while coming and was sad for them to navigate.

I had a fabulous French exchange visit when I was at school and, inspired by subsequent summers spent with my French exchange Adeline's family in their village near Montpellier, South of France, I went on to do a French degree. My first job after university was at the travel agent STA Travel in Cambridge, where I met Payne. Later I was lucky enough to get a permanent job at the British Council, the UK's Cultural Relations Organisation. It has offices around the world, and its headquarters is in London where I worked.

I lived in London for 14 years in various house shares with friends. I loved going out, seeing family and friends, my work, and travelling both for work and personally. I also loved open water swimming, the sea, nature, stickers, letter writing, Slush Puppies, romantic movies, watching TV in a rug, hiking, airports, reading, personal development books, the game Boggle and volunteering. I did dream of writing in a broader sense, but I never knew exactly what I wanted to write about.

I went on to work on the international team, followed by running the staff volunteering scheme, at King's College London, before returning to work at the British Council.

I travelled for work across my time at the British Council and King's: from Italy to Northern Norway in the Arctic Circle, to Greece, Turkey, Slovakia, Pakistan, the USA, UAE, Thailand and many more countries.

At the heart of all the international programmes I worked on at the British Council was the aim of broadening horizons, sharing knowledge, building trust and changing perspectives. I've carried those values with me ever since. The idea of sharing personal experiences to shift perspectives (which all the projects I worked on were about) is at the heart of my writing this book.

The last programme I worked on at the British Council was the eTwinning programme which connects schools across Europe and neighbouring countries through collaborative online projects. I worked closely with a network of 100 teachers who were "Ambassadors" for the programme.

During my career, being in control and being hyper-organised worked well for me. At least I thought it did. I felt good. If I went on holiday, I'd have my inbox down to zero.

I had a sense that I felt a bit flat sometimes, or that I wasn't getting all that I could out of life. I had not yet met a long-term partner but wanted to.

Through my old life coach Sophia, who I began seeing back in 2014, I discovered a different way to approach life. She told me: "There is this notion of 'I can't be happy until…' Happiness isn't external. It's a feeling inside you and does not come from a place or person. Happiness comes from your perception of things, and it is your choice how you see things." She went on to say, "You are not ready to meet someone yet, but you will be.

We will get your self-esteem to a ten out of ten and then you can go dating. But no dating before that. Then you can invite someone in who sees your worth and value as you see it."

Sophia said to me of my internal voice: "Imagine you had a friend who talked to you the way you talk to yourself. Would you want to spend time with them if they talked that way? If your value is kindness, then you're not being consistent with who you are by talking to yourself in any other way."

We set about building my life to be one where I had fun and valued myself. We made creating more joy in my life my absolute priority so then meeting a partner was based on wanting to, not needing to. She said to me:

> *Write down ten things which bring you joy, then make time to go out and do them and you will begin creating a great energy. Fill up your life with the things you love doing, prioritise your personal life, put yourself as a priority.*
>
> *That's where, and who, you need to be to make it happen, and it will happen in the right timing. It's all a mirror. There's no point trying to change the mirror. Change yourself to change the mirror. You have spent so much time focusing on what is wrong. What needs to change for you to have what you want is simply to focus your thoughts on what you want; not what you don't want. Focus your energy and attention on what makes you feel good. Like a camera, choose what you focus on.*
>
> *Hold your value, love yourself, and then you will meet someone who sees you the same way you see yourself.*

My new practice of kindness in my thinking and self-love began to form and they became my everyday habits, and it felt quite revolutionary in terms of how I experienced the world. That is when I began Internet dating again after the pause Sophia had suggested.

As part of my 39th birthday celebrations, excited about our hot dogs and Slush Puppies, Payne and I were having a grand time sat at an ice hockey game near my North London house share. Feeling brave, I gave my phone to her. "Right, you have a go and pick some people for me."

Payne swiped away on my Tinder app: "Done, done, done. I've picked this guy as he has all these snowboarding pictures. Excellent."

"Hang on! I'm not sporty! I don't know anything about snowboarding. I know you love exercise and the outdoors and all that, but I don't! He looks totally different to me. I'm not sure what I think about his photos."

"Too late!"

Payne had just chosen my future husband Kevin.

His messages began coming. They were so funny, and our messages back and forth had a real zip and an instant connection, chatting about topics from Jean-Claude Van Damme to the countries we had visited beginning with the letter "S". We began to set each other quizzes.

> Me: Ice breaker question. Is it easy to confuse merino wool with José Mourinho?
>
> Kevin: Very. Imagine if you bought a merino fleece online, and when you went away on a skiing holiday you realised that you had actually received a Portuguese football manager? Maybe he could still come in handy if you were skiing in Portugal?
>
> Me: I think this is why people don't mind too much when they confuse them.
>
> Kevin: Exactly.
>
> Me: Have Enrique and Julio Iglesias ever sung together?
>
> Kevin: Hmm. I don't think so.
>
> Me: Wow! I looked it up and that's what it said; that they haven't done so commercially at all. I think Enrique is amazing. I once made one of my friends a birthday cake with a photo of him printed on top onto sugar paper and called it "Enri-cake" except there was a whole corner chopped out when I presented it as I had burnt it.

Kevin: How big was the corner?

Me: Large.

Kevin: Well, that's not really a corner then. A large wedge.

Me: Next question. Is a beech tree deciduous?

Kevin: I would say yes but I should have paid more attention in geography at school. I learned about porous and igneous rocks in geography.

Me: Ingenious rocks. Those are the best.

Kevin: They are, igniting rocks are even better.

Me: These I don't know.

Kevin: Very few do.

Me: So, to more nature. Who am I? I shed my leaves in the winter.

Kevin: A non-evergreen tree?

Me: Also known as?

Kevin: Deciduous? Merino.

Me: Haha, yes! A wool tree.

Me: What is it easy to confuse an otter with?

Kevin: A branch from a deciduous tree!

Me: Name the number I am thinking of.

Kevin: Six.

Me: No, 12. You were half right. Excellent!

A week after we had begun texting, and a week after my 39th birthday in 2014, I found myself waiting for Kevin outside Charing Cross station on a Friday night after work. Kevin later told me he had been out to dinner with a female friend who encouraged him, "Go on, just ask her, don't spend all this time texting, ask her to meet up." After he suggested meeting up, I was far more spontaneous than is customary for me, as we had not been texting for long, and I agreed to his invitation straight away.

Walking down the road together, just minutes after meeting, I had a sensation that he was the one. This sounds hard to believe, but I felt this. I had come "home".

From Charing Cross we roamed to a wine bar and sat on some steps and chatted easily. "What do you want to drink? I'm having a Madeira," said Kevin. "Do you want to see my ice bucket challenge video?" And before I knew it, I was watching it on his phone.

We moved on to another trendy London bar and were sat on some stools, talking nineteen to the dozen. Well Kevin was talking more than me. He was very chatty. The people on the table next to us leaned over and began speaking, laughing away at things with us. One of them said, "So how do you both know each other? Wouldn't it be funny if you were on a first date?"

Kevin and I exclaimed, "We are!" They couldn't believe it. As we sailed off to our next venue we said to them, "We'll have to let you know how it goes." But we parted and never saw them again. I'd love to tell them now.

I said to my younger brother Ed after that first date, "I think I've met the man I'm going to marry."

Over the following days I basked in the glow of the date and how well we had got on. On the date Kevin had suggested a second date where he cooked for me as he had previously been a chef. I sat in work, and every now and then remembered with excitement that Kevin was going to cook for me.

Then my heart sank. Kevin texted and cancelled our second date saying he wasn't ready for anything serious at that point in his life. My instinct was to call him immediately to talk about it. I told Ed. He countered, "Absolutely not, you'll scare him off for good!" I felt devastated but, with guidance from family and friends, including my housemates and Sophia, I decided I had to let him walk away and be calm, as this was the impression I wanted to leave him with, if ever there was a chance he might come back. That was very hard.

Lo and behold, he texted again a week later: "I felt afraid of commitment even though we'd only had one date and you weren't asking me for commitment." We went tenpin bowling on our second date and clicked just as much as on our first. It felt effortless, and we have been together ever since. We both say that we are lucky in what we have found together. We laugh a lot, and we spur each other on. I find Kevin is exceptional, and a source of fascination for me, in that he remains so calm if ever we disagree. He does not go into a "tit-for-tat" mode in an argument, and he is over any disagreement quickly. He definitely speaks his mind and is honest. Challenges just increase his persistence, and he moves on from criticisms quickly.

Everything had changed with one date, one evening. And that's all it takes, for everything to change. A bit like 7th August 2017, the day Coraline was born.

Kevin was a sales manager for a fish and seafood supplier supplying high-end restaurants across London. He had daily visits to, and chats with, chefs across the city. He knew the streets of London inside out. His work tied into his expertise; he's passionate about food, as he had been a chef himself for 17 years beforehand. He was in innumerable WhatsApp groups for work, and he was lightning quick in responding to work matters.

At first, we had to adapt to our differences, like how social and chatty Kevin is, and how I am social but in a quieter way. Kevin's extroversion, loudness and forthrightness sometimes unnerved me, as one who had balanced a life of blending in. Over the years I have had to remind myself that I am just as valuable as an introvert in a social situation as he is as an extrovert. I feel both of us have a similar level of awareness of the tools which help us rebalance and connect to ourselves, e.g. mindfulness, gratitude or exercise.

I thank Sophia for guiding me to find myself before I found a relationship. It was a process, and it took time to rewire old habits. I am still rewiring them today and often need a reminder to look at the voice I use with myself. Am I being kind and loving in how I talk to myself? It is easy to drift back into critical ways of thinking and the first step for me is always awareness.

Kevin and I love being together and at the same time encourage each other in our pursuits independently.

I received this email from a friend a few years ago. He put into words how it feels for me with Kevin:

> *You don't realise the feeling you're looking for when you're looking for a partner. It's like you met your heart and soul.*

A couple of years after we met, Kevin and I made the decision to move in together to our beautiful little cottage in Surrey. We could commute into central London on a 20-minute overground train ride followed by a short walk.

In September 2016 I was attending an eTwinning conference in Rhodes, Greece. Kevin and I decided that we would go for a holiday together there before it began in honour of my 41st birthday being the week before. We had lived together for a month and a half at this point. We found an exquisite Airbnb villa by the sea. Kevin was in his element cooking seafood on the barbecue on our terrace.

We discussed trying for a baby now that I had turned 41. We thought "it's now or never". We had this feeling due to the fact that Kevin and I had met later in life just after my 39th birthday. We began trying in October. I found out I was pregnant in December much to our surprise and absolute joy.

Chapter 4:

My ordinary pregnancy

"I've spotted something with her growth rate…your baby needs to come out soon," said the consultant obstetrician, Susana, on a Friday summer morning at our local hospital. "We don't do elective caesareans over the weekend, so the soonest we can do this is first thing on Monday morning. I will arrange for you to come in then."

I was 38 weeks pregnant, and this was two weeks before my scheduled caesarean date. I already had a caesarean scheduled as our baby was in the breech position and would not turn, and this was the hospital's recommendation in this instance. Susana spared us from knowing that if we didn't take action – and soon – there was a possibility that we could lose our baby.

Throughout the time that I was pregnant, I wrote to our future baby in a diary I had called *Every Day Matters* in advance of her August due date. I wrote to her about what we were up to, recorded how I felt in my pregnancy and what I was thinking. As ever, writing just felt natural to me. In the December that I found out I was pregnant, I wrote to our baby:

> *We took an excursion today to see olde houses in Guildford for New Year's Eve. Just pottered and absorbed. We wandered into a church and were enveloped by the warmth of the people who welcomed us in. I think you'll like all the quotes in the leaflet they gave us. We each lit a candle, listened to a five-minute reflection and left our New Year's Resolution on a slip of paper*

in a bottle; all beautiful activities they had set up for visitors to mark the New Year. The times we've had have been all I hoped these past few days. They have been magical experiences. I am going to write for you here some of the quotes in the leaflet the church handed to us entitled, New Year's Eve 2016, New Year, New Promise*:*

"Do what you can, with what you have, where you are." Theodore Roosevelt

"Take the first step in faith. You don't have to see the whole staircase, just take the first step." Martin Luther King Jr.

I like that. Lately I've perhaps been over-reading about what might be to come for us, and this brings me back to what's important. The here and now. When I spoke to your dad about my mind racing away he said, "it's all about what is right here, and not imagining any more or less than that".

We then stopped in a traditional pub and wrote "Gratitudes", "people to toast" and "visualisations" for 2017 on little pieces of paper. I've stuck our gratitudes in here in this diary for you. We stuck all our visualisations onto a piece of card and put it up at home.

Our visualisations card faded in its place by the window at home as the sunlight kept falling upon it, but our dreams remained. We do this same thing every New Year: gratitudes, toasts and visualisations for the year ahead. Each year on Kevin's birthday I write a card to him about what's been happening that year, where we've been, our habits, plans we have and jokes we share, so that in years to come we can look back at what was at the fore during each particular year.

Walking down the road in Guildford that New Year's Eve, we received the news that a new baby had arrived on New Year's Day amongst our wider family in Australia. We felt so excited about his arrival and could not believe our own baby was due later that same year.

Coraline was lucky with all the family around her who were

all keenly phoning up to ask about my progress and anticipating her arrival.

In January 2017, my dad's partner Elisabeth had a stroke when they were on holiday abroad. She spent a good part of that year ahead in hospital before Coraline was born and we all went to visit her. After she was released from hospital, my dad began to care for her at her house in Shropshire, which he was to keep on doing, together with her team of carers, for the next seven years until she went into a care home after a second stroke. They lived in houses side-by-side which they had bought that way by choice. She could talk but move only one hand. She was a model of adaptation and looking on the bright side.

At the end of January 2017, I wrote to our baby in my pregnancy diary about an evening where I went to see a film called *Century: 10 Women x 10 Decades* drawn from the 1,000 Londoners project. My friend Flo and I went as our friend Susie, from our work, was one of the women in the film. Susie won a gold medal swimming at the Rio 2016 Paralympics. I wrote in my pregnancy diary to our future baby:

> *Here's some of the advice from the panel discussion which Susie was on this evening:*
>
> *"Anything is possible."*
>
> *"Dream big."*
>
> *"If you dip a toe in you may find the water too cold. If you jump, you'll be OK."*
>
> *"If you want to jump over an obstacle, do it running."*
>
> *The main thing I felt tonight was – love yourself, be true to yourself. Susie has shown me what you can do in life if you set a goal.*

When I was four months pregnant at an eTwinning conference, everyone cheered when my effervescent colleague John said at dinner, "Congratulations to Liz who is expecting a future global citizen in August 2017." I wrote in my pregnancy diary:

I feel so lucky that for 15 years of my life I've been involved in international cultural work and amazing worthwhile programmes. I hope the international, and other cultures, and love for them run through your schooling and life and that you have many an inspiring teacher like these ones.

In March 2017 I wrote in the diary to my baby:

16-week appointment with the midwife. All going well. We heard your heartbeat and she said you were strong.

"Strong" is a word we heard a lot when I was pregnant with Coraline. That was her little character.

I thought a lot about parenthood and wondered what it would be like to have a child, and if I could do it. At the end of March, we went in for our 20-week scan and found out we were expecting a girl. Kevin had written in our pregnancy diary book the day before:

We are going to see if you will be a boy or a girl – either way we are going to love you more than anything. Can't wait to meet you.

I thought, "Gosh will I be OK with a girl?" as I felt much more familiar with boys, having grown up with my two brothers. When I learned we were expecting Coraline I wasn't sure how I would relate to a girl, and I did some deep soul-searching around this fact.

It turns out this was the best thing that could have happened to me, expanding my horizons to know that having a girl was wonderful. The only way I would ever come to know that, and to reconcile this disquiet in myself, was to parent a daughter and to realise through parenting her what a gift it was. I understand my relationship with my own mother so much more as an adult. I understand how much she loved me. Sometimes when she was out of kilter, I took those feelings as personal towards me, but they were not. One hugely meaningful thing for me was that my mother loved, appreciated and celebrated Coraline fully for Coraline's first three years. My mother passed away shortly after

Coraline turned three.

On 3rd May 2017, Kevin proposed to me at Spanish Point in County Clare by the crashing waves of the Atlantic Ocean when we were on holiday in Ireland, staying in a beautiful stone cottage, together with Kevin's parents. What was hilarious was that I had an inkling it was coming as, on a visit to my father's house a couple of months previously, I had seen my father give Kevin a hug on a walk we were on in the Radnorshire Hills. The scenery was superb and vast and, as usual, there was not a soul around as the views stretched for miles. I was at the top of a hill, and they were at the bottom. I thought they must have been discussing something quite emotional to prompt this. Ed was also visiting that same weekend. I heard him exclaim in the kitchen when Kevin told him something and I thought I heard the phrase, "No, no, not a word."

When Kevin proposed to me there was no one around, apart from a far-off artist painting the craggy rocks and tumbling waves. I wondered if he had seen our moment, but I don't think so: Kevin on one knee, nature and its beauty surrounding us. We went on to have lunch together, a seafood platter. I told the waitress we had just got engaged. I felt so very happy. Kevin presented me with a ring he had chosen. I was a little unsure of it. The ruby stone felt larger than I might have chosen. It would stand out and I did not like to stand out. Over the years I have absolutely come to love it. Pushed out of my comfort zone I could realise I actually loved a ring like this.

Shortly after our trip to Ireland we went to Sicily for Payne's 40th birthday celebrations. There we climbed Mount Etna! Christina, one of my previous managers at work, wrote to me at the time: "You can tell your little daughter she's been up a volcano before she's even been born!"

Once back home from Italy and the hot days, swimming, meals out and sightseeing, I resumed my daily routines in life and at work. I began reading a book called *The Magic* by Rhonda Byrne (of *The Secret* fame) all about gratitude in life. It has a gratitude exercise to do daily for a month which I did. I felt I was seeing differently.

I did ten gratitudes quietly out loud, walking up the street to the station on my way to work each morning, and then said out loud the names of people I was thinking of and sending love to (I thought of different people each day). I then pictured something I wanted for myself, Kevin and our baby in the future. At the end of each day, Kevin and I would look back over the things we were grateful for and we would ask each other, "What are your top three things from today?"

At the end of June 2017, I wrote to our baby:

> *So we went for your 32-week scan today and you're doing so well. We could see one of your eyes and part of your face and the midwife said you have 3cm of hair and she saw your eyelashes. Both kidneys are now great and you're exactly average for growth at this stage. Wonderful. We're really grateful and blessed!*

I wrote about our baby's kidneys as the only thing which had come up earlier in scans was some fluid on one of them.

The screening tests we had earlier in my pregnancy hadn't really registered with us. I had been offered a test, maybe three months or so into my pregnancy, to test for Down's syndrome, Edwards' syndrome and Patau's syndrome. I had the two-step screening: the combined nuchal and blood test, which has an 80% detection rate for Down's syndrome. At the time I had no idea about the 80% rate or what that even meant (that 20% of the time it won't pick up if your baby did have Down's syndrome). The blood test was quick and non-invasive. I read in the literature provided, that if you have a 1 in 300 likelihood, or under, of your baby having Down's syndrome, they offer you a further test to confirm.

For me it was a tick box: take the test and trust the result. The letter with the results of my test arrived in the post and I opened it, sat on our sofa. It said that our probability for our baby having Down's syndrome was maybe 1 in 400 or something similar which, to our untrained eye, felt like no possibility really. I put the letter away in my file where I kept information about our appointments for our baby, without a second thought.

I actually had heard that our hospital was doing a trial of the Harmony test so that was the test I believed I had had. A friend had recommended I get that test. The Harmony test is non-invasive, like the one I had, and was a simple blood test. Yet it detected over 99% of pregnancies with Down's syndrome. In fact, I hadn't had this test at all.

This is another funny coincidence as, if I had realised that I hadn't had the Harmony test – or if I had fully understood about how accurate the different tests were – I would have got the Harmony test privately and then, I imagine, I would have known that Coraline had Down's syndrome. Life had its plan.

Had I known, I'd have been full of worry and doubt and fear of the unknown. I didn't know then that love replaces fear. If I think about it, perhaps life brought me Coraline so that I had no choice but to learn this every day of my life parenting her.

Overall, I found my pregnancy joyful and fascinating. I felt like my universe changed when I was pregnant; when I was out and about people cared for me, chatted to me, and got up for me on trains and buses.

"Haha, you don't know how much life is going to change," a commuter on the train said to me one morning when they got up for me to offer me a seat which was met with laughs and nods from the people around us.

I had all the usual feelings during my pregnancy, which really hit me, especially tiredness and tears from the hormonal changes. Sensations I remember towards the end were the lack of sleep, heartburn, needing the bathroom a lot and the wonderful sensations of her kicking. I went on maternity leave at the beginning of July 2017, seven weeks before my due date of 19th August, as I wanted a relaxed run-up to Coraline's birth.

Kevin encouraged me avidly to do this. He felt it was really important. "When will you get this chance again?" I worried about what people would think about me taking such a long time, but it was the best feeling to have that time to really relax and savour the days. Of course, nobody thought anything anyway, or they had better things to think about.

The old chestnut of "what will people think?" is often in evidence for me. I think the difference now is that although it still comes up, I hold the thought and look at it, instead of latching right into it. As Ed says to me, "You don't actually know what people are thinking and you can't presume to guess."

The other thing is that I have found that the more time I spend loving myself, and being true to myself, the less I worry what people think.

I loved the weekly pregnancy yoga at our local hospital held alternately by Rhian and Licia. The "Noobies" antenatal classes we took to make local friends who were expecting babies were also fabulous. Classes took place in the evening in a function room off the main part of a local pub and were relaxed and fun. That was why they chose that setting. I had agonised over making the right choice of group. I wanted the group to be "just so" and thought perhaps by poring over all the different options, I could make it just so. But, of course, you can't predict who is going to be in your group, so I am not sure why I spent that long deliberating. We lucked out with our group, and we are all firm friends and still chat in a WhatsApp group as some of us have moved to different locations. I think that all of us expecting our first baby, and being in a group together centred around that, has bonded us in a strong way. I really feel that when I am with them or on text with them.

The Noobies course was advertised at our hospital and was run by professional midwives. We became friends with the organiser and the midwife Amanda who led our course. Both were so personal and emailed me after we had Coraline, and Amanda even came to see us in hospital afterwards as she happened to be in that week. The course content was excellent: open and embracing to all our views of how we each perceived our journey ahead and it was run with spot-on professional knowledge.

We also did the NHS (National Health Service) antenatal class over two mornings which contained a wealth of information and we have kept in touch with a couple of lovely friends from that too.

I enjoyed pregnancy and the heightened emotions. I was

doing some volunteer dog walking which was great (I had done this for years in North London too). We had a hilarious baby shower in July with friends. I read a lot of parenting books. I went out for dinners with friends, and Kevin and I went away for weekends. We imagined the future.

Two weeks before our baby was born I wrote:

> *I was really tired today (pregnancy fatigue). You are such a blessing and have been so easy, but I do get wiped out with tiredness some days and I am making an effort to cancel things and not be so social so as to take care of me and you. Sleep is disrupted. Your dad is incredible, taking care of dinner and positive, happy and supportive. He said last night, "I have a new goal. To be the best dad I can be." "You already are," I said.*

Each day that I was pregnant I talked aloud to our little baby. My abiding emotion, once I got pregnant, was one of trust. Perhaps it was naiveté, but I simply thought, "I am pregnant now, I will eat well, I will rest, I will do what I can. I will let the emotions run wild, I will talk to my baby and play my baby music whilst I am pregnant. I feel nervous about what it will be like to be a new parent, but I know I want to be a parent." That's pretty much how it was.

I planned to go back to work at the British Council at the end of my maternity leave. As it turns out I never did go back.

When we discovered that Coraline was in the breech position in week 36 of my pregnancy I was offered an External Cephalic Version (ECV), a procedure to help turn her. If this worked, we could keep our wish for me to give birth naturally.

If she didn't turn, they said I would have a scheduled caesarean, as they told me they don't tend to deliver babies in the breech position naturally these days. An ECV involves manual hands on the abdomen – a process they describe as uncomfortable but not painful – accompanied by monitoring of the baby whilst they are doing it. They said our baby was the perfect size and position to turn. She didn't turn.

I wrote in our baby's diary that day, Monday 31st July 2017, my dad's birthday:

> *They got you halfway, but you didn't turn. I was really proud as both you and I were nice and calm and relaxed, and your dad was there and great.*

We were told that we could either try a second ECV in a few days or leave it there and come back for my scheduled caesarean on Tuesday 15th August, when I would have been 39 weeks and 3 days pregnant. "Week 39 is the best time to do an elective caesarean section when everything is going well," they explained. Our baby's due date throughout my pregnancy was Saturday 19th August.

We decided to come back four days later to give an ECV a second, and final, go because, being a conscientious type of person, I wanted to try again. That decision proved to be a pivotal one.

In the meantime, we tried moxibustion, acupuncture and reflexology as they are said to work for turning babies. Nothing worked.

On the morning of my second ECV, Friday 4th August, I woke up in tears as I was not managing to keep up with social commitments in my latter pregnancy weeks and was worried about this, and my hormonal emotions came full tilt! After we arrived at the hospital, for that whole morning I said to myself, "Don't cry, don't cry," whilst talking to all the hospital staff. It was nothing to do with the ECV, just that morning's feelings. Kev led me in loads of deep breathing and affirmations which we had learned at the active birthing workshop day. He also promised me a Slush Puppie and a pizza afterwards (ever the nutritionist, he put that aside and showed me photos of Slush Puppies as we waited so I could stay on track).

Little did we know that one of the duo trying to turn our baby that day, Susana the consultant obstetrician, would be a significant figure in our baby's arrival. This was the first time that we met her, and she had not been involved in any of our care before that day. She was clear in her explanations, kind and so knowledgeable. During our appointment she spotted that something was not quite right with our baby's growth rate whilst looking at the readings on the scan report which forms part of the ECV. She saw that something was unusual with the placenta and that it was not working well. She later explained that she probably only noticed this because she was an obstetrician with a foetal specialism, and it could easily have been missed.

On that same day, immediately afterwards, she rearranged her schedule to personally conduct further scans for us. She wanted to check that indeed our baby's recent growth pattern was not as it should have been. It was not. She said that she felt it was wise for our baby to be delivered sooner than 15th August. Straight away in fact. It was a Friday, so she booked us in for a caesarean at the earliest opportunity: first thing on Monday 7th August. "Wow," we said, "so that means she will come the day after Kevin's 40th birthday on Sunday. That's almost two weeks before our baby's due date. OK, yes, we trust you, thank you."

We had a lot to prepare for over the weekend. I didn't mind that I would now be having a caesarean and not giving birth naturally. I was just happy to go with what we were advised was right for our baby. I wasn't alarmed when Susana said we needed to come in for a caesarean as soon as they were able to do one next. I just trusted it would be all right.

Kevin's 40th birthday was spent racing around department stores picking up items for our baby. He didn't have time to reply to his birthday texts. I had been compiling numerous videos from his friends wishing him a Happy 40th Birthday and had been so excited to reveal them to him on the day. We didn't really have the time for him to properly view them either.

Hanging both our clothes and new little baby clothes on the washing line late afternoon in the summer sun in our tranquil little garden in my favourite black and white polka dot dress, I said to Kevin, "Take a video of me here, so I can speak to our little baby before she arrives tomorrow." So, we did a video as the sun went down, the light dancing behind me and the leaves of the tree fluttering in the breeze, presiding over the washing for us all hanging on the line. I poured out all our wishes for our baby whom we would meet the very next day. We could not quite get our heads around that fact.

In a meeting with Susana two and a half months after Coraline was born, she explained to me the ramifications had we not returned for the second ECV, and had she not spotted what she did in terms of our baby's growth rate. I realised when she spoke about the growth rate and my placenta not working well, what might have happened if we hadn't come back in again but instead just waited at home for our initial scheduled caesarean two weeks later.

Susana said that it didn't cross her mind that Coraline had Down's syndrome, however. "I'm sorry we didn't anticipate this antenatally," she said. She explained that the baby and the placenta are made of the same cells and both, therefore, had Down's syndrome, so Coraline's placenta also had an extra chromosome. I looked at Susana at this meeting with her, which I had come to with Coraline: "We were so lucky."

"I was lucky I met you," Susana replied. "I am very proud to have been Coraline's obstetrician! I carry her in my heart!"

How kind it was that Susana invited me in for this chat, to talk through and explain everything. She made herself available to me and to have this one-on-one time with her was very important to me as we began our journey as parents.

I look back now and do not take my pregnancy, or Coraline's arrival, for granted, but with an appreciation for how life directed it.

The midwives and staff we met were friendly and caring during our pregnancy appointments and the care at the hospital was exceptional before Coraline's birth and continued to be so after it. There was one more member of this cast of characters that I was to meet.

Chapter 5:

Meeting the mentor

Considering my reluctance to fully enter into our new reality the week that Coraline was born, the importance and influence of the attitude of our main medical point of contact, Dieudonné, the Consultant Paediatrician at our local hospital, cannot be overestimated.

Kevin had met him almost immediately after Coraline was born when she first went into the NICU, and had been saying to me, "Oh just wait until you meet him, you have to meet him."

I met the force of energy that was Dieudonné about 48 hours after Coraline was born. We were stood by Coraline's bed, after she was transiting out of the NICU to come to our hospital room with us. From the moment I met Dieudonné, his perspective began to influence my own. Dieudonné translates from French as "given by God".

Dieudonné is from Burundi. When Coraline was two days old, I had my chance to ask him all the questions I had filling up my head. I fired them off from my list. He smiled whilst he talked, so I found that I was smiling when I listened intently.

I couldn't help but blurt out, "I could listen to you all day." Any concerns I had were allayed when I asked him about them.

"Um, I've noticed her eyes are rolling around in her head, is that OK?"

"All babies' eyes roll."

"Your colleague told me she could have issues with her thyroid."

"Oh, that's easy to manage with medication if required."

It's more than words how he made me feel. It began with his words, but it was about his smile, relaxedness and his way of talking to us, making us feel seen, valued and important.

Still absorbing the news, still tears, but stepping into myself and life again. I felt like big things could become small. Supported. As though I was held metaphorically in his energy. That everything was OK. That Kevin and I were great people. That Coraline was cute. That Coraline was doing well. Centred. Hopeful. A deeper feeling about life. Connected.

When I have this memory, I am fully in it. I am stood inside myself remembering it like that and I have a good feeling.

When the paediatrician and her silent colleague told us the news Coraline most likely had Down's syndrome shortly after she was born I felt separate, self-conscious, as the other couple were behind the paper curtain, and alone taking in the news (though of course very together with Kevin). Like the bottom had fallen out of anything I ever knew about life. Incomprehension. Lack of connection. Afraid. Overwhelmed. Unequal to the road ahead. A mismatch in time, moments freezing.

When I have this memory of her talking to me and her colleague standing unmoving next to her, I remember it not as myself, but I am seeing it play out in the room, and my mind looks in on us all.

Coraline's initial tests in the NICU had been the blood tests and an ECG to check her heart as they suspected a heart murmur. This led to a trip to see the Paediatric Cardiology team at Evelina London Children's Hospital, also on this second day after her birth, for a heart echo ultrasound. Kevin and Coraline were transported to the Evelina by staff from our local hospital in an ambulance, but without any flashing lights. I did not feel up to going. They told Kevin at the appointment that Coraline had an atrioventricular septal defect (AVSD). This meant she had a hole in the wall between the two upper chambers of her heart (atria) and a hole between the two lower chambers (ventricles). It also affected her atrioventricular valves, the mitral and tricuspid valves, as she had a single valve instead of two separate valves. They said that she would likely need surgery when she was around three months old unless the holes closed on their own. They told Kevin at this first meeting that it would be so beneficial if we could keep Coraline healthy in advance of her surgery. This would mean we should always check if people were well before we saw them and not to take Coraline to baby groups for the months before her heart surgery, so she wasn't exposed to illness. They told Kevin that if she was to get ill, her body might not be able to handle it, and she might then need to go into hospital.

I had drawn on the words and affirmations Rhian had shared with us in the active birthing workshop during Coraline's first week. "Trust, breathe," she had written up on the flipchart.

It so happened that Rhian was in the reception of our local hospital as Kevin returned from this appointment with Coraline in a mobile neonatal incubator.

Kevin bowled up to Rhian (to use the word "bowled" is to use his phraseology) and gave her the news that Coraline had been born and that she had Down's syndrome, whereupon she gave him a massive hug. Later she came and found us all in the NICU. Her hand rested on my arm as we spoke, and the three of us had a group hug over Coraline's bed.

Rhian said, "She chose you."

That evening, after her 48 hours in the NICU, Coraline came to sleep in a little cot in the same room as us.

When I had first been wheeled in my hospital bed to this large, quiet, room where we would then stay for some days, I had been told: "Here's your room. Soon another mother and her baby will arrive to share the room with you."

My tears and protestations were strong. "I can't," I told them simply.

I was in too much shock and, for me, I needed solitude and our own space to process the news we had been given. I know for others it might have been different. Perhaps they would have liked the company and the conversation and the connected feeling of others around. We are all different. I am forever grateful that they respected my request, as they must have been pressed for beds and space, and they allowed us our own room for the week that we stayed. For me the peace of the room was a crucial part of my beginning to process how I was feeling and to regain myself.

Coraline was such a peaceful little baby, nestling into us or quietly sleeping in her bed. I'd watch her at night and sometimes her chest rose up and down particularly fast which brought on a rush of care and love, that her breathing was OK. It was. The midwives were on shifts and popped into our room to give me a daily injection and painkillers every few hours, and they checked on Coraline.

We had been told that we could press the call button for the midwives, the infant feeding team and feeding support teams at any time of day or night.

As the colostrum turned to breast milk on day three or four, we began to buzz for assistance in getting Coraline to latch on and breastfeed. Whenever a nurse came in and Coraline didn't quite latch they would then say routinely, "So if you just express a little milk".

Each time I replied to them, "Ah, Kevin helps me to do this!" I was still befuddled.

We were told by the paediatric team that Coraline had to have high volumes of milk to maintain her weight. This meant we had to use formula in addition to my expressed breast milk for about two days during our week in hospital. After those two days or so, we were allowed to lower the amount she consumed and we moved to a solely expressed breast milk diet for her as we, in particular Kevin, knew this would benefit her immune system. I continued to express breast milk for her for the next six months. The team also explained to us this was important for babies with Down's syndrome, if at all possible, as they can be prone to respiratory and viral infections.

There we remained in our local hospital for six days in our own room. The midwives said to us, "We've just been talking about how cute Coraline is at the nursing station."

We buzzed for them with our questions. One day I asked, "Is

it normal that she doesn't really cry?"

The midwife replied, "She has no need to cry; you're anticipating all her needs."

One of the midwives left us a note in our room during that week: "Elizabeth and Kevin, I have left for the day and wanted to say goodbye and wish you well. Kevin, you are an amazing support to your wife, and Elizabeth, you should be incredibly proud of yourself for how strong you are, and you are doing an amazing job. Coraline is a very lucky little girl. Take care and best wishes, from Natalie x."

We had wanted to give the midwives something for all they did for us. In our room we had birthday cakes which we offered them. I had made the cakes the weekend before Coraline was born, in a rare departure from the trained chef of the house inhabiting our kitchen. I had made one for Kevin aged 40, and one for Coraline, aged 0. The cake I made for our baby, who had not yet arrived, featured a large heart made out of cream icing in the middle.

My wonderful friend Pippa, who had been one of my housemates before I moved in with Kevin, came and visited us during our week in hospital and I asked her if she could bring me in a card so I could write it for Kevin. She brought a little blue one in which said on the front in gold lettering, "You're awesome". I wrote it to thank him for all he was, and all he had done that week. Quite aptly I was writing it whilst he had driven home to cook me a meal and bring it back to the hospital! This card is up in our bedroom today. What did Kevin do that meant the world to me?

He loved Coraline and was by her side.

He listened.

He accepted however I was feeling.

He said to feel what I was feeling fully.

Whatever I said was OK to say.

He was compassionate.

The force of his love was strong, and accepting.

He let his own joy abound, and this rubbed off on me.

From that space of love and understanding, my feelings had a chance to be heard and it allowed room for the love I was also feeling.

We did not have any more visitors that week in hospital, as we realised we needed to keep Coraline well and not expose her to any chance of getting ill due to the holes in her heart.

Having been in shock (I've since learned this can sometimes be the case when parents receive the news that their baby has Down's syndrome) I began to feel more like myself as the week went on. I still felt unsettled, but I also felt like I was inhabiting myself again. The more time I spent with Coraline, the more love I felt as I looked at her. I made a little video for our family of myself and her with her settled on me in our room, marvelling at how sweet she was and the little sounds she made.

During that first week, I announced to friends Coraline's arrival on my personal Facebook account with a photo of Kevin, me and Coraline in our hospital room taken by Pippa on her visit. Just as Kevin had set the tone with his phone calls to our family and friends, I wanted to do the same with my announcement. Debs and Chris had let us know that what we wrote for our family and friends would do this.

I wrote:

Here is Coraline, born on Monday 7th August 2017. Life already felt beautiful, but now it feels filled with beauty wherever we look. Coraline very likely has Down's syndrome and has a few heart problems which may require surgery in a few months. We are so proud of her and she is mesmerising – we simply couldn't be any happier.

I had begun to enter into the love I felt for Coraline. I loved this comment from one of the eTwinning Ambassadors I used to work with, Drew: "Liz, that is one of the most uplifting Facebook updates I've ever read." Comment after comment of congratulations and good wishes flooded in. In fact, we received over 400 comments of love on this post from our family and friends.

Dieudonné came to see us personally on the Friday, the day before we were due to go home from the hospital, to let us know that Coraline's genetic tests had come back and that they confirmed that she had Trisomy 21. He talked to us about feeding and about skin-to-skin and eye-to-eye contact with her when we were doing it.

We came to learn that Down's syndrome is one of the most common genetic conditions, and it has not been worked out fully as to why it occurs. It is characterised by a global developmental delay, i.e. a delay in all areas such as walking, talking and speech. It is also characterised by low muscle tone (hypotonia) and hypermobile joints which mean that considerably more effort is required for gross and fine motor skills. In effect, Coraline's muscles are "floppy".

Dieudonné said to us in a beautiful, gentle, positive way that we would need to support each other and, on occasion, handle reactions in the world. He said this was important. "We all have challenges," he said, "but sometimes nobody knows." He gave us his personal work email address and smiled, "When you give people access, they take less. When you hide, they want more."

I told my manager Christa from my first job at the British Council about Coraline's arrival and about Dieudonné, and she said, "It sounds like you have two Dieudonnés with Coraline as well."

"Ah," I said, "in fact three with Kevin."

Chapter 6:

Writing

In the hospital we did not receive a pack specifically for parents of children with Down's syndrome although I did receive some official pamphlets about it. My head was filled with questions as I wanted to read personal experiences. I needed to grasp onto some surety and I looked to the Internet to provide it. I went from link to link, post to post, to find the reassurance I was looking for. Now I can see that what I needed to know was that surety comes from within.

I began to look up what books were out there to read, either by people with Down's syndrome or their families. I wanted to read articles which gave me hope and, if I found one that did, I wanted to read another. I needed hope and lots of it. As regards books written by a parent with a young baby or child with Down's syndrome, I thought to myself:

> *Let me find a book where the parents are flying, where the parents are happy, where they love life and where their child is flourishing. Let me find a book where they tell me everything is well, in fact better than well. Let me find a book where I can read that their child is fabulous and adored and that great things are headed our way. I know, you can't generalise, I know that every experience is different, that life isn't all one thing, or all another thing. I know that life does not exist without challenges. But let me find this book.*

Then a clear thought came to me during that first week in hospital: "One day, I will write this book."

When I was thinking I might write the book I wanted to read back then, I had a different definition of "flourishing". I was imagining our daughter hitting all her milestones early, and that she would engage with everyone around her. But now I have a different definition.

For many of the first years of Coraline's life, she kept to herself and did not interact with others in the room. This is changing ever so slowly nowadays. But if anyone says "Hello" to her in the street or when they walk into the room, she does not respond; not with a sound of recognition, and not with a gesture. Coraline has many sensory considerations and stimming (self-stimulatory) behaviours, such as hitting her face and flapping her hands, and she actively resists transitions, even those from one room to another. In her early years she loved to press buttons in musical books, or hold a musical microphone to her ear, and could spend a long time doing this. Kevin and I did not really read too much into these things; they were just part of who she was. Other than that I had hoped she might engage with people more, or see what was around her apart from her musical books and musical toys, but she didn't. Coraline's paediatrician referred Coraline for an assessment for suspected autism at age seven and a half and she is currently on the waiting list for this.

Coraline is happy in the moment. That moment for her, aged eight, is in flapping her hands to music. It is in bouncing on the sofa to the TV. It is in looking at pictures in her books. These are the activities she likes to do. She does not see, or engage in, a playground, a soft play, a party and so on. In fact, she gets actively dysregulated at a soft play and cannot engage with it, especially if it's a new place. Yet now that she is older, when she does make that tentative move towards a visitor to our house, when they connect, the deep feeling I have is beyond words. When she sits on me stroking her hands and cosy, these are the most heart-melting moments. When Coraline makes a new development, my heart soars at how sweet it is. When I see how she has remembered where she placed a book and has gone to find it the next day, my heart leaps at her memory. When she laughs as Kevin jumps up and down in front of her doing exercise (as for some inexplicable reason she finds it hilarious), I feel joy.

Today my definition of flourishing is her being herself and us all being in our everyday just as it is, and truly seeing her and loving her for her, whatever she is up to; whether it's challenging, whether she's verbal or not verbal, whether she's hitting her face repetitively and we're trying to figure that out, or whether she's not hitting her face. Flourishing is us allowing her to be herself and not setting expectations as to how she has to be. Flourishing is in celebrating ourselves just as we are, because it is not about doing, it is about being.

Part of flourishing too is the challenges, the days where it all feels tiring, and in learning to be honest about that with others and recognising that tomorrow is a new day whatever the situation. For a long time, I was not honest with others about how much energy our parenting can take. But the reward is immeasurable. Coraline has gone through various phases of screeching, of refusing to eat unless we put music on and then pushing our hand to change the song a hundred times, of us questioning how we got into this habit with the music and of dysregulated days, which have left us searching for answers as she had no words to tell us.

I have long been conscious of not being able to articulate to guests that, yes, if I was in their shoes, I might think, "What on earth are they doing?" And of equally being unable to articulate that parenting a child with special educational needs is just a whole other ball game, that I could not explain the layers and layers of sensory needs and considerations that led us to putting on music for her to eat. And bowing to her will for me to change the song repeatedly until we hit upon one she is happy with.

All of this is OK! This is our life, just as it is. All of us evolving and all of us people to be loved and understood. Flourishing is to do with my having learned that feeling overwhelmed is valid, and that this comes and can engulf me, but it doesn't last forever. Flourishing is about validating how I feel emotionally and being who I am, and Coraline being who she is, rather than any particular need to be or do things in a certain way.

So, I have written the book I wanted to read, and in fact I have written the book that I didn't even know I wanted to read – about celebrating who we are just as we are, with no need to be anything in particular other than ourselves. I have written the book of hope that I wanted. But the hope comes not in conjuring up or controlling the exact scenario I had been looking to read about. Or imagining there is even some typical scenario. Every child with Down's syndrome and family is different, just as with typical children. The hope, for me, comes from loving ourselves as we are. And that challenging moments in our parenting, or moments when we feel we can't get on top of anything, are OK! These are the moments which come to us all, and which I have found have developed me as a person. These moments have taught me how to really value and look after myself as I know this is key now. I can fully feel my huge emotions in those moments, allow them, and then find my pathway out of them with awareness of my thought patterns. I can draw on the support around me. I can love my child just as she is. I can do my best and I can let go of my rigid expectations and trust life and my daughter.

If I could go and visit myself in hospital back then, I would hurry down the corridors and knock on the door to our hospital room and say to the me of 2017:

> *However you're feeling is OK. It's fine to feel this way. It's natural as it's a shock so just feel it and don't judge yourself. Be compassionate with yourself. It is emotion and all emotion is to be honoured because that way you can process it. Oh, and she's eight years old now and, yes, there are challenges and, yes, you are happy. Where you are right now just after she was born, and how you are feeling, that's entirely OK, and let me tell you, life is about to expand just as it was meant to. So be as you are, feel what you feel and trust that all this is to come.*

For me, the closest book to giving me the feeling of reassurance I was after, was *Expecting Adam* by Martha Beck, which I only found a year after Coraline was born. Martha wrote it whilst she was pregnant with her son Adam. She describes how she found out he had Down's syndrome before he was born. She wrote about her intuition and about her feelings about her son-to-be and her love for him. Her knowing was so strong about the deeper meaning he would bring to their lives. That gave me the hope I was looking for.

I have always trusted my gut instinct as I believe it is a guide as to what is right for me in life. I have learned that my instinct is the first thought I have, and then I begin to talk over that thought with my mind. Throughout my life, I paid attention to what my gut instinct was and mostly followed it because I could see an explanation for why that instinct was coming to me, but at times I didn't follow it and let my mind override it. But things never quite worked out when I did that.

In years to come, when Coraline was approaching her fifth birthday, I read a book her Auntie Roxy recommended to me called *The Horse Boy* by Rupert Isaacson, about his autistic son Rowan and their journey to meet shamans in Mongolia. In this book, Rowan's father Rupert talks about following your gut instinct but not needing to know why at all. Just knowing to follow it. That was a revelation for me.

A song I like is *Comeback Story* by Kings of Leon and I have listened to it over the years on walks with Coraline. There is a lyric in it that plays on the idea of walking a mile in someone else's shoes. By writing about our lives in my posts, I felt that next time my family and friends saw or met someone with Down's syndrome, or heard about it, they would feel familiar, as though they were wearing my shoes. Of course, no two children with Down's syndrome are the same. Likewise, no two children with a dual diagnosis of Down's syndrome and autism are the same, as we are learning in later years. But when I began writing in our hospital room I hoped what I wrote would give an insight into our new world parenting a child with additional needs and an insight into all we were learning about Down's syndrome.

It's as simple as that. My writing is not political. My writing is not making any statement. It's just about understanding. I do feel that broadening horizons and contributing to understanding are what life is all about. That's what my decade-long career at the British Council taught me. It is through knowing people and their personal stories that perspectives shift.

Chapter 7:

Crossing the threshold

Every experience and belief I held brought me to the point that I was at after Coraline was born. A life spent in perfectionism and control and managing events to be "just so". I had an awareness that this way of being actually left me exhausted sometimes. My mode was to *control what is* rather than to *adapt to what is.*

Into this way of being came the news of something wholly unexpected: the news that our daughter had Down's syndrome.

Up until Coraline was born, and for some years of her life afterwards, the association I had with the words "change" and "unexpected" was fear, and a feeling of being destabilised. I have since begun to entertain the idea of a new association with these words and it is about being open to what they might bring. That is pretty revolutionary for me.

I was to learn through Coraline that I could not control the world and its events. What is the opposite of deciding how a situation must be? Trusting in life. What is the opposite of controlling situations? Letting go. What is the opposite of keeping it so that I never had to feel uncomfortable emotions in the first place? Feeling them.

The revolutionary concept which has come to me over the last eight years is: if I am not controlling events and circumstances or, dare I say it, trying to control other people (which is a pretty tall order when you try to), then funnily enough that frees up a whole lot of energy. And that energy can be used to surf the waves of those unexpected events. That ability to surf the waves comes from inner validation of myself which gives me strength and surety.

What is the alternative I have now come to know? That when unexpected events turn up, I realise that the secret is not to deny difficult circumstances or to deny my associated feelings, but rather that it is OK to feel uncomfortable and that it's a part of life. Also, what if life has an even better plan than that which I can conceive or believe should be what's happening? How do I know where something that happens is going to lead? I recently listened to an amazing audiobook which Kevin encouraged me to listen to called *The Surrender Experiment* by Michael A. Singer. It is about this very point. He describes situations in his life to which he "surrendered" and by doing so quite incredible things happened to him as a result, which he could never have engineered or predicted with all the controlling in the world. And these happenings to which he surrendered often led to deeply fulfilling ripple effects in his life years later.

I like to listen to the messages of Abraham Hicks, via Esther Hicks, and she communicates the idea that when you feel good you are going with the flow of the stream, and when you feel bad, you are not going with the flow.

If I take Esther Hicks' analogy of the flow of life being the stream, I wasn't even *in* the stream at the point Coraline was born. I was *above* the stream on a bridge. My old life coach Sophia said to me during our sessions together:

> *There comes a point where your old beliefs don't serve you, but you stay in them because they are what you know. It's like carrying a really heavy load that's really uncomfortable and then walking across a rickety bridge carrying this heavy load. The bridge is high up above a stream below. You keep going because it's what you know and because you are afraid of what it would be like to jump down into the stream. You keep going until the point that what you are carrying literally becomes too heavy to keep going and you have to drop down into the stream. And when you drop down you realise the water isn't as cold and bottomless as you had imagined.*

Kevin did not feel as I did when Coraline was born because he held different beliefs. He told me that through 17 years of working in kitchens as a chef that he was used to the unexpected and to adapting on his feet and taking a different approach quickly. He had trained this habit of quick adaptation through practice every day in the kitchen. He also has a different association with the words "unexpected" and "change". There is no fear in it for him. He embraces them in a matter-of-fact way. So, his whole system was conditioned differently. But for me, my system was precisely tuned to balance everything gingerly.

When Coraline was born, I was propelled off that bridge and into the stream. That baggage I was carrying, of old beliefs of perfectionism and control, could not work for me here. Now that I was in the stream of my new life, I could stay stuck on the boulders in it, I could desperately try to go upstream, or I could go downstream.

Upstream was clinging to my expectations, entering into a dialogue around that, and then indulging in comparison. That's the ultimate ticket to upstream! As long as I held on to the expectation I had of life parenting a typical child and how our version of life was not matching that, I was going upstream. And believe me I've spent a good bit of time upstream.

Each chink of my accepting our experience was me turning slightly in the stream. Esther Hicks explained that you cannot control others, or conditions; the only thing you can control is your direction in the stream which is determined by your reaction to what is happening around you. One surefire thing that kept me going upstream was holding on to how I had decided things were meant to be and fuelling it with comparison.

The way to go downstream was to *allow* those emotions, not *wrestle* with them; to be gentle with myself and at the same time to get into my heart and my instinct as a mother, and to think about Coraline. To see her as a child who required love and to focus on loving my child and to trust that I could put one foot in front of the other and do that.

I was fully in my head when Coraline was born. I was

thinking about myself and my concerns and there, in front of me, was a baby to love, who was here for reasons greater than the workings of my mind were trying to figure out.

I love these two quotes from Joe Dispenza:

> *When you can't figure it out, it's bigger than you.*
>
> *The unknown has never let me down.*

I have become aware of my thoughts and know that I can choose to latch onto them or not. I can see that when I choose the better-feeling thoughts, they turn me around in the stream. I have learned that when I let go, and step back and trust in life and what it is bringing me, that life is easier and, in fact, lighter.

These thoughts that I had in the years since Coraline's birth led to my biggest teachings and growth, because it was more painful to hold onto them all (clinging to a different expectation and comparing), than it was to let them go.

As the years have gone by, I have seen beyond comparison or expectations, or "What will others think", or "What will others say", to seeing the essence of both Coraline and myself. And to validation from within. This, to me, was my endpoint, downstream. Connecting with my heart as everything else fell away. Seeing that the ultimate in life is to truly be ourselves and shine. This book is about how it fell away.

Many years after Coraline was born I had a session with a Creative Kinesiologist, Tini, where I recounted that, after hearing the news that Coraline had Down's syndrome, I was "frozen" inside. She said to me:

> *The sideways, unexpected nature of the news was a trauma for you. Look at the word you used. You described yourself as frozen. We have a "fight, flight, freeze" response in traumatic situations. You froze. Your body shut down. That's what the body does in a stressful situation. It disconnects, to protect you.*

On the Saturday afternoon, six days after Coraline was born, it was time to go home, and we did just that. Our little house, tidy and ready, had been waiting patiently for us to come back, up the path, through the door, under the roses and horseshoe.

We knew that there was a certain way we wanted to bring Coraline over the threshold into our house. Not literally the one moment of crossing the threshold, but the whole experience of her entering our home. I had read before she was born about how it's great and reassuring for a baby if you talk them through what you're doing and what's happening. So that's what we have endeavoured to do since Coraline was born. We explained every procedure, from the hearing test to the heel pricks to take blood, as they were happening in the hospital.

The thing we had often talked about, and were looking forward to, was doing the "house tour" when we got home. We left the hospital. We said our goodbyes and a multitude of "Thank Yous". We took the most adorable photo of Coraline in her car seat in the hospital corridor, and we carried her in this out to the car. Kevin drove us home so carefully with a muslin cloth draped across the rear side window so Coraline didn't get too hot, for it was high summer after all.

When we got home, we carried her in and talked her through her new surroundings from the path to the front door, and then explained each room of the house to her and what the room was for. The books I had read said babies understand more than you think. I am so pleased we did this as it was a lovely thing to do and has set up the way we talk to her. Sometimes we forget to do this now that she is eight years old and does not have the receptive language (understanding of language) to know what we are saying. Sometimes friends will come to our house and we won't have prepared Coraline with a photo of them to show her who is about to arrive. Then we remind ourselves to tell her everything. What I mean by receptive language is that at age eight, if we talk in sentences about our days and about the days of the week or about occasions like Easter, she will not grasp these concepts or understand our sentences. She understands some single words and we can tell by her behaviour that she has understood, for example if we say "food" she gets up and moves to the kitchen. She probably understands more than we know.

But each day we use pictures to show her what we are about to do and hope that she understands.

On the Sunday morning, after our first night back home from the hospital, two lovely, warm midwives appeared on a home visit as part of our "return to home" care. One of them, from Ireland, had been a midwife for 40 years and the other was a new midwife finishing her training.

The wonderful Irish midwife chatted us through everything whilst her colleague sat with her and encouraged us with nods and smiles. The longtime midwife looked at Coraline and said, "You're just perfect." This duo were doing 11 visits that day and said they were struck by how tranquil Kevin and I were and how Coraline was too. We could see they really meant it. We were peaceful in our manner with Coraline, but my head was all over the place.

The longtime midwife said, "She was born into the right family. You're calm so she's calm. Keep that attitude, she's a very lucky baby. She's a well baby."

I replied, "Oh thank you. That's really kind of you to say. It feels really odd to us as we have a baby with Down's syndrome, but we hardly know anything about Down's syndrome."

"You don't need to know anything about it. You just need to know your baby. You can begin reading about it in a few weeks' time."

"The only point of reference we have is our friends Chris and Debs in Australia and their one-year-old daughter Elsden, who has Down's syndrome. We sat at their table at a wedding."

The longtime midwife said, "Well that encounter was meant to happen." She continued, "I know a little boy called Oliver who has Down's syndrome. He has a beautiful disposition. At a wedding, everybody wants a dance with Oliver."

In that first conversation with the first professionals who had visited us at home during Coraline's first week in the world, the title of my book was presented to me. I absorbed the words the midwife used, and thought to myself instantly, "when I write my book about our lives that is going to be the title".

Bit by bit, we began to learn more about Down's syndrome.

For the biology of it, I learned that each cell in our body has 23 pairs of chromosomes, so 46 chromosomes in total per cell. One chromosome in each pair comes from the egg and one from the sperm. So, when the egg and sperm cell meet, they have 46 chromosomes each and divide in half. But sometimes the egg or sperm cell keeps both copies of chromosome 21. That extra copy is in every cell of the body. People with Down's syndrome have this extra copy of chromosome 21. This is referred to as "Trisomy 21". It is also why World Down Syndrome Day is on 21st March each year. I learned the 23rd pair is the XX (female) or XY (male) pair of chromosomes.

Some people say Down's syndrome. Others say Down syndrome. We personally say Down's syndrome. It is named after the Victorian physician John Langdon Down who characterised the condition. The Langdon Down Centre, where he lived and worked in Teddington, Surrey, is now the premises for the Headquarters of the Down's Syndrome Association in the UK. It's coincidental that we lived a 20-minute drive from it. In fact, Kevin drove there to talk to them almost straight after Coraline was born.

The extra chromosome gives rise to a number of characteristics in the development of the body and the brain, and the presence of these characteristics varies for each child with Down's syndrome.

I read that speech is delayed for children with Down's syndrome, and that it was likely that Coraline would start to talk from about 24–36 months old, as was the average for a child with Down's syndrome. For typical babies it was likely to be from 10–18 months. She is not yet talking, aged eight, whilst many of her peers with Down's syndrome are, though some are not. And those who are, do so to varying degrees, from saying a few words, to speaking in sentences. And so on. The fact that Coraline is not yet talking is a potential characteristic of her suspected dual diagnosis of Down's syndrome and autism. Typical children begin to walk from between approximately 9-18 months old; for children with Down's syndrome, it is from between approximately 18 months to 4 years old. I have friends with children with Down's syndrome who were walking at two and a half, or before. Coraline took her first independent steps at four and a half years old. By five and a half years old Coraline was not yet walking for more than five minutes at a time (and during this time she would sit down repeatedly). At eight years old we can go on walks of about 20 minutes in duration, but Coraline does not walk readily on demand and can refuse to move. We often encourage her with music or singing.

Babies and children with Down's syndrome develop at different rates, just as typical children do. Every child is an individual and it is about us seeing, and responding to, that individual.

About 50% of babies with Down's syndrome are born with a congenital heart defect, as Coraline was. I did not yet know what this was going to mean for her and us.

Chapter 8:

Navigating our first month

When Coraline was born, and in the weeks afterwards, what we wanted to hear was: "Congratulations, your baby is beautiful."

During our first week at home a health professional came to our house and joked, "For most people they have that moment their child leaves home, but of course you won't have that."

Kevin replied, "I don't know about that. This may be the case, this may not be the case, but either way I do not want to make assumptions."

The key for us, then and since, has been to meet any comment which is said with good intentions with equanimity and love, and also to push back in a calm way if we don't quite agree with what is said. Speaking up doesn't come naturally to me at all and it is something I continue to learn how to do but it is a lesson Coraline has brought to me.

My friend Nina from Switzerland who had also worked on eTwinning had messaged me coincidentally that first week to say, "When I moved into a house I shared with four others, one of my housemates had Down's syndrome. It was great to have him as a housemate. Back when he was born, his parents were told he'd never be able to do anything independently, but they started to teach him whatever they felt he could learn. He was a full member of our shared house, although his brother helped him with 'official' things. For me, and certainly for everyone who experienced sharing a house with him, this was a great time. We are currently on holiday with our baby, sleeping in our tent with him. People were telling us that camping with a baby was crazy, but that's how we love our holidays, and we didn't see why we shouldn't do it with him. And it's awesome. So – you'll soon know Coraline well enough to tell what's possible with and for her, whatever others are saying, and this is a wonderful feeling – it gives me a lot of confidence."

Another health professional who visited us in our first week said: "So compared to normal babies... Ah hang on, I don't want to say 'normal', I'm struggling here, and I feel bad that you're the ones helping me."

Kevin replied, "What about 'babies without Down's syndrome'?"

We were new to the wording too. We appreciated her showing her vulnerability, just as we too didn't quite know how to phrase things, but would learn, and we would learn together with those around us. We learned the phrase to use is "typical babies".

At two weeks old, we had a phone call from a visiting health professional. She began, "I'm sorry to hear your baby has Down's syndrome…"

I felt a jolt at her words and thought to myself, "Perhaps we don't need to have 'sorry' in that sentence." It immediately made me feel taken aback. And yet I didn't say anything as I had not developed my ability to speak up having lived a life of appeasing people. It just wasn't something I did.

She said she would bring round centile charts particular to babies with Down's syndrome to record Coraline's weight and height growth, as growth velocity can be different (slower). It was interesting to learn that this was the case as I had not known that there were different charts. She brought them round a few days later, and the two of us stood there together, both looking at Coraline whilst she was measuring her, and she said: "There are baby groups in your area, but you may not feel comfortable going to them."

On this second occasion too with her, I didn't speak up in response. I felt a smarting feeling rising through my body and my immediate internal reaction was, "of course we are going to go and of course we will feel comfortable."

I knew that the baby groups would be whatever we chose to make them. The experience would be whatever I chose to believe it would be. Our attitude would create our experience. I had the power of thoughts, of feelings, of reactions, of perspective.

The health professional also had a power in the language she used around me at that time to contribute to my perspective about my future experience, and I believe she could simply have said, "There are baby groups in your area, which you can go to."

Her words had an effect long after she left our house. I felt crushed and sad, and pain in my heart. Perhaps she did not realise that things can shift on a dime with what people say to us and how they say it. It is that important.

I don't wish I hadn't received these comments, because I can't control what other people say – only my own response. The real leap is in hearing them, not letting them take root in my mind, and finding validation from within. As I have said, my worth is not derived externally, it is derived internally. And another leap for me has been to counter them when I hear them, in a gently assertive way.

I think it's a fascinating conversation to have and, personally, I would welcome and love it if people asked me, "Talk to me about terminology and what you've learned through parenting Coraline," just as I have now learned to ask someone else to talk to me about terminology in other areas, and to take my lead from them and mirror the language they use in that area. I know that now Coraline has a suspected autism diagnosis that I do not know as much about the terminology here and very much wish to be led by – and to learn from – others.

In time to come, after Coraline was a year old, a friend told me: "My friend reads your blog and she is glad she does because she said it helps her know what terminology to use, otherwise she wouldn't be sure." I found it really interesting that what I wrote could actually be helpful in this way.

Kevin and I went on to learn a lot about terminology during Coraline's first year and the importance of it. We learned that the generally advised terminology is "a baby with Down's syndrome" as the baby comes first. As opposed to saying a "Down's syndrome baby". We also learned that the only abbreviation would be DS, otherwise the full two words said together and not shortened to "Down's".

During Coraline's first couple of weeks, I received a phone call from a cardiac nurse on the team at the Evelina London Children's Hospital. It was to give us the number for a dedicated phone line for a team of six of them to call if we needed anything or if we had any concerns about Coraline's heart. They said to me, "You will have a lot to do with us over the following years. Coraline will have lifelong follow-up every two to three years and into adult life."

For a moment I reeled and thought, "Wow, that's how things are going to be..." Then, as the lady went on, I began to consider the fact that we were lucky to have that contact, to be supported and to have medical experts caring for Coraline and us.

The cardiac nurse finished our call with the words, "We will look after her heart and your local hospital will look after the whole of her."

We were getting used to our new reality. We had ordered the large book with photographs which Chris and Debs had recommended to us, and it sat on our coffee table whilst we sat with Coraline beside us, looking through its beautiful pictures and the moving words from parents next to their children's photographs. Their words spoke to us from across the pages.

We began to think about a suggestion that Chris and Debs had made in their early messages to us, that we might like to write a letter to family and friends. It was an excellent idea. Kevin wrote a letter on Facebook in late August in the same vein as my initial announcement after Coraline was born, sharing his feelings about all that had happened over the previous three weeks. He began it:

> *We are just getting to know Coraline and all the fun and beauty that entails (plus the endless rounds of nappies and early morning feeds) – we can't stop looking at her as she is just so cute. This letter is definitely something that I felt would be a really useful process for all of our wide range of friends and*

family throughout the world. Reading it back I now know that it is also good for me to write it personally so that people understand the immense joy and happiness fatherhood brings, even if it happened not quite as I expected…

In rather a fortuitous coincidence, Chris, Debs and Elsden were on a planned trip to the UK from Australia when Coraline was about a month old. They made a detour to come and see us, and we are grateful to this day that they did, just as we were for their initial messages after Coraline was born. How good it felt to sit all together in person at our house and in our garden, and to meet beautiful little Elsden. They were full of warmth and humour and love for Coraline.

On the first Monday morning in September, we registered Coraline's birth. In the afternoon, we took Coraline to the Evelina for an appointment with paediatric cardiology, her first visit back since she went there with Kevin at two days old.

They confirmed she did need open heart surgery and that they would see us again in four weeks to determine when, but that it was still likely to be in a few months' time. I felt a rush of emotion, of care for Coraline, as the prospect of this surgery became real. At the surgery they would close the two holes in her heart and do some repair work on her leaking heart valve. She had one atrioventricular valve instead of two, but they said they could divide this into two. The team were remarkable in their skill and care, taking great time to answer all our questions. We were very grateful to them. They said Coraline looked strong and that she was moving nicely. They said that everything looked as they expected further to her initial heart scan at two days old. She was really good throughout! We also liked it when they said, "She's cute; we see a lot of babies but she's really cute." Yet I couldn't stop thinking about what was coming up for her.

Chapter 9:

The hands appear

We received message after message of sharing, openness and suggestions of contacts from our wide network of friends and family.

I had powerful phone calls with friends of friends who have children with Down's syndrome and their words have stuck with me, like a vein of gold running through all I do.

A friend from the British Council put me in touch with Sangitaa who lives in India and has four children. Her third child has Down's syndrome and was 26 years old at the time of our phone call.

Sangitaa said to me:

> *Even though we've never met, I'm going to talk to you as if I've known you all my life.*
>
> *All good things come through my daughter's door. The niceness of human nature has come back because of her.*
>
> *Nobody knows as much as you do as a parent. Always remember, only you as a parent will set her up. If she's not learning, it's not because she can't, it's up to you to figure out how she can learn. Stop thinking, "She can't learn this"; think "How can she learn this?" Kids are so smart, and we presume they aren't. Don't worry about her responding, ignore that, it's all going in. It's not linear. It's not incremental. She won't show results immediately. One day it's triggered in one moment. If I had listened to what people told me, I would have held back.*

It's all getting registered. Neurons are triggered. She won't show results immediately. One day my daughter just stood up and walked.

This is a big grand adventure, full of pleasant surprises. It changes you. Not just you, but every member of your family. We are much closer. She holds us together. She is the glue. She is very intuitive. We have forgotten intuition. Don't kill her radar by imposing your world view. Don't say she must be like everybody else. She is on a different vibration. Allow her to shine. She has the gift of a love one doesn't receive from anyone else, I can tell you this with all my heart.

Another message that I loved came from Ian, one of the energetic eTwinning Ambassadors I used to work with. It read:

I had a cousin who lived next door to me who had Down's syndrome...he was the nearest I had to a brother. The love and joy and blessings he showered us with...is a gift I will never forget. I honestly think he was a major influence in making me the man I am today. I learned so much.

Another eTwinning Ambassador, Michael, wrote to tell me about his brother, Keith, who has Down's syndrome and sent me a link to look at photos of their annual holidays together in Finland at a truly stunning cabin on a lake. As I sat there in those first few weeks with our newborn daughter, I reflected upon the fact that whatever paths we choose in life, they are all crisscrossing to take us to moments we are meant to have. That is my belief anyway. And that sometimes you can't work out the reasoning behind something that happens, and you might find it hard at the time, but it will be leading you somewhere you are meant to go. I often say that to others, that perhaps their life to date has all led up to what they currently tell me is happening. I was still processing the news, and still caught in alternate realities in my head, but I also had that belief in the corner of my mind.

The network of eTwinning Ambassadors with whom I had worked have been instrumental in their encouragement, knowledge and championing of Coraline and us since she was born. As have previous colleagues in the field of education from the British Council and King's.

That hands appear to guide you along the way is something I have come to know, such as how it was for me in the form of the people writing to us and sharing insights, contacts and warmth. I had already begun to feel a connectedness to the world on a deeper level due to people opening up to me. People have continued to open up in this way across all Coraline's years, and not just friends but people I meet in the street. As I began to walk around with Coraline in the pram or sling in our local area, at the supermarket or at the bus stop, people would come up to me and it was like a shortcut to conversing with them on a deeper level as they offered me their life stories without so much as my asking.

I am thankful to each of the people to whom I spoke as they all encouraged me. I first took Coraline out in the sling when she was about a month old after we'd finally worked out how to use it from YouTube videos. Three people came up to chat to me on this walk, which felt really exciting. The sling was so easy. Coraline always slept in it, so it was very convenient to have my hands free at the tills in the local supermarket, a ten-minute walk from our house.

When she was a few months old, I took Coraline on the train in the pram into central London (half an hour) on the old route I used to commute to work. We were going for lunch to meet Fatima, one of the eTwinning Ambassadors. It felt brave to negotiate the pram on the train.

This time four people came up to me to offer to help Coraline and me on and off the train with her in the pram, and the guard followed us on our way home and said, "Excuse me, what station are you getting off at? I'll keep an eye out for you." Coraline was wide-eyed for her trip in the pram into London.

This journey we had set out upon after Coraline was born reminds me of the winding path up to the Wisdom Tree in Los Angeles. Kevin and I had been out to Los Angeles the year before she was born to visit Ed and we had loved this iconic hike which takes in the Wisdom Tree and ends underneath the letters of the Hollywood sign. The path began on the pavement where we happened upon some painted white letters saying, "Stand here and consider what makes you happy." Then the ascent began. At the top of the long and scenic trail to the Wisdom Tree, with staggering views, we arrived to find people who had made the journey before us had left notes under rocks by the tree. There were hundreds of notes under individual rocks in the dusty earth, so I upturned the rocks to read as many as I could. The notes contained whatever sayings or words people wished to share with others. I suppose it works as it doesn't rain too much there.

I took a photograph of one of the notes which particularly appealed to me, and when we got home, I printed and framed it and we have it hung on the wall. The note reads:

> *No matter where you are in life, no matter what you go through, you are in the right place at the right time. The Universe is taking care of you.*

A Spanish friend of mine, Rony, one of the eTwinning Ambassadors, had told me when I was pregnant to look up Pablo Piñeda, a Spanish writer, actor and lecturer with Down's syndrome, as she found him inspirational. This was before I knew that I would have a child with Down's syndrome.

He came back to my mind again after Coraline was born and I looked him up and watched a video of him on YouTube. Pablo Piñeda was the first student with Down's syndrome in Europe to obtain a university degree. He said he expected this of himself as this is what his siblings did. I can't find the exact video that I watched, as there are quite a few of him, but in it he said something like this: "Our parents should expect more of us, and we should expect more of ourselves." This stuck with me. I love this quote. He also said words to the effect of, "Your parents have to teach you, and encourage you. After that, you can do anything."

Early on we had been told by Coraline's cardiology team to wash our hands, use antibacterial gel and dry them with kitchen towel (not a tea towel which may have bacteria) to keep her healthy. I mentioned this in passing on a phone call to Coraline's godmother Payne. The next day a large delivery of handtowels and antibacterial gel arrived on our doorstep. Payne also sent us Caroline White's great book *The Label* in the post where she writes about simply seeing her son, and not his diagnosis.

I had seen our neighbour Margaret in the street not long after we brought Coraline home from hospital, outside her and her husband's beautifully presented house with its gorgeous back garden. I invited her to come in and meet Coraline.

It is hard to put into words the look on Margaret's face when she first met Coraline. It was complete and total love from that moment; her face lit up when she peered into Coraline's cot. It was straightforward and simple. As opposed to my mind which was running in all sorts of directions. Margaret turned her head towards me, from looking into Coraline's cot, and said smiling, "I'd love to help you look after Coraline." I am not sure she knew where the words came from. She often reminisces about this moment and how she just had a feeling when she met Coraline.

At that point we didn't know each other that well. When we had moved into our house Margaret had thoughtfully posted a welcome card through our door from her and her husband Dave which was there when we arrived. I spotted the card on the doormat in our empty porch and kept saying to Kevin, "Wow, how lovely is this card?" Margaret had gone to the trouble of finding out our names from our landlords.

We began the arrangement when Coraline was about five weeks old that she would spend a few hours at Margaret and Dave's each Monday. Kevin encouraged me, although I wasn't so sure about letting go. But it was a wonderful thing, as Coraline was happy and these few hours made all the difference to me. I would always check with Margaret and Dave that they were well and didn't have a cold before Coraline went round, given what the cardiology team had said. All the time Coraline has ever spent with Margaret and Dave in her life has been for free with no payment from us and they offer it simply because they love to spend time with Coraline, which has touched us deeply.

Meanwhile I kept blogging and I was overwhelmed by the amount of messages and comments I received from friends and family in response to each post I wrote about what we were learning with Coraline. Their encouragement and positivity was the catalyst for me deciding to write more widely and to open up my blog publicly. I received so many insights, stories, contacts and comments that I felt it was larger than myself.

With the wind of this encouragement in my sails, I made my blog and Instagram account public in October 2017, our first Down Syndrome Awareness Month. My friend Joseph created a website for me to host my blog posts, www.coralineandus.com.

Here is what I wrote for the website.

Why I am writing this blog:

To celebrate Coraline
To share our love for Coraline
To learn from each other
To change perspectives
To raise awareness
To create understanding

I also put up a section on the website called "My Values" as I felt it was important to write based on the values I had defined as key for me in my life back in 2014. Until Sophia asked me to sit down and think about what they were, it had never occurred to me to do so. Surprisingly it took me a long time to realise what they were.

At the time of working on them, Sophia said to me, "I want you to immerse yourself in these new values so that you become passionate about them and so that they become the blueprint of how you live. They will be your grail and will guide your decisions." Here they are:

Love
Health

Acceptance
Kindness
Gratitude
Trust in Life
Appreciation
Joy
Openness
Authenticity

It was actually scary for me to write publicly, for people who I didn't know. I was afraid of doing it. When sitting down to write this book, I also thought, "Why me, what right do I have to write a book?" However, what made me think, "Go on, do it!" was: it has felt so right to write, it is my instinct to do it, so I wanted to be brave and honour that. I can say to myself, "who am I to write this book?" but I suppose there is the other school of thought which says, as expressed by Marianne Williamson in her poem *Our Deepest Fear*, who am I not to?

Chapter 10:
Just Mum and Dad

In October 2017, when Coraline was two months old, I was changing her upstairs and we were getting ready for a peaceful weekend day going out for a walk. I called out, "Kevin, can you come and look at Coraline's hands?"

"Coming."

"Do her hands look slightly blue to you?"

"Yes."

"I'm not sure what to do? Should we call 111? I guess they will just tell us to go to the hospital?" It was a Sunday so we could not ring the usual weekday cardiology team phone number we had been given at the Evelina London Children's Hospital if ever we had any queries.

"I'll drive us in."

We made a snap decision to drive to A&E, 15 minutes away, who then referred us to our usual paediatric ward.

We had gone in being conscious of Coraline's heart condition and because we were new parents. In the hospital after doing some tests they explained to us that she was fine. They said that in our situation it was only if Coraline's lips turned blue that we should worry, but that it was always the right decision to come in or call up for medical advice straight away to check if we noticed something which seemed out of the ordinary. That we had been right to do so, and to always do that.

To our surprise Dieudonné rang a couple of days later, as he hadn't been there when we went in, which I think is amazing in itself for a consultant paediatrician to take that personal care. I was stood in our living room, and I couldn't believe it was him on the other end of the phone.

He said in his usual lovely manner, "I see you were in at the weekend, tell me what happened."

What a line. It's all I ever want to hear when something happens. I faltered, "Umm, I think we were being hypochondriacs."

"No, just Mum and Dad."

Just like that he made me walk tall.

I had subscribed to a couple of different email lists destined for new mums across the first year of parenting saying, "Your baby is up to this at two months old," and so on. The emails detailed what to expect developmentally.

Inspired by Down Syndrome Awareness Month, I wrote to a couple of the organisations sending out the emails to ask if I could be a guest blogger and be another voice in the emails saying what my daughter was up to at the same age. One of them replied to say they could only include official content from health professionals, and I didn't pursue it.

I wanted to add my voice to these developmental emails so that I felt included as a mum, so that Coraline was included, and so that the emails gave some idea of what it might be like if your child had additional needs and a developmental delay. And to convey the message that every developmental journey is unique.

A few weeks later Coraline had her next appointment with her paediatric cardiologist at the Evelina, who said she was doing "very nicely". They said they would keep checking Coraline monthly and felt it was advisable for Coraline to keep growing bigger and stronger before her heart operation which they now felt was likely to be at some point the following year. Coraline was good as gold throughout this appointment and did about four rolls on her mat in the morning. At 11 weeks old Coraline had rolled for the first time from her front to her back; a new development which we absolutely loved seeing.

Not too long after this appointment, I rang the Evelina cardiology team's phoneline as we had noticed Coraline was eating much less than usual and taking longer to do so. Her first morning feed had been pronounced in this respect. The cardiac nurse on the phoneline told us to go into our local hospital, which we did.

It so happened that we bumped into Dieudonné in the corridor. He was there because he had swapped a shift with someone. He stepped in to help on our case even though his shift had not yet started. We were in a side room, and I was sitting feeding Coraline from a bottle as we talked. For a time, we talked about recent personal life events, and he chatted to us about how he was that day, as we had not seen him in person since Coraline was born. He then said, "You see in life people think it's about giving things to people. But it's actually about listening. You have listened to what I have told you about my life today, and I have listened to you and we both feel appreciated."

After this we got onto him assessing Coraline's feeding. But actually, he'd had one expert eye on her feeding all the time we had been chatting. He said that it was either a virus or her heart and told us what to do for either one of these. As a precaution he gave us diuretics for her to take for her heart. On this day in hospital Coraline snuck in a roll for Dieudonné at the last minute. He duly marvelled at this, as we had hoped he might.

We also asked him about the fact Coraline had reflux and he explained: "Coraline's low muscle tone is present internally too so the ring of muscle joining the oesophagus to the stomach can let the milk up again. Reflux improves with a change in body position, if you hold her upright more. Babies tend to grow out of reflux by the time they are a year old as they are more upright generally by then."

He explained things so beautifully and we felt supported. A smile was on my face again.

Coraline began to do much better the next day; eating more speedily than before, and she was lively in a new way. The diuretic which Coraline took daily in the morning and evening was to help ease the pressure on her system from her heart – we used a syringe to drop it into her milk.

At the time of this impromptu trip to hospital, we were getting used to attending all Coraline's many appointments with healthcare professionals. We were continuing to keep Coraline well and check around us that people were not infectious as far as we could. This vigilance around her health was ongoing.

What we had to do then was what people would do the world over during COVID times some years later, and even more so with isolation rules in place for long periods of time. That had not happened in the world yet and our reality felt quite different to us, to how it was for others with babies around us. I knew in future that it would make me grateful for a time when we were able to do what we liked and see who we liked without having to limit contact with people. We had to limit who we saw, and did not attend baby groups at all – and if ever I did venture to a café with her, I was constantly conscious of whether anyone sat near us had a cold.

When Coraline was eight weeks old, I wrote down what we had learned about Down's syndrome so far:

1. It's not a longer tongue; it's a smaller mouth. So says our doctor.
2. Babies with Down's syndrome find it harder to latch and breast feed due to this; however, it absolutely is possible.
3. About 50% of babies with Down's syndrome have heart problems. The teams who surround you to take care of this are exceptional.
4. The care on the NHS in the UK in our case was amazing, thoughtful and superb.
5. Babies with Down's syndrome can have lower muscle tone.
6. Babies with Down's syndrome can have a lower immune system.
7. There are some inspiring bloggers, books and TV shows out there.
8. Each baby is totally their own person in terms of the developmental and physical characteristics of Down's

syndrome that they have. In Coraline's case, we are led by her as an individual and our aim is to give her love, love, love.

9. There is an educational home-visiting service for children who have additional support needs called "Portage". They will visit us when she is ten weeks old to see what support may be required, e.g. speech development, motor development.
10. Babies with Down's syndrome are social and this is a strength.

Portage did indeed come to visit us when Coraline was two months old. I had not heard the term "Portage" before having Coraline. I first pronounced it as though it were a French word, akin to how you might pronounce "potage", the French word for soup, but Portage is actually named after the town in Wisconsin where it first began. It is a preschool home-visiting educational service for children who have a delay in development, or particular conditions. It's free, not statutory, and offered to parents or carers to choose if they'd like it.

Pam, the sunny manager of our local Portage service, and Director of Playwise Learning CIC, came to our house and suggested we get a "see-through" cot for downstairs as she felt that Coraline was so alert that she would like to see what's going on around her. We did this on her advice in the weeks to come and Coraline loved it and settled really well after looking around everywhere.

I think at that time we had been putting Coraline to sleep in her pram "bassinet" which we had unclicked from her pram and put on a stand downstairs. We would then put the bassinet back onto the pram at other times whenever we went on a walk. Pam told us it would be wise not to do that, as Coraline would associate the bassinet with going on a walk, so this would be confusing for her if it was also her downstairs place to sleep. These were amazing insights for us, as new parents, and made sense.

Pam brought materials for Coraline to play with too. Coraline's new selection of toys included a spongy ball, beads, dangling mirrors and a shower loofah. Pam explained that it was all about textures. Coraline loved all the items. Pam had a wealth of knowledge.

Pam also told me about Home-Start, a voluntary organisation which supports parents with young children and whose volunteers come to give home-based support for two hours once a week. She let us know that our fortnightly Portage visits would begin from January 2018, and that she had just the lady in mind to be our Portage worker.

We told Pam that the appointments and liaising with healthcare professionals had begun after we brought Coraline home from the hospital, and she said, "You might want to keep one day free where you have no healthcare appointments at all." Pam is another of those people whose energy rubbed off on us, who makes things happen, who creates opportunities and, some years later, she was awarded an MBE for services to children with special educational needs and disabilities (SEND).

We recorded Coraline's developments and milestones just as parents of typical babies do, but my notes about milestones were peppered with medical appointments either side. We had visits either from professionals to our house or from us to professionals in medical settings. We ensured they were all in good health before our appointments. That was what was different for us as new parents. Our home was not just our home where we played with our new child and had friends to visit. So began my diary management and keeping tabs on all Coraline's appointments, and what was said at them.

Sharing how we are feeling is what Kevin and I have always done, and I do believe that by simply listening to each other we help one another a lot and validate each other. For me having the space to verbalise a thought immediately lifts some of the intensity in my head.

I was open with Kevin: "Sometimes I just want the simple milestones trajectory without all the extra liaison and appointments with professionals, and without having to always think about keeping her well."

"I know. Me too. And that's OK to feel that way. That's totally natural."

"Sometimes I just wish it wasn't that way."

"I know. But that's not our journey."

Kevin often uses this phrase, although I don't particularly warm to it. I realise that the way to peace is to be present with what is our journey, and every time I am wishing for a journey that is not ours, I am not at peace. Our journey is equally valid as a journey, it's just different to what I had imagined.

We continued to talk: "OK, let's think about this. Can we change this situation?" Kevin asked me.

"No," I replied.

"So, what can we do?" he said.

"We can allow the thoughts, welcome and acknowledge them. We can validate what we are feeling and where we are at. At the same time as that we can look at what we are grateful for. I am grateful for all the care around us."

"Yes, it's true. Me too."

"I am grateful, I mean that. I have gained more appreciation of considerations or appointments others may have in their day-to-day lives, now that we have them in ours, and I feel that's opened my eyes."

"Totally," Kevin agreed.

"And it makes me conscious of, and grateful for, simple pleasures which I don't think I would have been otherwise. Not to this extent. I adore the cosy, unfettered days when we can choose what we want to do when we don't have any appointments."

"Absolutely."

This reminded me of a Maya Angelou quote which I had printed out long before this time, and which has sat on our chest of drawers for years:

> *What you're supposed to do when you don't like a thing is change it. If you can't change it, change the way you think about it. Don't complain.*

For me, I have to let those complaints out first, air them, then make a choice to not sit in them.

I went on to make a call to Home-Start a few weeks later knowing I did need a little support. I also wanted other influences for Coraline, given we weren't going out too much. One of Home-Start's coordinators, Bev, answered the phone and her manner was bubbly, caring and friendly. She came to visit Coraline and me at home whilst Kevin was out at work and told us there was a wait list of a couple of months. I knew I would just need to keep going as we were until that time.

Kevin's father died that October. Kevin managed to fly back to Ireland, together with his brother Mick, to be there with their mother at the hospital, with their father when he died.

Chapter 11:
Our new world

Kevin came back home. Our day-to-day life continued, and memories of his father, and thoughts of his mother back in Ireland, were at the fore.

Kevin, Coraline and I met up with our wonderful Noobies antenatal group for a Sunday pub lunch when the five babies in our group were about three months old. We had checked everyone was well and ensured the room in the pub was well ventilated and we all sat apart from each other.

We'd been a bit cocooned in terms of how Coraline was getting along and, as we sat at the table, I looked across at one of the beautiful babies in our group who was born only a few weeks after Coraline. She was sitting up straight, able to balance herself upright on her mum's knee. I felt surprise descend on me. I could not pinpoint how I felt. I felt a sadness, I think, and a wistfulness. It was not until that point that I understood the fact of Coraline having low muscle tone. We were first-time parents after all.

I wondered whether to talk to Kevin about it because I didn't feel he'd have even remarked upon what I had noticed, and I did not want to voice aloud the beginnings of the restive voice in my head. I didn't mention it to him in the car on the way home.

Later that evening, back home, I was hanging up some washing and casually, in a roundabout way, I finally aired those thoughts which had taken root in my head, eyes focused on the washing.

"...So, I just felt sad when I saw she was able to sit like that, so straight. I had no idea that was possible."

"Oh yes, I felt that too," he said. "It was actually a seminal moment for me because I hadn't really thought it was an option for Coraline to be holding her head up, and I had been feeling a bit down about it that it was an option for other babies her age."

It was such a relief to hear him say that. A relief to know he'd felt it too.

Then we said to each other, "Why do we feel this way? Why does it matter?" And there lies the question for us all perennially in life when the hooks of comparison catch us.

So, looking back the answer was self-love. For myself and for Coraline. To know that Coraline is her own person and to celebrate exactly who she is, and to release these thoughts to the winds of life. The only benchmark is Coraline to Coraline.

I know what our awesome antenatal group would have said if I'd told them at the time: the message would have been about embracing each of our children as individuals. What I love about our group is that we encourage each other and celebrate our children. All I have heard from them is celebration of Coraline just as she is.

As we approached Coraline's first Christmas, at four months old, her weight was plateauing. My friend Rachel, who is a biology teacher, explained this to me (as did the cardiology team at the Evelina).

Rachel said, "Coraline is taking in the same amount of food as a typical baby, but she is burning more of it to keep her system going due to the holes in her heart, so as a result she is putting on less weight."

"Can we give her more milk?"

"No, giving her more food won't rectify it, as there is an optimum volume of feed for her size and stomach."

"Oh yes, we've been told the volume she's meant to drink each day."

"Another point is that due to her lower muscle tone, she is working hard to produce her sucking reflex to drink her milk, which is also using up energy."

One of the local health visiting team began to make a home visit to weigh Coraline each week. This was above and beyond what they usually did but they were doing it so that Coraline did not have to come into the children's centre and be exposed to any potential illnesses. The cardiology team from the Evelina called to check on Coraline's weight gain each week.

A dietician from the Evelina prescribed a high-calorie formula in order to help her gain weight, which Coraline began taking in mid-December to supplement the expressed breast milk she was having. Ted at the local chemist had this ready for us with a smile when I came in for it: "We'll take care of her," he said, and continued, "If ever you can't make it down to pick up a repeat prescription from Coraline's cardiologist I can drop it in to your house when I'm driving home." This made me leave the chemist's smiling at how kind he was and how cared for I felt.

Coraline's godmother Payne said, "Haven't we all got a high-calorie diet prescribed over Christmas?"

After a week on the high-calorie supplement, Coraline put on 200 grams (she had 100ml expressed breast milk and 30ml high-calorie Infantrini milk per feed). We had also been doing what Dieudonné had suggested, i.e. to keep Coraline upright for 30 minutes after a feed so that she didn't bring the milk up again and it worked; pausing a few times during each feed really helped too.

Rachel also explained why the paediatric cardiology team had advised us not to attend groups and classes: "When we get ill, we have reserves of energy to fight off an illness and to raise an immune response, but Coraline does not have the same kind of reserves. So, this is why the cardiology team are asking you to do your best to keep her healthy and well."

It was a carefully calibrated decision for us: to ensure Coraline was social and stimulated but for us to do everything possible so that she was not exposed to risk of infection. We noticed that she loved to meet new people and had a beautiful, endearing flicker of a smile for them, but we knew we had to be careful about where we took her.

The days and weeks continued in a similar pattern. I pottered about with Coraline, a few friends came over (but not many), I met friends in coffee shops which had plenty of space and sat off to the side, checking people were well around us. Coraline and I went on lots of walks, and we went to the various appointments for her development and health, or they came to us wherever possible. All the while we continued to make sure everyone we were around was in good health.

That Christmas we rented a beautiful house in Suffolk together with my mum, Kevin's mum who had come over from Ireland, Ed and Payne. We checked everyone was well before we all went. Everyone loved holding Coraline, sat around the fireplace. Kevin's mum loved to sing songs to her, with Coraline nestled in close. Julian and his family joined us for a walk in the frosty air on Boxing Day in Framlingham, Ed Sheeran's hometown. I carried Coraline in the sling and we walked up to Framlingham castle, the inspiration for his song *Castle on the Hill*. I love Ed Sheeran's music. Kevin's engaging and fun mum came back to Surrey with us and we spent New Year's Eve together toasting family and friends.

In early 2018 an NHS speech and language therapist and a physiotherapist began working with Coraline at our home and Teresa, Coraline's Portage worker, also began home visits. They all set objectives for Coraline for play, behaviour, motor skills and so on. Teresa came fortnightly to work on developmental goals with Coraline through play. Pam, the Portage Service Lead, had been right to say that she had someone special in mind for us: someone who listened and who celebrated with us and who was as calm and bright for us as a clear and cloudless blue sky; and someone who also made us rather love the cloudy days too, knowing that the blue sky was always behind.

I loved it when Teresa presented me with the sheet of goals early on for us to work on with Coraline and said: "You see this goal here, 'Have fun!' – that's always on the sheet of goals."

We did indeed do fun things with Teresa, like play with see-through hot-water bottles with toy fish in them. Her visits were about sensory stimulation and development through play, delighting in Coraline and giving us ideas as her parents. I found Teresa's terminology fascinating too, for example, "Coraline tolerates...", which Teresa wrote in her notes regarding Coraline's reaction to certain textures and activities.

It was also very interesting to me how a few months later in March 2018 Teresa set a goal centred around responding and anticipating. That month Teresa sat down with a developmental checklist with me, which was great for benchmarking the things Coraline was, and was not, doing so we could see what to work on and track her progress.

"Does Coraline smile in response to you?"

"Not really. She does sort of smile of her own accord, but not in response to us smiling."

In time to come, at eight months old, Coraline was smiling sometimes in response to us when we smiled. It was a really big change. It was a fabulous feeling. At ten months old we noticed that whenever we yawned Coraline smiled back as she thought we were laughing! This period of smiling lasted a year or so. We have found this has been the case in many areas of Coraline's development. It was as though the smiling went away and came back again after Coraline was about four and a half years old.

In January 2018 we were also matched with a Home-Start volunteer, Tracy, who began to come once a week and would feed Coraline her milk, play with her and take her for a walk in the pram. I could choose how I spent those two hours. I looked forward to her visits, and I enjoyed chatting to Tracy. Each time Tracy came I thought how lucky we were that organisations like Home-Start existed, for ourselves and other people. Such an impact do time and kindness have. Tracy was a lovely presence: calm, enthusiastic and encouraging.

I used my two hours for continuing my doing, organising and racing to get things done rather than on self-love and self-care. I did the washing, tidying and emails. At the time, however, I felt it was self-care to try to get on top of my list. And those hours really did help me.

Tracy was a wonderful addition to the weekly support we had from our neighbours Margaret and Dave, and a couple of other great babysitters who we had every few weeks. Even though we were limiting our social outings, we wanted Coraline to be comfortable with others and to have other influences.

That January was a busy month. In addition to all these home visits, I also went on a local six-week Makaton sign language course on the recommendation of Coraline's speech therapist in case Coraline took a while to begin speaking. I met a host of parents and carers who were all there to learn Makaton to use with their children for different reasons. Until then I had just been chatting to parents and carers of children with Down's syndrome. Here I met parents and carers of children with a range of conditions. Our neighbour Margaret even came with me to one of the classes as she wanted to learn Makaton to use with Coraline. After each class they gave those of us who had attended cards depicting the Makaton signs we had learned and they began to send one pack home for Margaret too each week for me to give to her. Margaret generally looked after Coraline whilst I was at the classes. I did not bring Coraline to them so as to minimise exposing her to any illnesses.

I found the home physiotherapy sessions fascinating. Coraline's hypotonia (low muscle tone) meant that everything felt wobbly for her, such as her ankles and pelvis, so she was working harder all the time just to sit up, or in future to walk. This extra effort meant she could tire more easily. Coraline would build muscle memory of movement and strength in her muscles through physiotherapy. Her muscles are "floppy", and her lax ligaments mean that she is extremely flexible. Her favourite way to sit now that she is eight is with her feet behind her ears, but our therapists suggest we encourage her to sit in a traditional way otherwise this will put pressure on her hips. She also sleeps folded over in two. I could feel this floppiness in Coraline's body as a baby: when I held her, she just seemed to melt into me. When I held a typical baby, I could feel the spring in their movements and a totally different tone to their muscles. We saw her physiotherapist about every two weeks.

Meanwhile Kevin and I also began "goals coaching" with our Irish friend Declan, who ran a brilliant online coaching group centred around personal and professional goals. That January I set my professional goal as getting my blog out there and Declan's weekly group coaching helped me to work towards this with targeted steps, focus and belief. Kevin's goal was to put the foundations in place to start up his own organic, natural handmade soap business using only natural, wild-harvested or organic ingredients. Declan told us our goals should both scare and excite us. For us, these really were big goals.

We had found that Coraline had sensitive skin which often reacted to products that we bought despite them saying "natural" or "organic" on the label. We discovered that a beauty product can have one organic ingredient and say that it is organic on the packaging (the term is not as regulated in the UK in this industry as it is in the food industry). Kevin had been making soap as a hobby over the past year after our friend Ali had taught him and when we used his soap for Coraline in the bath and to wash her hair her skin was fine. Kevin felt that others with dry, sensitive or itchy skin could also benefit from his soaps.

I also contacted and met up with Lu from Get on Down's and Tatty from 21&Co, our local parent-run charities for families of children with Down's syndrome. They both gave us a warm welcome. Coraline and I met with each of them personally, checking they were well first, and knowing they were ready and waiting for us whenever we could join in group activities.

That January, when Coraline was five months old we, and our wider family, each wrote a reflection on what Coraline had taught us.

January 2018: Things Coraline has taught us all.

1. Me: Acceptance. I used to sometimes search to be somewhere other than I was or that I "should have" done this or that, but she's taught me to let any of that thinking go, and it is liberating to release thinking that way. And whatever moment you're in is just right.

2. Kevin: Love is all that really matters. Coraline is just the most beautiful baby I could ever have hoped for. It's a level of love I could never have imagined. Coraline has taught me that loving her is everything!

3. Uncle Mick and Auntie Roxy: Awareness. Noticing more grown-up children and adults with Down's syndrome and seeing how they are integrated and just enjoying life/society like everybody else. We're looking forward to the journey and seeing and helping her grow into the best person she can be. We think that she will teach us plenty more as we go, the best is yet to come!
4. Godmother Payne: She's made me learn more about Down's syndrome and nothing is what it appears to be. Why do we put limits on others when we truly have no idea of what they can achieve. She's taught me to read (not literally she's only five months) but read and learn more about children and adults with Down's syndrome, that have stood up and said (like Coraline's parents and Obama) "Yes, we can" and have gone on to achieve extraordinary things, profoundly enriching the lives of those around them. She has taught me so much, where do I begin. Babies aren't scary. Watching my friends become loving, selfless parents is a joy to watch. I can hold and feed a baby. I've never been so excited about teaching Coraline to ride a bike. P.S. She also taught me to like Christmas this year! Didn't see that one coming!!
5. My old life coach Sophia: What it is to surrender to what is. And to express what I need. She also taught me to be open to new people and to give them my trust. (She's taught me a lot!)
6. Nana (Kevin's mum): The power of attitude. Coraline has made me realise the need to foster a positive attitude/approach in people who are socialising or working with children or adults who have Down's syndrome.
7. Uncle Ed: She's taught me about my need to strive for the perfect life, and by accepting "what is" it can be even better than your own idea of perfection.

8. Grandpa: Wonder. The wonder is about all the love, joy and affection that Coraline has already inspired and about being deeply moved by the way her parents, in particular, have responded to this little miracle.
9. Uncle Julian and Auntie Chris: The path less travelled hides wonderful surprises and interest. There's the "wonder" bit! What at first seemed a fairly daunting route is so much due to being the unknown, and it's been filled with all the love and excitement you'd have hoped for, plus a little more.
10. Grandma (my mum): For hers, chose to quote a Christmas card she had received from my cousin Melissa in Australia; "beautiful Coraline has been born adding further love and depth to our family."

We were finding our feet. Yet, as all Coraline's therapists were suggesting therapy through play, it was only a matter of time for me to start to feel I had to be doing something for Coraline's learning every time we played. It meant that my head was always switched on, and it also meant that I felt guilty when I wasn't doing something during play directly for Coraline's learning. For example, from early on in physiotherapy we were asked to put Coraline's toys where she had to reach for them, or in speech therapy we were asked to do flashcards with her during playtime. Looking back now I would like to have known the simple fact that sometimes you can just switch off, play for no reason other than to play and to really enjoy that.

It was a fine balance for the paediatric cardiology team at the Evelina to work out when Coraline's heart surgery was going to be; and they felt they would be able to know more by doing a sedated heart echo. The idea of sedation for a small baby unnerved me a little. The reason for the sedation was because Coraline was often moving about during her monthly heart scans, so they wanted to have a look at her heart when she was still.

It was scheduled for the end of January 2018, when she was almost six months old. She didn't have any food for seven hours by the time everything was finished and was so well behaved. We were asked that she have no expressed breast milk after 4.30am before our 8.30am appointment. One of the nurses there said, "She's so chilled out."

The appointment went well. The cardiologist at the appointment thought her operation now looked like it could be four to six months away but that they would know more at a meeting when they analysed the photos with her consultant. Whilst they had originally thought Coraline's operation would be at three months old, the bigger Coraline was when they operated, the better, they said. They told us there was some tissue around one of the holes in her heart, so it was sealing it a bit.

They also emphasised, "Please do keep asking everyone you meet if they are well, or if they have a cold, and avoid crowded places so as to protect her. If she catches a cold, it is likely she will have to come into hospital." The implication was that she would need support for breathing and feeding because even a cold would have made her heart work harder and would have put strain on her system. Due to her heart condition, Coraline already had to work harder to breathe and to circulate blood delivering oxygen through her body. A cold would have made breathing more difficult. If she got ill, she might have fed less, which could have led to dehydration and weight loss, stressing her heart.

Our regular cardiology check followed a month after this sedated echo. They told us:

> *The top atrial hole has closed itself and the bottom ventricular hole has almost sealed due to tissue growing around it; there is just a 1mm gap. She does only have one valve instead of two; however it is functioning like two, but it has a small leak. It could be that the only operation we need to do is to repair the valve, and we will keep tabs on the valve and delay this as long as possible. The valve leak may cope OK due to the holes now not putting that much pressure on it. We don't think she will have an operation in the foreseeable future, though she*

> *will have one at some point. We will now move appointments to every two to three months instead of monthly.*
>
> *Please keep protecting her from bugs as she will still be compromised if she catches something, but you can probably relax things in about April/May when she is a bit bigger and the illnesses season is less. We will let you know at your next appointment.*

We saw another cardiologist that we knew in the hallway and told him the news, and he said, "That's great, but what are you going to do about her cuteness?"

I had read that breastmilk would be good for Coraline's immunity and wanted to do whatever I good to get her strong for her operation in the future. In terms of the practicalities of our lives, whilst we had had many midwives come to our house to try to help Coraline to latch on to breastfeed we were still unable to manage it.

At each daytime feed in her first month or so I tried her on the breast for five minutes before the bottle of expressed milk, but each time she did not latch on. Perhaps it was due to her lower muscle tone or her sucking reflex. I continued to pump breastmilk for Coraline. Right at the beginning Kevin made me a bra to hold the pumping device hands-free. As I progressed, we bought a proper hands-free pumping bra online, when we found out they existed.

I had invested in a double breast pump (after using them at the hospital). I expressed milk for Coraline for 20 minutes, eight times a day to keep the milk flow coming. I arranged my days around this schedule. I pumped two hourly in the day and then had a five-hour break sometimes at night (the longest you can leave it in the first 12 weeks before milk supply is established). Kev got up to bottle-feed Coraline the expressed milk alternately with me. After 12 weeks I had begun to drop the number of pumps slowly and was now down to pumping milk twice a day.

Kevin suggested I look at the time positively as a chance to read as otherwise he saw that I could get caught up in "OMG I am doing this how many times?" thinking. For me, it was bigger than me, as it was about her development and so, personally, it was my decision to do that. The hospital had said it didn't matter that the breast milk was coming from a bottle not the breast in terms of bonding, as they said it was all about how I talked to her and did skin-to-skin when I fed her.

I went on to pump breastmilk until Coraline was seven months old but gently slowed it down over the last month. I had initially aimed to pump for three months but continued. I finished up pumping in early March 2018 and we celebrated in style when Payne was visiting us for her birthday that month.

I loved chatting to Roisin and Ted at the local chemists up the street each time I went in for Coraline's little bottles of Infantrini to help her to put on weight. Whenever we came in Ted would say, "More milk?" He'd have it out the back in a special place for us.

Roisin, our pharmacist, was brilliant. Friendly and funny, she had the most wonderful knowledge and way of explaining things that left me feeling well-informed and confident.

In early 2018 something occurred to me about how I wrote my blog. Was I being a bit too positive?

I do believe that the way I express myself creates my experience, which is why my writing is positive. Yet it is also how I feel. My predominant life approach is positivity. When I tackle, or am submerged in, difficult situations and low emotions, I spend a lot of time overthinking and definitely believe in accepting and inhabiting whatever emotion I am in. Then I get to the positivity eventually.

Back in 2014 I had a pretty negative script running in my head and I was unaware of how I was talking to myself. That is why I began work with my life coach Sophia. She asked me to imagine that I was hanging out with myself, and if all I said to myself were unkind things then it would be hard to be around myself and I would start to believe these things.

She also said: "Imagine if you were looking after a child would you speak to them like that?"

"No."

"Are you an unkind person?"

"No."

"Your thinking is not consistent with who you are. Even if you believe those things about yourself, it's not kind to say them."

Through this work with Sophia, I made a change in how I talked to myself, and I came to feel so much better in life.

Of course, I still dip back to unhelpful thoughts, and also rapid escalation of feeling like I can't handle things. I suppose my long-term programming is fear and worry and self-criticism. As ever, awareness is the first step. I felt I was sharing this side too in my writing.

Like when we went for Coraline's sedated echo and the team said: "Yes, you must keep being vigilant not to expose Coraline to anyone who is ill."

I immediately thought, "Do we have to? I can't keep doing this. Why is it so different for us than for everyone else? We can't do what everyone else does."

And that's totally OK that I went down this path of thinking. It's valid. Even if I stayed in a feeling off and on for weeks, or even months, I tried to *allow* the feelings but not to *latch onto* them in a dialogue in my head. I came out of them much more quickly due to the work I had done with Sophia.

I loved Coraline, and that was a constant, and my overthinking put layers on top of that.

This is the root of my positive attitude, as it's honestly how I feel, but I do of course have unproductive thinking too. I wanted to convey authentically what went through my mind that troubled me, and when things felt challenging, I wanted to share how I had moved through it. The alternative was to stay stuck.

Years later when Coraline was four or so years old, I spoke to a friend, Jacqui, after her son was born and had an undiagnosed condition. I came across positively then in keeping with who I was as a person. I asked her recently if perhaps I did not allow her the space to be with what was, with how lost she felt at the time or for her to inhabit authentically just how she was feeling.

I said: "I was probably overly positive when I spoke to you, and I've learned so much since then when people come to me of really listening and being aware of where someone is at when I speak to them. To find out where people are at and to validate their feelings."

Jacqui replied:

> *Getting the balance is so important right? I sometimes worry that I am overly positive now but crikey I'd much prefer to be in the positive space in comparison to where I was. I needed your positivity at the time as I was in such a low place.*

Changing my inner voice has been the first step for me towards finding safety and love within.

My sister-in-law Chris emailed me:

> *In a world of 11+ exams, tutors and competitive parenting, Coraline's arrival has shown me that love and care for your child reign supreme when considering their needs.*

I replied: "Oh I love this. I recently listened to an excellent podcast from Lewis Howes interviewing professional surfer Mark Mathews who said something along the lines of not to compare yourself to anyone else, only to how you were yesterday."

Over the years I have heard this same sentiment many times about only comparing your progress to yourself, especially in the sporting world, and that is an anchor for me.

I am happy that Coraline inspired that thought for my sister-in-law that it all just comes back to love. As that's what it does come back to, and it's the abiding thing of everything Coraline was teaching me; that all things come back to love. This started with loving myself. That's the biggest lesson I have learned parenting Coraline. It is about learning to love myself just as I am, and our life just as it is. Though, I'll add that line in again: if there's something I want to change in life, and it's something I can change, then I change it.

Chapter 12:

Learning from those around us

We had a check-up appointment with Dieudonné and all was well. Our continued contact with him at routine appointments infused our first year with Coraline with the same feeling of relaxedness as when we first met him.

Due to all the insights we continued to receive from family, professionals and friends, I asked a few of our friends to write guest posts for my blog. I wanted to share with others their words which had meant so much to me, to give a flavour of the backdrop that had been around Coraline since she was born. I looked forward to Coraline reading their pieces when she was older.

The first one I received was from one of the eTwinning Ambassadors, Sharon, a lecturer in Education, and she wrote it all about Dr. Seuss's book *Oh, the Places You'll Go!* which she had given us as a gift after Coraline was born. She said of it in this excerpt from her piece:

> This book is my life book and one I gift to all I know due to each page being a different page of our lives. It is not a linear book as one can stay stuck on one page, jump to another or revisit a previous page, just like life.
>
> Dr. Seuss's book sits in my bag and at different times I take it out to see which page I am on. The book is not a linear story of life where each page represents a different chapter in life. Instead, it is a book that represents the sudden changes in life that are passable, returnable and fragmented.

> The reason I gave Liz this book for her, Kevin and Coraline, was to let them see that no matter what they will face there are places to go.

Sharon, a talented musician, had said to me in an email, "Always sing and use music as it is a way of communicating, recognising sounds and words, etc. and most importantly connecting with each other. Remember rhythm and music are the foundations to the development of language."

Funnily enough, we had a song we sang to Coraline from her speech therapist, to be sung twice a day whilst also touching her face in directed steps, which was to normalise sensation and "warm up" for speech. Music had formed a huge part of Coraline's life since she was born and does to this day. In fact, the central part; her whole demeanour changes when she listens to music. This began as nursery rhymes and now that she is eight her number one is Taylor Swift. She does not have an awareness of what a pop star is, or who Taylor Swift is, but she bounces up and down to her music or rocks back and forwards to it in the car. She is fully in the moment.

My first Mother's Day came around that March. I had travelled a lot for work, to the extent that people would often be saying to me in my 20s and 30s, "I can't believe you're off again." I threw myself hugely into every trip; immersing myself from the moment my feet stepped off the plane (or even on the plane – I love planes!) and getting excited beforehand. I have been so fortunate in the jobs I have had that I travelled often for work. I come alive with travel. I adore it to this day.

I saved up and travelled at any opportunity for personal holidays too. In the three years before Coraline was born, I took an annual trip to Los Angeles. I wanted to maximise the fact that Ed lived there for those years.

On my visits to his sensational house in the Hollywood Hills, with its balconies overlooking the cityscape of Los Angeles, I felt aglow. I had my morning coffee next to the hummingbirds on his balcony; jogged down Mulholland Drive, marvelling at the houses there; delighted in ice from his fridge's ice machine;

and sat on his sun-drenched balcony gazing at the view of the cityscape in the distance beyond the hills. That is really how it was! Not to mention all the hilarity and escapades we had on my visits. The first time I went to visit him in America was with Payne and her partner; the second time alone; and the third time with Kevin. On each of them we took stunning road trips to places like Yosemite, the Grand Canyon, Zion and Sedona National Park. These were dream trips and my heart burst with how amazing it felt to be there.

I realised that I had not been on a plane in ten months. And this was all still before COVID. For me, this was a long time.

Ed had moved back to London in early 2018. I thought to myself on that Mother's Day that had he still been living there and, if I were to go again on a fourth trip, who would I take? My daughter Coraline, because in March 2018 I could say, for the first time, that I was a mother on Mother's Day. In reality, though, I would not have been able to take her due to her pending open-heart surgery. I had a catch-up with Ed, Sophia and little Coraline. We sat together in a Dim Sum restaurant near Waterloo station.

"One thing I am a bit nostalgic for is the travels," I said to them, "but I don't mind too much as I know we will resume them. We will wait to go on planes as a family until Coraline is older and stronger, given her heart checks and such. Plus, I know we will go all out when we do go; we will take her on the wildest of adventures and explorations!"

Sophia replied, "If you want to go away on travels, what is the feeling you're looking to get?"

Without missing a beat, my words tumbled out: "Excitement, wonder, can't wait to explore, love everything, love everyone I meet, so many new sensations, so happy. Of course it's not like that all the time; they're just the overarching feelings."

"Can you create those feelings right now?"

True enough, when I stopped to notice, I could have all those feelings about my life, and all that was around me. I could look at Coraline and marvel at her. I could stop and look at nature. I knew that I felt for Coraline a kind of deep love that I had not experienced before, like another geological layer in soil! Being a mother had also made me appreciate my own mother and realise what her love for me might have been like.

The other thing about Coraline was that I was learning about life through her. Every day I was brought back to what matters in life, and that presence in my life could bring about those sensations I felt when travelling. That is if I chose to notice what I already had around me instead of wishing for what I did not have.

I replied to Sophia, "It's about enjoying, noticing and being present in the little things and seeing them with the same eyes as I do when I'm in the Hollywood Hills isn't it?"

Our first Down Syndrome Awareness Week was coming up that March, and the theme for the week was "Inclusion Matters". We invited friends and family to join the #LotsOfSocks campaign for World Down Syndrome Day, which takes place during Awareness Week, the idea being to wear colourful odd socks since when chromosomes are lined up some say they look like lots of socks hanging on a washing line.

When people wear odd socks on the day it sparks conversation. If people ask us why we are wearing odd socks we can help raise awareness and tell them about World Down Syndrome Day. We received so many pictures of our friends and family wearing them that first year in 2018 and we have taken part every year since.

I continued to share my friends' words during Down Syndrome Awareness Week:

March 2018: "Yes you can!"

Friend: Susie (Susannah Rodgers MBE)

Tell me about yourself

I am Susie Rodgers, a former Paralympic swimmer who competed in two Games in both London 2012 and Rio 2016.

How do we know each other?

I know Liz from the British Council and our overlap on the Language Assistants team many years ago, my first job at the Council…Pretty much the whole time I knew Liz I was training regularly around my job and she watched me go from winning three bronze in London to a gold and two bronze in Rio.

She also was there for me when I decided to retire from sport and Liz, Bryony and I would meet to do a regular meditation every day in the office. It really was helpful when I needed to get my head around such a huge change and transition.

Liz at the same time, found out that she was pregnant with Coraline and we continued our meditation throughout.

Talk to me about "Yes you can!"

I have a disability myself. I have a congenital deformity of my right foot and a through-knee and below arm amputation on the left side. All of this occurred at birth. My parents had no idea and when I was born, it was a huge shock for them. I don't know what they went through of course, but I know it changed their lives.

However, 34 years later, Mum and Dad both say how amazed they are at how much I have packed into my life and the different challenges I have taken on. I told Mum about Coraline when she was born and she immediately said, "She will be fine. They will be fine". I passed this on to Liz. I think life can throw a lot of unexpected things at you but my parents often tell me how my challenges that I faced growing up, just helped them develop and learn. On a practical level, problem solving skills, lateral thinking but on a deeper emotional level, it opened up their eyes to something else, to a whole other world of joy.

When I raced at the Paralympic Games and won gold, I looked to Mum in the stands and mouthed it was for her too. I looked at Dad as well and smiled knowingly. I met Mum the next day and cried as I hugged her – the first time I had cried since winning. They have given me the best possible start in life and that is all any parent can do. To encourage, to love, to support you to become who you are meant to be.

What would you like to say to Coraline?

Be yourself, be happy and thank your parents, because they will give you everything you need to start your journey in life.

Susie was one of the friends who wrote to us in the first month after Coraline was born. Kevin had said he planned to take Coraline snowboarding in the future. She said to us: "Having a disability won't stop Coraline. She will be just fine with two strong parents behind her. Like mine! I reckon you can get her snowboarding. Everything is possible. I live my life by that motto. When I'm told 'can't' I think 'no, you're wrong'."

Susie had given me a little book for our baby when I was pregnant. She wrote an inscription inside it: "If you can dream it, you can do it!"

After Coraline was born she gave her one of her "ParalympicsGB" red swimming caps from Rio 2016 which we have framed and put up in Coraline's bedroom. On the cap, Susie has written in pen, "To Coraline, this is one of my racing caps from the Rio 2016 Paralympic Games. It reminds me of my gold and the realisation that you can achieve anything in your life – just follow your passions and dreams! You will always succeed if you try! Lots of love, Susie xx."

The next piece I shared was from another colleague at the British Council:

March 2018: "The world is Coraline's oyster"

Friend: Susan

Tell me about yourself

My name is Susan Douglas and I've worked in education for more than 25 years. I'm lucky enough to have two jobs! One at the British Council as Senior Schools Adviser meaning that I work with policy makers and practitioners in lots of countries around the world and secondly as CEO of the Eden Academy.

The Eden Academy is a group of five special schools in West London catering for children with complex needs.

How do we know each other?

We met each other at the British Council. My overriding memory of you is that you were always so positive and you were always smiling!

What did you write to me/say to me in the early days of Coraline's arrival?

I told you that my key piece of advice was to avoid, as far as was sensible and possible, the temptation to join in with those who would want to categorise Coraline.

I told you that I had been inspired by, and completely subscribed to, the social model of education. In that model, we take a look at what a child's needs might be and ensure we adapt ourselves to suit them, removing barriers that we might come across in the process. This is in contrast to the medical model which seeks to identify what is "wrong" with a child and then looks for ways to change them to suit how we see the world and its systems.

I told you that I thought it was easy for people to say "this is the best thing to do for a baby born with Down's syndrome" but that that was a dangerous and potentially damaging thing to do. It would be like saying "this is the best thing to do for a baby with a certain hair colour…"

So, my advice was to focus on these two questions:

· What does Coraline need now?

· How do we adapt the way that we see the world to ensure we enable and empower her to be the best that she can be?

Talk to me about "The world is Coraline's oyster"

There will be medical things that are similar across the piste because of the chromosomal make up. But there are children with Down's syndrome who will be beautifully suited to mainstream education (and who will get qualifications) and others suited in a special school setting such as ours. That's a way away. The key thing to ask now is what does Coraline need? What can she achieve?

"How do we adapt the way we see the world to ensure we enable and empower her to be the best that she can be?"

The social model of inclusion is surprisingly simple and obvious and yet when someone first explained it to me (far too far I should say into my teaching career!!) it changed my outlook on education but more importantly on life really. It may sound a bit melodramatic but it really was true...all I had done to that point was try to ensure that all the children I met filled a particular space, got particular levels, achieved a particular grade...

What utter nonsense! If we had achieved that – and fortunately we haven't – we wouldn't have the brilliantly diverse, brilliantly eclectic society we have. What a terrible thing it would be if we forced everyone to be the same and yet that's what much of our society (and certainly our education system) seeks to do. If you can free yourself from those constraints then the world is your (and Coraline's) oyster.

So...the key question is...what is the barrier that I need

to remove to make sure that Coraline takes her next step successfully?

What are you passionate about?

Education – and ensuring that all children get the best possible deal in terms of accessing and engaging in that education. Oh – and I quite like my husband and my dog too!

What would you like to say to Coraline?

Anything is possible!

Anything you would like to add?

Just how much I have enjoyed reading your blog and seeing you and your family growing together. I have no doubt what a happy family environment you have created and I can't think of a better start for Coraline. She's a lucky girl. This is parenting plus – so it won't be without its challenges but will potentially be even more rewarding as a result.

I received messages from Susan when Coraline was about three weeks old encouraging us in the same way she has in this piece she wrote, and it was almost like changing a lane in a motorway after reading her messages in those early weeks. I also felt honoured Susan had written to me as she is someone senior I had very much looked up to at work and is a lively and captivating public speaker.

In 2021, Susan received a CBE (Commander of the Order of the British Empire) for Services to Education. When we did come to a time when we, together with Coraline's lovely local mainstream school and therapists, felt that a special school would be the best move for Coraline when she was five years old (though the move did not happen until she was seven years old), Susan was there. She gave her time freely to me to talk it through on a phone call. In our conversation then she reminded me, "it's about removing the barriers to communication".

That March when Coraline was seven months old, I went into the hospital together with Coraline and a member of our local parent-run charity 21&Co and one of her daughters. I was still not yet taking Coraline to any of 21&Co's groups but had formed a connection with them. We met with midwives from the hospital on behalf of 21&Co. I had also been invited to do this by Susana, Coraline's consultant obstetrician.

The meeting was to chat through all our thoughts around language used when giving news to parents based on our own experiences, and a document of suggestions for maternity unit staff drawn up by members of 21&Co. We also gave them new-parent bags to give out when new babies were born who had Down's syndrome which was brilliant – the kind of personal bag I'd have liked to have received. 21&Co is involved with a national initiative written by parents for parents called Positive about Down syndrome (PADS). PADS has an excellent website of parents' stories, for parents and parents-to-be, and we gave the hospital posters and postcards from them.

It was a privilege to be involved in this meeting at the hospital and to be able to have an open discussion and share how the experience had been for me personally. What is interesting is how everyone, and as such their experience, is different too. The lady I was with from 21&Co said she wanted to be in a ward with other families after her daughter with Down's syndrome was born, whereas I said all I wanted was to be in a room on my own. This prompted the midwives to think to ask parents what they needed. On the point of language, we discussed things like at the screening tests using the words, "chance of Down's syndrome" as opposed to "risk of Down's syndrome" as each choice of word shapes the associated feeling.

PADS went on to print a beautiful book called *#NobodyToldMe: The truth about Down syndrome* in summer 2020. It is filled with parents' own stories. In fact, Coraline snuck into it as there is a little picture of her on the collage of photos on the back inside cover.

There is another beautiful book too, *Wouldn't Change A Thing*, by the charity of the same name with photographs and quotes from parents, published in September 2019 when Coraline was two years old.

Our Home-Start volunteer Tracy saw Coraline change from lying on her baby activity mat, to reaching up for her toys. She then got a full-time job so had to stop volunteering, and she said to us during her penultimate week, "I've never heard her cry. She's so content, isn't she?" On her last day she said, "She's adorable," just as she said every week to me and to Coraline whilst Kevin was at work during the day. This is exactly how Coraline was as a baby, very easy, though I did not realise it at the time. Now that she is older, she has many quite pronounced sensory reactions and behaviours, but she did not have these as a baby. We missed Tracy.

After Tracy finished up with us, we were appointed a new volunteer, Christine, and Kim – brilliant and lively – became our co-ordinator for Christine's visits. How lucky we were that Christine was thoughtful, wise and kind, and I could open up to her in our conversations generally, and especially in the run-up to Coraline's prospective open-heart surgery.

Organisations like Home-Start spread such great energy. I realise now that Home-Start changed my resilience and appreciation of what I had during a time when I was not free to do much due to Coraline's health considerations.

Chapter 13:

Confronting comparison

When Coraline was seven months old I received this email from my pregnancy yoga teacher, Licia. She had met Coraline at the hospital when she was two and a half months old:

> *I had a look at your website and it is amazing…Coraline looks lovely. I feel privileged to have met you as your experience has reminded me to watch out for judgemental moments.*

I understood what she meant as I myself was navigating the biggest word of them all, "comparison".

We had recently begun weaning and Coraline was now having purées. Coraline's physiotherapist explained to us that gross motor skills underpin fine motor skills for eating; everything was connected across the therapies we were doing. Coraline had a tomato chair to support her body when she was eating as she did not have the muscle tone to sit up in a highchair. We were examining and working on each stage of development, as opposed to not particularly thinking about how it happened. I saw that other babies were reaching milestones effortlessly, and that we were working on each one.

At eight months old Dieudonné said that babies with Down's syndrome can be three months behind developmentally and that at 18 months old, as paediatricians, they might expect development to be up to six months behind. But that it was important not to generalise.

At this stage Coraline's development was a few months behind other babies, so it wasn't so much of a marked difference.

I compared on a high level, but I was relaxed as I felt she'd still be meeting all the milestones, and I'd see life wasn't that different after all. But as the years went on, she hadn't, or didn't, or her sensory set-up was quite all-consuming.

What I have learned now that Coraline is eight years old is that whether she meets a milestone – like speaking, swimming or riding a bike – or whether she doesn't and never does, it doesn't matter. What matters is her being herself and loving herself.

In years to come, my companion since Coraline was born, *comparison,* was perhaps at its most virulent for me when Coraline was about five years old as the developmental gap had continued to widen. Our private occupational therapist said that Coraline's motor skillset was developmentally the equivalent of a 14–15-month-old. Every day my eyes trained on what typical children were doing, "Oh they are walking to school, they get up themselves, they get dressed themselves, they are watching movies, they know what Easter is, what Christmas is, they can unwrap presents, they are scooting around, they are riding bikes, they are speaking, they can draw, they go to after school clubs, they can sit and eat with a knife and fork at restaurants and chat to those around the table, etc. They can conjure up games together, and chat them through, they sing rhymes to the games." The crescendo of this voice in my head was like a record playing in the background. A broken one.

And what was wrong with Coraline not doing these things? Maybe it was all about me and the fact I longed for this kind of engagement? Maybe I longed for things to be quick and effortless? Maybe I was still trying to control how things were meant to be?

Now, I do honestly feel free of it, and that has only happened in the past couple of years as I have invested in my own self-love and self-care, which has the ripple effect of me releasing any feelings of comparison. Don't ask me how that works, but it's the case.

When Coraline was about eight months old she began babbling and her speech therapist told us to mimic the same sounds back to her so she would learn about copying sounds and turn-taking. She would also feel confident that we were listening to her and understood her. Just as with other developments, Coraline's babbling stopped and then reappeared when she was five years old, when we mimicked back to her the "b" and "d" sounds she was making. Now at eight years old Coraline is making loud sort of grunting noises and ever so occasionally the "b,b,b" letter sound but no other letter sounds and no words! It is not linear, there is no predicting.

The answer, when Coraline was eight months old, is the same as it is now that she is eight years old: that I just needed to engage with Coraline on an energetic level. It was not about what we were doing, it was about being.

So, what is the opposite of my day-to-day comparison? To me, an opposite feeling is acceptance, trust and embracing ourselves as we are.

Sophia used to say, "There's a reason you are where you are. There's a bigger picture going on. Life puts you somewhere. Trust. Be in the flow. Trust life is looking after you."

One of the most oft said things by people to me since Coraline was born is, "Trust your instincts".

From my mum to the midwives who visited when Coraline was a couple of days old, to a friend who said to me when Coraline was eight months old, "You know what is right for you and your child."

My mum told me to remember Dr Spock's first line in his book *Baby and Childcare*: "You know more than you think you do."

I like that the first chapter that line is from is called, "Trust yourself and your children" (I don't know enough about Dr Spock to comment on his philosophies, but I know I love this line).

I was shopping in the local supermarket, and a lady called Caz came up to me and said, "I am a childminder, and I would love to babysit your child." It was so funny! When you recognise that somehow life engineered this timing. Caz babysat Coraline for about six months, including at our upcoming wedding that we were starting to plan, before she got a childminding job with longer hours. She had a fabulous energy and attitude which inspired us.

The little WhatsApp group I was in with my antenatal group friends was very much the backdrop to my day-to-day life. I said to her one day when she was at our house babysitting Coraline, "I love my antenatal group because with them I feel like I am just one of the gang."

Caz picked up on my tone and replied, "You *are* just one of the gang."

Her words made me stop and reposition my own thinking. Until she said that I had enjoyed the idea of "feeling" like one of the gang, but actually underneath I felt conscious of being a little different. But her words were as simple as turning that around for me and were pretty pivotal for my thinking. We were, quite simply, a part of the gang!

As Hamlet says:

> *There is nothing either good or bad, but thinking makes it so (Hamlet, Act 2, Scene 2)*

Or, as Sophia used to remind me, "It's all about the story you tell yourself, and you can choose to tell yourself a different story."

At the antenatal classes, it was important for me to be, first and foremost, a mum in a group of mums who all knew each other from pregnancy, and who all chatted away about their children, one of whom was Coraline. I was one of the gang, as was Coraline.

Looking into the topic of comparison, and the feelings it creates, has shown me that the way to experience different feelings is by choosing a different perspective.

Perception is a tool I have, and one I can actually use to great effect. I can stand back from my thoughts and think, "What is my perception of this situation bringing me? What am I feeling in my body? How am I feeling about myself and about life because of this perception?"

That's another thing about perspective; I can look at all the ways I feel I'm not doing the right thing. I can come up with a list of 20 things in my head that haven't gone right. Or I can list 20 things that have gone well. It's a simple choice, and it leads to a completely different feeling. It's about what I focus on. Sophia said to me during our coaching years:

> *You can't think a good thought and feel bad. You have a conveyor belt of thoughts, and you create an experience with those you choose to pick up. You have always got a choice to simply let thoughts go and allow new ones to come in.*

Chapter 14:

Coming into ourselves

A place I loved to dip into during Coraline's first year were the "Dear Mom" letters from Dear Mom Conference on Instagram from mums to other mums who have a child with Down's syndrome. This is one of my favourite Instagram accounts to follow as each letter is beautiful. Kevin and I were delighted that they featured letters from both of us in May 2018, as they had been inviting dads to write letters that month too. I began my letter as follows:

> Dear Mom,
>
> I love you! That's all you need to know, and all you need to know you will know! Love is what it all comes back to. And love will be all around you…

Kevin told our story in his letter and wrote about how I was as Coraline's mother. He finished it by saying:

> Liz already knows what I think of all that she does, but I want to shout it loud as I am so grateful and in awe of all that she is, and all that she does.

It wasn't just Kevin and I who were writing pieces. Coraline's Grandpa, my dad, also wrote a musing that May as a guest piece for my blog:

> I remember clearly talking with Liz and her younger brother Ed before Coraline was born. What did I think she would be like, they asked? A surprisingly vivid image came

> to mind. I said that I thought she would be unusual, with a distinctive presence, and would influence many people in unforeseen ways. She would be gentle and idealistic. She would be self-possessed and have a deep inner calmness. Those were not the exact words I used but, I think, reasonably close to what I said and felt.
>
> The extraordinary thing is that Coraline's little life is already evolving along precisely these lines. People respond to something special and unusual in her. I love her little, gentle cry and the way she can fix her gaze on you as though she is peering into your very soul. Her sense of wonder, concentration and connection with the world around her are beautiful.
>
> What would I want to say to Coraline? That she is a blessing, and that she has chosen her parents wisely! And that we will love each other deeply.

I can still see that moment my dad describes in my mind's eye, sitting in his kitchen, in the Shropshire Hills, one I had visited so many times, one where I felt so at ease and could admire the nature and clear air all around, when Dad said the words, "She's going to make a bit of a splash." Ed and I both laughed and laughed at that as Dad is often prone to exaggeration! It turns out he had chosen just the right phrase.

A friend, Annari, wrote to me regarding my blog: "I suddenly remember among the gloom that your site is like a resource hub for when I feel lost."

What a thing to hear, that the website where I was storing my blog posts and my writing could work on many levels for people generally. It felt like a reminder of our value in life, and the value of our words and relationships, especially as I was still adapting to how our life was different to how I had expected it to be. "So just keep doing what you are doing. So much love and wonder Liz. Keep Writing. The strands you spin stretch out way beyond your field of vision."

All went well at Coraline's cardiology appointment that

month. "She's doing really nicely," they said. "We will see her again in three months' time. We would like to keep an eye on her leaking valve which has not changed since your last appointment. Her operation will not be in the foreseeable future."

They also said we could halve her diuretics which was a good sign. Plus, that we could take her out and about more as, if she did get ill, she would be strong enough to deal with it, and she could start building up her immunity. This was big news as it meant we could relax a little on checking everyone's health before we saw anyone. So, we now had the go-ahead to take her to a class once in a while as she'd never been to one – we contemplated a sensory or music class for her! In the end, I chose one which combined the two: Baby Sensory which I lined up to go to soon.

The world began to open up, as we came into ourselves as a family, and we booked a little trip to Dorset. It was utterly beautiful. It was one of those times where the accommodation, the setting and the experiences all worked beyond our dreams. We went on clifftop walks and took Coraline in the sling and had sundowners by the sea.

Coraline promptly caught her first cold after we began to take her out and about more. It was inevitable that she did.

It came, she managed with it, and it passed, which was so good. Apparently until about this time she had been covered by my immunity with my pregnancy antibodies in her system and, at around about nine months old, now that we had the go-ahead from her consultant cardiologist, it was a key time for her to develop her own immunity and for her body to fight infections itself. We learned that colds, and illnesses in general, can last longer for people with Down's syndrome. For Coraline, this first cold lasted two and a half weeks. Her low muscle tone extends to things like being able to clear colds, and this is compounded by her having smaller eustachian tubes.

Coraline had her first audiology appointment at nine months old to check her hearing. Children with Down's syndrome have regular hearing checks scheduled by the NHS due to the possibility of hearing loss. The readings were a little inconclusive as Coraline didn't sit for what they wanted her to do, which was why we went back every few months for her first couple of years.

Behind the scenes of all this, we were also planning our wedding for July 2018, and I had my hen do coming up. We had previously asked the cardiology team if all this was OK and they had said yes. We were even planning a flight on a plane for our honeymoon. We picked a destination which was both close (on the cardiology team's advice), and close to my heart: Montpellier, France.

My hen do happened to be on the day that Prince Harry and Meghan got married. There was a real buzz around London which we were lucky to coincide with. Payne had flown in from Scotland, where she was living at the time. She had organised the day and about a dozen of us spent time on a boat on the River Thames playing hen do games, then on to a table tennis bar, and out to dinner afterwards. Payne knew I loved table tennis and had rather sweetly bought a lot of table tennis bats and had glued printouts of celebrities I liked onto the bats so we each had one with a different person on. Ed came too for good measure; I had a great day doing my favourite activities, with the sun shining. Kevin was at home with Coraline.

In the last week of May, Coraline and I went to the children's centre for the first time. Our health visitors had been great about coming to our house weekly to weigh Coraline, even when it was not something they would normally do. Now we could go to have them weigh her there which was novel. We appreciated their kindness in having come each week. A few days later, Coraline and I went to Baby Sensory.

Whilst comparison reared its head and I noticed that other babies were sitting up by themselves, but Coraline was not, my abiding feeling about my first taste of a baby group was that in one rush I understood what those past nine months had meant not going out too much or to classes. I had thought we didn't miss it at all, but after going I felt a connection and sense of fun. I even met a mum with a toddler there whose older daughter, who was not with her, had Down's syndrome. I also made a fantastic friend and Coraline and I began to meet up with her and her daughter outside the group.

I explained to Kev: "I hadn't realised what it has been like these past months. I hadn't realised it had been isolating. I feel like the world just opened up."

"It's a bit like driving," he replied. "You think you're fine, and you don't need it at all, but then once you get your licence you think, wow, this is liberating, this is great." It was a good job I was taking refresher driving lessons as I had my licence but didn't drive since I had lost my confidence!

Coraline had a calm energy as a baby. She cried for the usual things – like when food ended, or when she got startled by something – but she was very contented. She loved to chew on things and to roll and to feel textures like the walls inside and outside.

She also loved to blow raspberries. Her cousin James said before we stayed with them one weekend, "Will Coraline be doing her signature raspberry?" This was the sound she made at that time. On that weekend visit to see Julian and his family, he took a series of photos which captured Coraline's essence at nine months old. He is an editor and has fantastic photography equipment, nous and skills!

Kevin said to me, whilst looking at the photos, "I think people think Coraline is cute because of her spirit." It's interesting Kevin said that about Coraline's spirit. A good few years ago I was in a time of working too hard on a temporary promotion trying to please everyone and had been signed off work with exhaustion. I felt lost. I had gone to stay with my dad at the time and said to him, "But why would people like me if I don't always please them and always make sure I get everything done?"

He replied, "For your essence. They like you for your essence."

Coming into my essence and connecting with it is key to me shining in life. Experiencing life as my true self means I experience it with joy. Coraline does not think about inhabiting her essence. She simply is. Now that Coraline is eight years old I feel I have come home to inhabiting my essence by setting boundaries as to whether I do or don't wish to do something, and honouring myself.

"I love that bonsai tree; it symbolises our life," Kevin said of his little bonsai tree when Coraline was ten months old. "They're the same age, they both came back from an initial adversity and they're both flourishing."

Coraline's "adversity" had been going into the Neonatal Intensive Care Unit for 48 hours straight after she was born, then our staying in hospital for a week for her to have other tests. The bonsai, meanwhile, had been in our conservatory for an impromptu week in the August sun whilst we were at the hospital. Its leaves went brown and crisp and so Kevin pruned it all carefully and kept watering it until its leaves began growing again. They became rather massive, not like you'd expect a bonsai's leaves to look, but we rather liked it.

I had presented the bonsai to Kevin on his 40th birthday, the day before Coraline was born. I'd adorned it with alternate quotes from Mr Miyagi in *The Karate Kid* and our wonderful active birthing workshop leader Rhian, which I'd hung off its small branches on little tags. The plan was for Kevin to guess which quotes were whose. There was a lovely one from Mr Miyagi about drawing on our own strong roots to grow and not needing anything apart from what's already within us.

How funny that the quotes, and wisdom from them, applied to our lives in meaningful ways now. I hadn't imagined this when I sat quietly crafting up which quotes to write out and hang on the bonsai for Kevin, ready to present to him the day before our daughter was born.

I had been looking forward to our appointment with Dieudonné in mid-June since the time we had made it. This was our last appointment with him as he was going to move to another London hospital. How else to put it but to say I felt my energy (even if I already felt good on the days we saw him) lift that notch higher from a moment spent with him. He had made an unquantifiable difference to us in this respect. After this, our paediatric appointments were also changed from the hospital to seeing a community paediatrician, who turned out to be absolutely lovely.

With all of the recent opening up of activity for Coraline and us, I began to enter the world of travel again!

Payne and I went on a pre-wedding daytrip to stunning Jersey in mid-June 2018. We had champagne on arrival at a breakfast venue and sat outdoors overlooking the sea with a friend who lives there. It was such a precious day. We went for a daytrip as I wasn't quite ready to go away from Coraline for the night. This was my time to be back in an airport, and back on a plane, which I had not done in a year. It was pure heaven. How precious a day could feel and how much I realised I could do, and appreciate, in a day.

Coraline was doing well. She reached out and ate her first solid food of a crisp at ten months old. At the same age she sat up for the first time (all in her own good time). I wrote myself little lists every now and then of the main things Coraline was up to and what she was like so we could remember how she was at certain ages. My notion was nothing is on schedule, all is in its own time; it comes or it doesn't come and we handle the challenges and love the developments just as they are.

I wrote this the day after I returned from my magical day in Jersey.

24th June 2018: Things we love about Coraline at ten months old

1. That she sleeps through the night from 7pm–7am and self-settles. This never ceases to amaze us.

2. We are in contact with medical professionals through Coraline who care for us and inspire us, plus people in the community and at local groups who all spread their energy.

3. She inspires so much love in friends and family.

4. She is starting to really move herself around on her

activity mat – she can move from one end to the other, and she loves to chew the crunchy leaf at the end of the mat.

5. Her babbling – she says a lot of "da-da ba-ba-ba", and smiles so much at us whilst she looks at us intently.
6. Her little laugh which, when it comes, is amazing. You have to work for it! She's much more into smiling at the moment than actual laughing.
7. How she loves to eat, and loves all the purées we give her with enthusiasm and that she has just in the past month started to pick things up from her tray.
8. That she has managed to have a nap from 8.45–10am in the morning on her own and settles herself. This has been for the past couple of months.
9. She sat up for the first time a few weeks ago.
10. That she is going to look incredibly cute in the wedding outfit we have for her for our wedding, which is in a few weeks!

Now, as part of our life opening up, I took Coraline on a train. We had a five-or-so hour journey to visit my dad and his partner in Shropshire, with various changes of train on the way. I hoped to swim in a river when we got there.

This journey felt, to me, like such an accomplishment because it was the first time Coraline and I had done a big journey together on public transport. We were normally with Kevin in the car so that we were not exposed to illnesses.

Those hands we had come to know during Coraline's life kicked into action again that day. They belonged to a succession of different people, people we did not know who we encountered that morning. They took Coraline's pram up escalators for me, whilst I had Coraline in the sling, and up even more escalators, and held lifts for us, and various people lifted the pram on and off trains for me. I saw an amazing dad with his three children and the empowering words he used with them, and I noticed this because I now had a child and was aware of how I spoke to her and around her.

One woman whispered to me, "She's perfect," as we got off the train. Coraline was a great travel companion. She smiled a lot. She was relaxed. That is not the case now. She's loud. But it was the case then.

Coraline and I heard people's life stories on the escalators which they told us whilst holding her pram. One was from a man on the London Underground, him holding our pram, me on the escalator step just below him with Coraline in the sling, whilst he told me about shared custody of his child.

Later a lady told us what life was like in France where she had moved. People felt motivated to share their lives with me. I looked back at them and smiled and asked more with interest.

I wanted to tell them: "We were late this morning and ran here," "We don't do this much; she wasn't allowed to get ill for nine months because of her heart so this is new for us," "I needed you to help because getting on the escalator with both her and the pram scared me," "I'm getting married in three weeks and my head is spinning with all we have to do still, so thank you."

But we only had minutes each time a hand helped. I think my eyes told them anyway. We all have a story and we all have a kindness.

Back home from Dad's, before the impending fizz of our wedding day, surrounded by cardboard boxes containing everything we needed to set up at the venue for our DIY wedding, I spent a night watching TV whilst Kevin was on his stag do. It was the cosiest night, thinking to myself how lucky I was, whilst Coraline slept upstairs in our little cottage.

Chapter 15:

The honeymoon period

Our wedding day approached. Ed had given Kevin and me a wedding gift of two nights at the Petersham Hotel in Richmond. I stayed there on my own the night before our wedding. Payne and Ed joined me for a walk, dinner and a drink that evening. It was stunning as the room had a wide balcony overlooking the river in the middle of an ongoing heatwave.

Kevin and I were to get married on Thursday 19th July 2018 at Twickenham Town Hall. We were going to have a small ceremony for about 30 family and friends, including family from Australia and Holland, and friends from Canada.

It's funny that "Savour the moment" was written in the tiny breakfast jam jar lid which I had with my croissant! After breakfast, a lovely lady named Sylwia, who had been recommended by a makeup artist friend, arrived at the hotel. Whilst Sylwia was doing my makeup in my room overlooking the meadows and river, I could see a wasp at one of the windows repeatedly trying to get out of the glass in front of it, but the window was closed. It brought to mind a story which was part of the goals coaching I was doing with Declan, and I told Sylwia about it.

> *You see that wasp there? It reminds me of a story from the book* You^2 *by Price Pritchett. Have you heard of it? It's about a fly who just keeps on doing the same thing, trying to get out of a window in the same way again and again, but it's shut; and if only it looked a few feet away, there's an open door.*

A few feet away in our room were the open balcony doors. As I finished telling Sylwia the story, the wasp turned and soared out of the doors. Something to remember from the visiting wasp for me about choosing different thoughts.

My dad arrived, ever so proud, and off he, Payne and I set for the wedding venue in a pre-booked car which picked us up.

Coraline was our flower girl together with my niece, and my nephew was our page boy. After we got married, we went on for our reception at a local restaurant and bar. Dad's speech brought a tear to the eye, and he shed a tear during it too. My mum had come, even though she did not usually travel this far, and we noticed how our Dutch relatives, who she had known for decades, sat with her to ensure she felt alright. Some of us went on to a riverside pub in the evening, whilst Coraline went to stay at Margaret and Dave's. The next day was going to be a busy one.

We spent all of the next day setting up for our large DIY wedding celebration party at a former converted church and its halls and garden in Kew Gardens, London. The following day we were going to hold this wider celebration for 150 family and friends during the daytime and then a further 50 guests would arrive for the evening, making a gathering of over 200 of us. I can't quite believe those numbers but that was what we were setting up for in one day!

Family and friends from across the world helped us set up the venue. So many pitched in selflessly. Payne and Ed at the helm and there day and night. When we got to late afternoon, we were all still flying around. Ed declared, "I've worked on enough TV shoots to know that this is going to go late into the night." It did indeed.

The next day our guests gathered in the early afternoon in the garden in the continued heatwave. We had a selection of fabulous canapés, including an oyster stand run by Kevin's bosses, and a huge pork pie generously made by Chef Calum, who was then Executive Chef at Holborn Dining Room, London. Kevin knew him from his job working with chefs across London. Calum had created a 15kg pie for us as one of the canapés. What a pie!

"The food at your wedding was phenomenal. I sometimes find myself daydreaming about that pork pie...," wrote a friend to me afterwards.

Friends handed around drinks and all the different canapés to everyone gathered outside in the summer sun. Some of Kevin's friends from his snowboarding days acted as waiting staff for us and were so cool and smooth, gliding around, making everyone feel welcome.

Declan said to us, "We are ushering everyone into the main hall for the meal and speeches but stay here outside and take a moment just the three of you." Kevin, Coraline and I sat down and looked at each other. Coraline in her sweet little silky dress with a pink bow at the waist. We felt lucky that Declan had suggested this to us. A moment of stillness.

Inside, guests from the UK, Europe and other parts of the world from all corners of both our lives had sat down together. Everyone simply sat where they wanted to spontaneously, and we loved the fact that people made new, unexpected connections and friendships due to where they sat. We had portable fans in there and just hoped everyone wouldn't get too hot.

As the three of us came in and they clapped and cheered, their combined presence in the room cannot be put into words. We had heartfelt speeches and for my bridal favours we ordered small discs about the size of a 5p piece which were for guests to hang on their keyrings. All different colours, each one read "Down right awesome".

Every element had a personal touch, from chef friends providing ingredients for, and cooking, the food. From guests bringing desserts for the dessert table, homemade games on the tables to a friend who owned a brewery bottling us beers with our own personalised name labels on them.

Coraline had her green light for socialising from cardiology and sat right next to us at the wedding. Caz, who'd come up to me in the supermarket, was her babysitter for the day and night. So many of the guests gravitated to Coraline and held her: not least Margaret who never seemed far from her side! Coraline was wonderful throughout, and happy.

We received a wedding message from Dieudonné:

> *Coraline is lucky to have you. Go further. Yes, go further! Be even better in your approach to everything in life. You need no knocking as all doors are open and all ways are clear for you. Keep up the magnificent, joyful, happy life with lovely Coraline.*

On the Monday, we left our house stacked full of presents and set off on our weeklong honeymoon to Montpellier in the South of France. Kevin said once we were on the plane, "If there's anything our wedding week has shown, whatever life throws, just roll with it," just as we'd learned to with Coraline.

We loved our honeymoon trip and all the French friends we saw on it, including Adeline and her family. They adored Coraline and shone love on her. Adeline has sent Coraline a thoughtful gift for her birthday ever since she was born.

In early August, once we got home, we had our two-year anniversary of moving into our house together, followed by Kevin's 41st birthday and Coraline's first birthday.

The day before his birthday Kevin said of Coraline, "She's everything we dreamed of and more, isn't she?"

"She is," I replied.

We celebrated Kevin's birthday and, funnily enough, that evening a ladybird visited us, just as it had on his birthday the previous year, the night before Coraline was born. I looked up again what the ladybird symbolised to remind myself: "…being open to receiving gifts if you get out of your own way."

"Thank you for getting me out of my own way Coraline," I told her on her first birthday the next day.

I wrote to her in her birthday card: "On this day, the day you were born, my heart cracked, and the tears fell when we received the news you had Down's syndrome. Since then, my heart is fuller and deeper than ever. You bring me to my best self. 'My heart's best treasure' – that's what William Wordsworth wrote in a poem about one of his daughters, who is thought perhaps to have had Down's syndrome. You are helping us all to find the treasure in our hearts. You are our girl, you are a joy to be with, and we love you dearly. At age one you possess an equanimity and an equilibrium."

Even when writing this at the time, I had recurring thoughts of how our journey was not what I had expected, and I sometimes dwelled on that. Today I see just how much Coraline is "getting me out of my own way" – I do believe that I am now in a place of embracing our life, and who we all are, just as we are. I am truly living from the heart.

On Coraline's first birthday afternoon Kevin suggested we go back to the ward at our local hospital where we were for her first week. We wanted to go in and thank them for the brilliant care we received. We received such a heartfelt welcome. Many of the staff remembered us which was amazing as we were just one of the many families they must have come across that year and taken such personal care of. Completely by chance, Susana, the consultant obstetrician, was there, and we could spend time and take a photo all together which makes me smile each time I see it.

We thought about what we wanted for Coraline in the years to come: to feel love around her. We knew at one year old that she had it; from friends, family, and from people we didn't know in shops and on trains. We felt it. She, and we, were lucky to have been surrounded by it since she was born.

Coraline was the first child to be born in our antenatal group. At the end of August, Coraline attended her first birthday party which was for one of the babies from the group. Coraline was overawed by the noise and sounds, and Kevin decided to take her out of the room and upstairs at one point as she was crying out repeatedly and loudly. We were beginning to experience Coraline's sensory reactions to loud noise. We had dressed her in a lovely dress for the occasion.

Back home afterwards Kevin was saying to her, "You've got gorgeous hair, Coraline and everyone said it today. 'Like silk,' they said."

Kevin went out for work drinks later that week and when he got home he said, "I've been showing her picture to everyone."

I said, "Oh, to who?"

And he replied, "Everyone, just everyone. She's so beautiful."

Coraline began to hold a toy wand that she had been given and to look at its changing colours, whereas before that she would have tried to eat it. She began to lower the felt covers in the book *Where's Mr Lion?* which had animals hidden underneath them. She began to copy the way we pushed down the top of a spinning top Payne had given her. Her favourite toys were a crocheted octopus and a crinkly book. Already we were slowing down in what we noticed, and what we appreciated.

She loved to eat paper, or grass. Tried to eat, I should say. Kevin was passionate about what she ate; baked celeriac and wild turbot and such. He could bring home all sorts of fish due to his work. Kevin sang for her all the time, and she swayed. Ridiculous, made-up, loud songs. He still does today! We took her out and about in the sling a lot. She had navy blue eyes, and we wondered if they would stay this way. They have. She had 100 nicknames. She still does. We also think Coraline suits her beautifully and are really happy that is the name we chose for her.

Coraline had the best wardrobe of anyone I've met, gorgeous clothes all given to her by family and friends. We had received so many delightful cards and gifts across her first year welcoming her to the world. I had covered sheets and sheets of A4 paper with the names of everyone who had sent her a gift and what they had sent her. It was quite remarkable.

Coraline moved into her own room aged one and three weeks. She continued to sleep through each night as usual. She had a beautiful wooden "Coraline's Room" sign with bright coloured pom poms hanging from it which Greek friends had given her. It took me a little while to get used to the transition as I had loved hearing her gently sleeping at night when she had been in our room. But with the transition, I then loved seeing her again in the morning.

I spent too much time worrying that Coraline was not *playing* or *interacting* or that we didn't *do* a lot, as Coraline did not engage with much. Margaret was the epitome of being in the moment when she had Coraline and that has always been the way. Each time before she had Coraline to stay at her house, she had done everything around the house and on her To-Do list, so she could be fully present with Coraline. Whenever Margaret sent us pictures of Coraline during their time together, Coraline was beaming and glowing with happiness. Kevin and I were discussing why this was, and we said it was because when Coraline was with Margaret, Margaret was 100% in the moment with her, full of love for her, chatting and singing, off to groups or on outings together. Her husband Dave was so lovely with Coraline too and noticed all her interests and developments. All of this is the same today when they see each other.

Margaret encouraged me to use my time when Coraline was with her as time for myself; not running around after my To-Do lists and tidying. I only recently learnt to do so more, as I had always felt I couldn't stop as there was so much I had to get in order. But I see now that it is absolutely the best use of the time as I feel re-energised when I do that.

One afternoon that summer I dropped Coraline off at Margaret's and Margaret again said, "take some time for you Liz". I loved our chats when I went round her beautiful house with Coraline. So, this time I sat in our little garden under our oak tree having some quiet time. A squirrel was above me holding and eating an acorn. I could feel little shreds of the acorn falling onto me whilst I was reading, and it was the best thing in the world. My body and spirit could unfurl.

Ed and I watched a good documentary recently called *David Holmes: The Boy Who Lived*, about stuntman David Holmes who was Daniel Radcliffe's stunt double and was paralysed after an accident on the set of Harry Potter. In this documentary he charts his adaptation to this new reality. Such a huge part of his life was based on his movement before the accident. In the documentary, he looks at how he can truly inhabit who he is now. Something that stuck with me from what he said was that what happened brought him to being present in the moment.

Kevin and I went away for the night without Coraline for the first time when she was a year and a month old. Coraline stayed overnight at Margaret and Dave's. They had even got a little bed for her. Kevin booked our destination as a surprise. The gift of this time was Margaret and Dave's birthday present to Kevin. It was Margaret's way of getting us to do something for ourselves!

We went to a stunning Surrey village about 45 minutes away. We had coffee and cake out, a long walk through fields and went out for dinner. It felt so novel and fun. It was then brilliant to see Coraline when we got back. Margaret and Dave said she'd been a "model baby".

Chapter 16:

Finding my voice

Whilst I had done so well in rewiring my inner voice in my life before I became Coraline's mother, there was a habitual way I had of living my life which I had no idea meant I was not really being "me".

I never disagreed with anyone to avoid conflict. Likewise, I manipulated everything I did to avoid any situations when anyone was ever upset or sad or mad. I also tried to control situations, so they felt "just so". It was intolerable to me that I could ever upset anyone as I felt they would no longer like or love me. I could not bear that rejection. I had spent most of my life people pleasing, saying "Yes". I didn't ever call anyone out on anything that bothered me, as that kind of conversation was too hard to even contemplate. I actually thought how I was being was "me", but it wasn't. I wasn't being true to what I really thought or wanted. I had created a persona which wasn't truly me.

This control I was seeking was an illusion anyway. It's not possible to avoid any upset, ever! And the irony was that after suppressing my emotions so many times, they would then bubble over in a wild way onto those closest to me, past the point of being able to express myself calmly and in something of an alarming manner for the other person. So, my grand plan to keep everything harmonious backfired anyway.

At the root of this was that I felt it was a way for me to feel safe in the world and for me to feel love from people. But I was beginning to slowly see a different way. I began to see glimmers that a situation could be spontaneous, and not what I had planned, or that there could be an occasion with friends or family where someone got angry or frustrated, and whilst I would still dwell on it for days and days, I would eventually see that it was OK. I had moments where I saw that even if life around me was not controlled, or people were feeling emotions, I was still safe. I honestly had no idea before that I actually wasn't really being myself what with all my controlling and still not quite saying what I truly felt to people. I had no idea that this was placing a strain on me in terms of saying "Yes" when I wanted to say "No" to people. But my old life coach Sophia did say Coraline was going to teach me. If I let her.

"What if all you need to do is to be happy? What if all you need to do is be happy yourself? What if that's what you've been looking for?" Sophia said back in 2014.

This was quite novel, given my default in a social situation was to check everyone was OK, to look around, and steel myself to keep everything great for everyone with the result that then I would be happy. But just as you can't keep everyone happy all the time, you can't be happy yourself 100% of the time. That's the beauty of life, as all the emotions, all the moments, are valid and just are. And happiness, when it's there, is all the sweeter and more appreciated as a result.

This approach of just focusing on how I was feeling in a situation, and honouring myself within it, was coming at things from entirely the opposite angle. This approach frees up boundless energy which everyone around me feels, rather than a pent-up controlling energy which I think I am hiding but am not.

Sophia had reminded me in our sessions that what I am responsible for is my own happiness and it took years to sink in. She said: "Focus on you having the best time, really enjoy where you are, and everything else will come with that! You're looking in all the wrong places, the support is from you to you."

I continued to share pieces from people who had inspired me along the way. I was delighted to receive a guest blog post on leadership by Michelle, my old Marketing Department Director from King's College London.

I am fascinated by leadership. For me the key to performance as a team is in valuing the members of it, listening to them and celebrating them. People, and how valued and motivated they feel, are at the heart of any company or organisation. I believe it is intrinsic to the business's or organisation's success. It is about discovering how each person works and what motivates them. Never have I met anyone who could bond a team like Michelle did. I had the privilege of working in her team for two years. She has a nephew with Down's syndrome.

One thing Michelle did after Coraline was born, and for many years afterwards, was to post her stunning outfits from Australia, from one of our favourite brands, Bonds. Michelle was from Australia and had moved back there. This deeply touched us. We love to give little Bonds zip-up brightly coloured onesies to friends when they have a new baby.

In this excerpt from her piece on Leadership for me, in September 2018, Michelle wrote about earning respect in a team:

> I believe leadership is an important skill for all of us, for life, and it applies to parents too. And it's quite simple, or is it?
>
> I've had the opportunity to lead many teams in my career and my approach is always the same. I create an environment where people want to come to work, where they feel valued and safe and have an understanding of where we are going.
>
> My secret is to show respect to all my staff, at all levels. Respect really is the key to it all. The definition of respect talks about admiration for someone's abilities, qualities and achievements; regard for the feelings and rights of others. This goes for children as well as staff. But it only works if it goes both ways. And how do you earn respect? Well obviously you give it, but also you respect yourself. You increase your self-awareness, you gain a very clear

> understanding of what you bring to the table and you understand their expectations of you and set expectations of them.
>
> A really good leader is actually very similar to a good parent. A leader sets the scene for them, provides what they need to grow and achieve. A leader puts the effort in, they celebrate the good times, are kind in the bad times and doesn't take themselves or their position too seriously. You are in a great place, mentally, when you can laugh at your own mistakes. And you'll make mistakes, every day if not every week. And that never stops! But you learn.
>
> I was fortunate to be able to attend the Authentic Leadership Program at Harvard Business School which concentrated a lot on who we are as individuals, what is our purpose, what are our values.

Her words made me think how I was getting to know myself through parenting Coraline, how I was finding my purpose and becoming true to myself living my values.

Through parenting Coraline I was discovering my voice and realising it could have an impact. In 2018 I entered my first national blogging awards: the BritMums annual Brilliance in Blogging Awards (BiBs) under the Fresh Voice category for blogs started over that last 18 months. BritMums is a network of lifestyle bloggers and social influencers.

It was an honour to hear in September 2018 that I had been shortlisted in that category, along with seven other blogs. It reinforced my commitment to, and love for, writing my blog *Coraline and Us.*

More than 50,000 votes were cast across 11 categories for the awards. The fact that the category was called Fresh Voice felt so pertinent to my blog. For me it is all about the voice we use throughout the day every day, to ourselves and to others.

Everything I wrote about was underpinned by my values. I knew that the following factors, quite simply, created the world I experienced: beliefs, focus, language.

I wrote my blog with the belief that we were lucky to have our daughter. My focus was on the joy I saw around us, the love which came our way and on what I was learning. There were challenges, and days, when I felt exhausted and like I hadn't done things well, and it was also important to acknowledge this reality.

If there was a challenge or a problem, I felt all the emotions around it, and knew that tomorrow was a new day. I could then focus on the next best step I could take to feeling better.

Language was key as this shaped my reality. I was aware of the language I used when I wrote, when I spoke to Coraline, and in everyday life. My instinct was to use language that was affirming, respectful, fun, empathetic, interested and caring.

Just like everyone, I complained and blew off steam about things, but this was a state which came and went, and that is the same for me today. It was not a way of talking that I was in as a default. If I was airing something that had come up, that had bothered me, to a friend, I also gravitated towards talking with them about what I could do to help myself feel better or to change the situation, if that was possible. This was the nature of my "voice". It took me far longer to get past a situation or a problem than Kevin, or to override my default "worry mindset". And that was part of who I was. At the times I felt down, I allowed myself to stay in it and said, "This is how it is for now, and in time this will shift."

My voice, to me, is such a huge thing; I create my reality by how I talk. On a wider level I can choose to look at the world around me and see the joy there is, especially in the little things, and in that state that is what comes back to me. Or I can look at everything that is lacking, missing and wrong, and dwell on that. Then that is what comes back to me. And it is only my perception anyway that something is missing. It is as simple as that.

Through shifting my perspective, even by one percent, I have the power to change how I feel. There are no two ways about this. I feel strongly that the language we choose to use shapes our reality in every area of our lives. There came a time when we had a huge amount of paperwork and assertiveness around Coraline's provision between the ages of five and six years old. During that time I began to say to myself, "This is a fight, I've got to do this," and my language made me feel tired, resentful and frustrated.

If I stay stuck in difficulty or in complaining, then this is the energy that surrounds me. How can it not be?

One of the wise eTwinning Ambassadors, Lesley, summed it up in a message to me: "It's called 'reframing' your experience and you and Kevin have excelled in that and therefore the difference in your experiencing has been amazing."

The winner in my category in the BiBs Awards was determined by votes and a judging panel and was announced in October 2018.

Chapter 17:

Inhabiting my values

I didn't win in my category. I told my mum and she said, "Well done! We've always thought you the winner anyway."

Payne commented, when I relayed that to her, "That's a lovely multigenerational thing that your mum said that and that the awards were by BritMums and you are blogging about your daughter!"

Here's a funny thing: I would not have begun writing my blog if I had been going back to work. I would have been afraid. Afraid of drawing attention to myself. Of being seen. Of being anything other than not standing out.

As it was, there was a scheme for "voluntary exits" from my work and I had applied for it, and I was pretty sure I was going to get it. This thought was confirmed when I was approved for it some months after Coraline was born, and I knew then I would not be going back to work instead of returning after maternity leave. Whilst I totally adored my job, I had made this decision because we wanted to move to Devon, and I could not have worked there remotely.

I would not be going back to my floor of 100 or more people, in our building at the time of around 800 people just off Trafalgar Square in the heart of London. I knew so many people who I said "Hello" to in the corridors, on my floor or who I bumped into at the canteen in the basement for lunch.

As I wasn't going back, and wouldn't be seeing them day-to-day, I felt open to write. I was happy for people to read my words from afar if they wanted to and I wouldn't need to come across anyone in the office the day after writing something and posting it and feel a bit embarrassed about it.

Had I been going back, my beliefs around not standing out would have directly meant I'd have never started writing, and I'd have lost out on so much.

It was my belief coming up of "what will people think". Walls I built up in my mind that needn't have been there. But actually, the lesson was to simply be me and to follow my own instinct. I have loved writing about the connection to people on a deep level that Coraline has brought to our lives. I have embarked on something I always wanted to do. Writing.

I listened to an audio from Lewis Howes. In it he said there are three things which stop us pursuing our big goal: fear of success, fear of failure and fear of judgement, and that each of these leads to self-doubt.

It turns out many people I used to work with messaged me to tell me they loved reading my blog soon after I began it, and ever since. I am glad I felt the liberty to follow my heart and nowadays I feel that even if I was in a big office I would still take the leap and write, which is pretty massive!

My voice was centred around my values which I will list again here.

Trust in Life
Openness
Acceptance
Appreciation
Joy
Health
Kindness
Gratitude
Love
Authenticity

I think Trust in Life is a very interesting value; for me it is a case of taking action towards what I want but also having a general sense of trust if something unexpected comes along. Whilst I think I know what's best for me, actually sometimes it's good for me be open to other possibilities. I have learned that with whatever comes my way, or happens to me, life has a plan. There's the word "open" again.

For me I have come to live life with a notion that whenever I have a challenge, or a difficult situation, I know that something is going to come from it; a breakthrough that needs to be had, a direction I need to take or a new awareness of myself and my behaviour that is going to help me. At the time the challenge can feel insurmountable, but I can look at these situations as helping me to grow.

Many of the personal development books I love to read highlight this point. There is this quote I like from the author Byron Katie:

Life is simple. Everything happens for you, not to you.

There is a video where the author and motivational speaker, Tony Robbins, talks about blueprints. The idea in it is that we all have a blueprint for how we think certain areas of our life should be for us personally, e.g. relationships, career, etc., and that you feel out of sorts when your reality doesn't match your blueprint.

His message in what I listened to was that there are two choices here for your life to feel full: either to change your life, or to change your blueprint. Sometimes, however, you can't change your life. The notion he conveyed was that your blueprint is what you believe you need to make you happy, and if you update the blueprint, suddenly your life feels better. He put forward the idea that not achieving your original plan can turn out to be what guides you towards your "destiny". I wrote a lot about my expectations (or blueprint) when Coraline was born.

Sophia used to say, "You have your own idea of what's important but then trust what life brings you and leave space for it. So much more than you can conceive is available. You limit what's possible by putting a ceiling on how things should be. Be open for the creative force of life to come in, leave space for that energy to offer you what it has."

Whilst I was planning so tightly, my rigidity was closing doors. Sophia opened up my eyes with her interpretation: "Trust that life will bring what you need at the right time and make space for that. Trust that life is unfolding perfectly and work with it instead of pushing against it or trying to control it. Magic happens when you are living from the heart."

Appreciating where, and who, I am leads to joy for me. At the heart of that is self-acceptance, and acceptance of what is happening and what I am doing.

I was aware that if I accepted and loved our lives just as they were with Coraline, accepting and appreciating what we had and that we did different things to other families, then life would flow for us. It was a work in progress for me, as with everything, and as I began to do so I freed up a lot of energy.

When I totally and fully accept myself just as I am, and when I choose to be present with my experience and love what's in front of me, well the world blossoms and blooms all around me.

Acceptance also includes my emotions. Whenever I have a flat day or a tired day, as I do (as anyone does), I accept the feelings, allow them and let them be as they are. That's liberating if I've begun to entertain "should": *should* be feeling this, *should* be feeling that. By accepting it, I free up an energy for it to pass, that would have been spent wrestling it, and it really does pass. Kevin accepts it when my emotions boil over as he sees it as human. He feels all emotions are to be felt and expressed. If I had a vent about something, allowed it, felt it, raged against a situation, then I didn't stay stuck in the complaining.

When you begin to think about it, acceptance is everywhere. It is in acceptance of others without wishing to change them. It's about all the everyday experiences in life; those frustrating times when you are queuing far longer than you wanted, or stuck in a waiting room when someone forgot to call your name, or when your appointment was cancelled and you made the whole journey in and they say, "didn't you get the message it was cancelled?". Acceptance that it happened. Or when you drop something all over the floor and have to set about picking it all up. From these small incidences that happen across our days to the bigger happenings in our lives, it's then the realisation that you can't control life which leads to a calmness: "OK, this is what happened, and it happened, that's that; now I get to choose what I think in response to it."

If Coraline feels mad or angry or frustrated, we want to encourage her to feel those things as she grows up as any emotion is OK.

When Coraline was seven and a half, I had another realisation about acceptance. It wasn't that the feeling itself had to pass but that the all-consuming energy of it could pass whilst I could still have the feeling itself. I will try to explain. I was finding some days at the weekend or in the holidays difficult as I did not know what to do with Coraline. There were many things she would not engage with, or she would get angry in a setting that was not routine to her. Sometimes if she didn't like being in a new place or felt overwhelmed, she would go around biting down hard on wooden tables with a kind of rage in her face because she didn't want to be there and was in sensory overload. I had feelings of worry over how she was for her own wellbeing. I compounded those feelings by saying to myself wearily and sadly, "Ah, she could have hurt herself doing that and I can't stop her doing that. We have to go home because she is overwhelmed. We don't get to do anything." Not being able to get out and about for the reasons I have mentioned led to my thinking, "I'm not doing enough with her," but I was caught in the fact that many things she actively did not want to do and she did not engage with them at all. The range of things we did was limited. I often use the expression, "Groundhog Day".

My thoughts didn't help because I would say to myself, "This is hard," and then I would not only spiral into all my, "should be trying to do X, Y and Z with her," whilst simultaneously saying to myself, "you shouldn't be feeling this, you shouldn't feel this is hard". But I couldn't get to that place, and on and on my loops went. I'd get stuck on the fact that during half term many parents I knew could take their children to a museum, to an art club, to a dance club, to see something at the cinema. There were so many little activity sessions advertised in our town magazine, but we couldn't go to any of them as Coraline would not tolerate the new setting, and I had never done anything like craft with her. She simply wouldn't see it or engage with it. I had never held a pencil together with her or done any kind of mark-making or drawing with her. They were working towards that kind of thing with her at school, with all sorts of work to develop fine motor skills. If I took her for a short walk on foot, the level of hypervigilance and effort that would be required from me left me feeling exhausted before I had even begun trying to do the walk, due to her refusing to move on it. At some point Coraline would become rapidly dysregulated and I would be on edge trying to calm her.

Then I had a change of tack and I thought, if I actually listen and validate my own thoughts then it makes a big difference. If I say to myself, "parenting my child with additional needs feels hard because I am hypervigilant at every turn, because there are lots of sensory things going on for her and I worry when she is overwhelmed," then I do feel validated. My own acceptance that it can simply feel hard is, funnily enough, enormously freeing mentally for me. If I simply say, "it's hard," and don't fight that thought, or try to say it is anything other, it frees me up to parent her just as things are. This, instead of spending a huge amount of mental energy trying to tell myself "it *shouldn't* feel hard, you *shouldn't* feel this, you're not doing this properly."

Amazingly, once I've said to myself, "yep, this is hard," the freedom of that acceptance shifts energy in me and I actually feel lighter and click into another gear of, "OK, let's do this, OK let's go with how she is and where she's at, and whilst I might long for us to do other activities, she is not ready to engage with them. We only need to be where we are, we don't need to be doing all these activities, I just need to be with her where she is at."

Then I end up having a good day because of how my energy has freed up. So here is another nuance of acceptance: by accepting "this feels hard" the whole force of that feeling lightens up as a result of my acceptance of it, as I am not wrestling with the feeling itself. It's not that that feeling itself passes, but the intense emotion around it does, and I am able to let go a little.

To know the values of appreciation and joy better, I am going to write about what sits opposite them: comparison. What is the antidote to comparison? Appreciation and self-love. What does appreciation lead to? Joy.

I have mentioned the fact I compared what we were doing to what others were doing. I think we all compare. The funny thing is, whenever I do it, I don't feel good. So why do I do it? Perhaps it's just human nature.

Coraline was just over a year old. Fast forward to when she was two years old. Kevin and I saw other two-year-olds walking, talking and scooting, where Coraline was not. Fast forward to now at eight years old and we see other eight-year-olds going on long walks, talking, cycling, scooting, playing sports and more. So, what feeling does comparison promote? A wistfulness. A feeling of "lack". And nothing is to be gained from coming from a place of lack.

Now that Coraline is eight, if I find myself comparing, I allow it and think, "that's OK, that's human". Once I have allowed my feelings, I then say something Kevin has taught me, "who am I to judge this moment?" and I focus on having the best possible feeling in the moment I am in. I look for what there is to appreciate.

Sophia showed me that if I have such a structured rule foundation of how something must be, there's no space for something different. "What if there's something equally spectacular and wonderful?" she said.

When Coraline does little things, the sense of wonderment is immense for me. At five years old for example, our days were still a routine of walks in the pram, short walks in circles at the park, books, music and TV, and that was where we were at. Within those days she began peering over the tops of cupboards and stopping to look out of the windows in our house. I had to take a minute as I was so amazed at her new development. This amazement is one that takes my breath away each time I see her doing something different.

At six and a half she began to recognise the letters A-Z with the fabulous guidance from, and structured learning with, her 1-1 at school. She began to look intently into our faces. She took to banging her spoon on the table when she wanted more food. This was all new! She began playing with stacking toys for the first time; throwing them so they split in half and then putting them back together. Again, something her 1-1 encouraged. She then even began storing things inside them. "Wow," was all I could think. At eight years old we have added the local open-air swimming pool to our repertoire and I am so delighted that we have done that. On our first few trips there in the summer I felt like I couldn't go back as she was so vocal and loud because it was all new to her, but Kevin persisted and encouraged me to do the same. And I am so pleased we did as now she loves it and splashes whilst he holds her. We followed our intuition to push on because we knew she loved her weekly swimming at school. Now I have let go of what we do. I go by what is good for Coraline or what is of interest to her. She adores books with animals in them and loves to point at the animals. There is such beauty in doing that together.

If I let go, I allow room for life to hand its goodness to us. I enter into appreciation and then I find joy.

I got to talking with Ed. I said to him: "Why am I comparing? What's the purpose of it? And more to the point, what is it I am after with this comparison? What is it I am hoping for in our life?"

"I think it comes down to joy," he replied. "Being joyous in your life. That's why you're comparing, because you think that other person is really happy and doing so great."

"Yes, and I can just think, 'Hang on, do we feel joyous? Oh yes! Does Coraline in the activities we are doing? Yes!' There's no need to compare, then, as there are different routes to joy, and different expressions of joy, and joy comes from us all appreciating and loving who we are and being our unique selves with confidence and love. Aha! Joy also comes from not stifling myself. I have learnt joy for me comes when I allow myself time each day to do what I really love – to write my book, to walk in nature, to spend time with friends or to be present with

Coraline, instead of prioritising all my administrative work all day. If I feel full from within, then I am free to experience appreciation and joy. Joy comes from Coraline doing the things she loves to do and focusing on what we are doing together, not what we are not doing. Joy fundamentally comes from self-love."

If I do things that bring me joy then I create the feeling around myself, and subsequently that enters into all areas of my life. I am creating the feeling I want to feel first and then getting into its flow. I have found if I put aside a problem, and go and do something I love, I can then come back to it in a new state, and it leads to my seeing it with new eyes and it resolving more quickly.

Appreciation for me comes when I choose to be present, choose to go with the flow and to know that it is the biggest opportunity of my life to shift into appreciation. It changes the feeling of my whole day. There may be challenges, but once I have navigated them, or processed them, I can choose to see what they have brought me for my growth. The other thing is to let go of all judgement. I do not know where a challenge is going to lead me in the future. Or what a seemingly difficult circumstance might bring to me, so who am I to judge it?

My mind is full of thinking and my heart knows the truth. How do I know what my heart really feels? By spending five minutes at the start of every day checking in with it and how I feel in my heart, time sat in silence. It's amazing how this practice allows me to recentre myself. I will often rate how I feel out of ten before spending time in my heart, and I can leap from a 5/10 energetically to an 8/10 simply by checking in with myself and my heart for only five minutes.

These days I recognise the uncomfortable feeling comparison brings as one I no longer want to give time to. And I know the antidote. Self-love, gratitude and appreciation for what I do have. And laughter and joy.

As for my value of health, Kevin was passionate about what Coraline ate, the products we used for her (soap, sunscreen, etc.), and the supplements she took. His wish was to choose "organic" and "natural" wherever possible. He was then, and is now, very conscious of what you put into your body. I had not quite caught up with where he was at, but I knew how important it was to him.

For me the avalanche of advertising and attractive supermarket aisles meant I often wrestled with his viewpoint. "Well, why are all these things there in the shops, Kevin, if they are not good for us?"

"Money," he says.

Kevin has always danced to a different tune. He held fast to his own beliefs about what hidden chemicals in food or skincare are doing to our bodies. His approach was important for Coraline's health and immunity. We read that children with Down's syndrome can have problems with their digestive system and can have a slower metabolism (burning off calories at a 10–15% slower rate when exercising or, to put it another way, a lower resting metabolic rate of 10–15%). Kevin's preference of having very little sugar in Coraline's diet was good in the respect of her teeth having weaker enamel. I personally would have given Coraline sugar as it's what I saw in the world around me, but this was important to Kevin and something he wanted to do, and I respected his choice. When we went for a dental check-up when she was seven and a half years old and they said if she ever needed any dental work done she would need a general anaesthetic as she would not be able to sit for it, I realised the good stead Kevin had stood her in. Coraline has always loved to eat which is great and she likes the wholefood options he offers her. Kevin sees food as nourishing and taking care of Coraline.

In terms of my own health, I realised that if my mind was really feeling these approaches to life, then my body would feel calmer.

My mind influenced my body, as when I was stressed this presented itself physically in my body, such as the skin on my neck or eyelids flaring up with the stress. I could look at calming my mind to help my body, or a new notion of calming my body to help my mind. After years of ignoring my body, and living in my head, I was beginning to see that it was important to pay attention to my body, and to look at it lovingly instead of not even connecting with it. When I did physical exercise, my mind didn't go into overdrive so much, but it was funny how little I did this. One thing was for sure; I could not solve my racing mind with my mind.

I was beginning to become aware of the fact that mind, body and spirit are all connected. I believed that being loving towards myself did wonders for my health. And this was in terms of speaking with a loving voice to myself and eating foods which were taking care of my body.

I thought back on the times when I had been overwhelmed at work and I saw that I was basically living in my mind, working really hard but not exercising or taking care of my body, or paying it any attention. My mind and body were totally separate, and I had no awareness of this.

When I used to see my body as separate, I would do "diets" to try to get it into shape, but they were based on not allowing myself certain things and feeling restricted. I could see this but didn't really know how to move out of it. My eating was also led by comfort eating, which all originated in my mind, in terms of what my mind said would comfort me to eat with no regard as to whether it was any good for my body. The change that was coming about was that I simply wanted to get in tune with my body and listen to it. Kindness to myself and my body.

A few years ago, a friend put up a video on social media talking about kindness where he said, "Kindness is kingly," and that the people he remembers most in life are those who have been kind to him. I liked that Dieudonné said that he treats all his patients like he would treat his family. Kindness, kindness, kindness. It is one of the most important values.

Kindness to others is something I live by. I could see what a difference kindness made to others, and to me when people were kind to me. So why not be kind to myself too starting with the way I talked to myself?

Gratitude was something I had begun during my pregnancy with Coraline and had been aware of before. Each day I made time to either think about, write down or say aloud what I was grateful for.

I knew this had infused my outlook on life when, one day, in the morning, recently I was journaling, I looked down and felt very grateful for my cup of coffee, my water, the tray they sat on which a dear friend had given me, and the fact I was sitting in a safe house drinking them. I felt that my eyes were looking differently.

My hope before Coraline was born was that I would love being a parent, and my idea was that the key thing was to pour love into my child. I felt that it was all about love and surrounding my child with this. I had been interested in becoming a mother, and of course I wondered what it might be like, how I would be, and how life might change. I read so many books about parenting before Coraline was born.

What did I feel was important before I had Coraline? To pour love into my child. What I realise more than ever, when I am dancing in comparison, putting myself down, or tired, is that it boils down to love and celebration of my child for who she is, and love and celebration of myself for who I am. Both halves of that sentence are equally vital. I perhaps might not have realised that to the degree that I have had I not parented Coraline.

Everything is about love. Choosing the path of love over the path of fear. I still often chose fear, but I do my best to bring my thoughts back to love each time.

Everything I needed was within me. It was just about kinder thinking to myself. All I needed was self-love; everything shone with that. Everything shone when I was authentically me.

My brother Ed said, "You know what, it takes us 40 years of achieving to actually realise the goal of life is just to be happy."

Chapter 18:

Inspire Coraline

Life and practicalities continued. At one year and one month old Coraline went to the dentist for the first time, as they said it was good for her to get familiar with going there. She had no teeth.

I found it very interesting that Coraline, and other babies with Down's syndrome, would expect to get teeth coming through between the ages of one to two years old. For typical babies it's from six months old and usually in a certain order (generally bottom central incisors first). For babies with Down's syndrome, they come later and in a random order.

Our appointment lasted about a minute and thirty seconds.

It was good fun, and they said to start swishing a bit of toothpaste about in her mouth so she would get used to the sensation in advance of her teeth coming in, when we would begin brushing.

The later appearance of her teeth didn't affect weaning, which she began at the usual time of six months. As it turned out, Coraline's first teeth appeared when she was just over a year and a half old.

Physio became monthly when Coraline was about a year old. Coraline began speech classes with our local charity 21&Co at 13 months old. The idea was that early intervention then would have a positive effect on her later development. Early Intervention is a term we hear a lot about.

The classes were really sweet and fun with objects, word cards, matching things, turn-taking and sitting in little chairs. Teachers Tatty and Susie explained that there would be lots of visual activity and repetition in the classes and that this input would help Coraline's recognition progress and help her reach her milestones. I love that they said the most important thing to do at home was to just have fun together, just as Teresa from Portage had told us.

That October we even flew to visit Kevin's mum in Ireland and Coraline spent time with her Nana who read her stories at her house. Kevin's mother came back to ours too for an October visit; she was great then, and ever since, in making regular trips across each year to visit us and spend time with Coraline.

In mid-October 2018, Coraline and I did our usual journey to the Evelina London Children's Hospital for her regular heart check-up appointment. I brought Coraline in on the train in the sling. We were lucky the journey was so quick each time we went. The station was a ten-minute walk from our house; we then had a 20-minute train journey into London Waterloo Station followed by a ten-minute walk the other side to the hospital. Kevin met us at the hospital each time, as he worked in central London.

At this appointment, when she was 14 months old, Coraline's consultant cardiologist saw that the leak on her valve, which had previously been mild, was now severe. The left side of her heart had dilated, and she explained that with each heartbeat, a quarter of the blood was going the other way. The blood was leaking backwards instead of being sent to the rest of her body; this reduced how efficiently her heart could pump and had caused her heart to work harder and stretch (dilate). The valve leak meant that Coraline's heart wasn't pumping efficiently so less oxygen might reach her body's cells which affected her energy levels, growth and organ function. Repairing her valve would make a big difference. Coraline's consultant decided it was time to schedule her operation. It was set for 2nd November.

We were asked to keep Coraline well in October as she would need to be healthy for them to operate. So, we stopped attending baby classes and so on. Coraline had been going to her weekly speech class for a month and we had to stop going and knew we would need to pause again after her surgery. After this we went on some travels and decided to wait until Coraline was a little older before we began weekly speech classes again. We were also contemplating moving to Devon that year or the next.

We did not share widely that Coraline's surgery was happening beforehand. We didn't speak to other parents that October whose babies had had the operation.

Back when Coraline was three months old, I had spoken to other parents and am grateful to them for sharing their experiences of the operation with me. But what I realised was that everyone's experience was individual, and that actually all I needed to know was that I trusted the doctors, I trusted Kevin, I trusted myself – and I trusted Coraline. We felt instinctively that our experience would be our experience and that's all we needed to know.

One thing I never did – and was not drawn to do around Coraline's heart surgery – was to read accounts online or to Google anything, which is highly unusual for me! Now that the time had come that we had a date for her operation, we knew that we just wanted to experience this as it came. We wanted to feel calm. I felt nervous thinking about how her heart was functioning, as much as I could understand it from what they had told me and the diagrams they had drawn for us. But our process was to visualise her operation going well, and to calmly take care of her in the run-up to it.

We were going to bring with us a quilt that Val, one of the eTwinning Ambassadors, had made specifically for Coraline. Val made quilts as a volunteer for Project Linus which provides quilts and blankets – either new or homemade by volunteers – for children who could benefit from a hug in the form of a quilt, such as children going into hospital.

After we had received the news of Coraline's scheduled surgery, I reflected on our lives during our second Down Syndrome Awareness Month that October.

At 14 months old, Coraline liked rolling, babbling, looking in the mirror, family, our neighbours Margaret and Dave, our friends and Kevin singing. She also liked smiling and laughter. She did not, however, like sudden loud laughter!

I thought about Baby Sensory class. Most recently it had been "Baby Pirate" theme week. The very first time I took her to the class I had averted Coraline's bottom lip dissolving any further a few times, as it was so much for her to take in. I myself had looked at all the other babies about her age, sitting up. Coraline wasn't doing this yet, due to her lower muscle tone. We all sat in a circle, so my eyes roamed around it. How possessed of a strange sadness I was. I wondered if we would go back again to the class as it was a bit confronting what the other babies were doing.

But we did go back. For "Space" theme week, for "French" theme week and so on. And we began to love it. I loved chatting to everyone there and our teacher was superb and energetic. In the classes running up to that October, I watched as the other babies of a similar age were crawling, and Coraline was not yet. I saw babies crawl into the centre of the circle to become more involved. Of course, it was not about me noticing or caring about this, it was about Coraline. She had begun to wave her arms with joy at the start of the class, and this was her development.

I had to shed layers that I didn't know I had, and I had to lose them all in their own time. Sophia told me Coraline would teach me unconditional love when she was born, and she was right. That is what the layers revealed. Unconditional love is about Coraline being herself and me celebrating that.

So, I think awareness months are also about appreciating the parent, or the family, or the person, and the journey they have been on. Stopping to appreciate all that they might have been thinking or feeling over time. I am much more aware of that now for other people who I meet, or simply who I see in the street.

Dawn, who is based in America and writes the blog *Cedar's Story* about one of her children, Cedar, who has Down's syndrome, invited us and others to complete the sentence, "I am..." and take a photo for Down Syndrome Awareness Month. She made a video of the photos put together called *Down*

Syndrome - I am Worth it. Ours was "I am amazing". It had to be this word.

A few years before, we had a speaker called Action Jackson at an eTwinning conference. In his slot at our conference, he told all of us present to say to ourselves, "I am amazing!" Then we all sang it together in the conference room led by him. He even had tiny badges saying, "I am amazing" on them. My one floats around our house and whenever I come across it in a corner it brings a smile to my face.

Across October in 2018, I invited friends and family to write little posts for my blog to "Inspire Coraline" so that she could look back on all the messages to her in the future. I asked them to choose from three topics:

1. Best piece of advice you've been given which you'd like to pass on to Coraline.
2. What has Coraline made you more aware of?
3. Paragraph about someone you know/someone famous with Down's syndrome.

Here's what came back:

A very special little girl

What Coraline and the blog have taught me is how selfish I can be. I forget how lucky I am to have started life on a level playing field, I take so much for granted. It takes a very special little girl to make me realise how lucky I am. I feel very privileged to be involved in Coraline's growing up... albeit from a social media perspective.

Oliver

Joy and Wonder

Coraline. Through your Mummy's amazing blog you have made me aware of just how much joy and happiness one little girl can bring into the world. It's the domino effect you have Coraline: you pass on this joy and wonder to everyone you meet and who reads about you. Me and other mummies and daddies see your developments and beautiful face and we know that everything is going to be alright.

Helen (earlier in 2018 I received an email from Helen to say that she had found my blog online. Her daughter was six days old at the time and has Down's syndrome.)

Follow your heart

The best advice was given to me. Listen to everyone's stories and advice and then do what's in your heart.

Susan

Life is not a dress rehearsal

When I was first thinking about going to Tanzania to volunteer, a colleague of mine shared this saying with me, "life's not a dress rehearsal"...it changed my outlook on life.

Hayley

Can-do outlook

Advice for Coraline and family: Always listen to your dad, rather than your mum when it comes to food – otherwise you'll be eating boiled mushrooms. Fact.

Coraline has made me aware of how it's in our power to embrace all the good things that life offers if we try not to stand in our own way with self-doubt and negative, self-critical thoughts. Seeing Liz and Kevin's love ensure that Coraline has only a positive, can-do outlook on life as she grows up reminds me that I must do the same – for myself. Surround yourself with people who love you and support you to be your best and in turn, love and support those around you too.

Pippa

You can do anything in life

I love the Guatemalan designer Isabella Springmühl. She is so great because she has this personality of showing the world in a great way, and of showing that with Down's syndrome you can do anything in life.

Claudia

Life is about love

Coraline reminded me of what life is about; love. Genuine, unconditional true love. In life, throughout our journey, we usually meet and have different teachers. These are people who come and go in different moments and leave us with some kind of learning experience. They are usually grown-up people but Coraline reminded me that the little ones have so much to teach us and in such a simple, powerful, transparent, beautiful and loving way! Thanks Coraline for reminding me that life is so simple and beautiful because it is all about love, kindness and respect.

Ana Paula

Watch out moon

Coraline has inspired me to see the power of a loving family – instilling in her the belief that she can be or do whatever she wants. That belief that anything is possible. With such strong, loving, supportive and nurturing parents like Liz and Kevin she can go to the moon if she wants. That inspires me to reach for my own moon, and to embrace that same sense of support, nurture and love from my family and from myself. Watch out moon – here we come!

Ed

Rainbows

Look for rainbows. Be brave, be a friend, read, love, trust yourself.

Kaddi

Be patient

Your story is one of love, gratitude, inclusion, celebration and self-belief and it is touching hearts far and wide. So, I have been giving some thought to the best piece of advice I can pass on to Coraline. I have arrived at two little gems that I come back to time and time again when I'm feeling a bit stuck.

The first is "What's for you won't pass you by"...It doesn't get more Irish than that now does it! The second is "Feelings pass". I guess it comes down to being patient, being patient with others but more importantly being patient with yourself, knowing that in life the difficult feelings, the disappointments, the challenges don't last forever, they will pass. They are paving the way for you to shine. Stay encouraged. Trust that staying true to yourself, pursuing your dreams, doing the things that light up your soul, living your very best life will lead you on a path of adventure compassion and contentment.

Karen

A source of love

In order to be loved you need to become a source of love [and] "You never regret a run."

Rachel

There is no better you

When I first heard of your birth from your daddy by email, I swear I could feel the joy in his words from across the ocean, all the way from England to Canada. He was so proud! When I finally got to meet you your daddy bounced into the house, again with a face full of pure joy. At your parents' wedding I could see their faces light up whenever they were near you. You are so loved little girl. Always remember that there is no better you.

Sarah (she sent five quotes from Dr. Seuss for Coraline, all about being yourself.)

Embrace life

Coraline has taught me to slow down and embrace life. It is photos of her magnetic smile that can brighten my day instantly and is a daily reminder to stop and enjoy the little and big things going on around me. Watching Liz, Kev and Coraline and the love and dedication they bestow not only on each other, but to all of us they share their precious life moments with, is aspiring and heartwarming. We need more of this amazing love and perseverance out there!

Kerry

Lessons

At my first job in London, I had a colleague named John who worked in the Facilities department. He has Down's syndrome, and when new staff met him they often made assumptions about his capabilities, not recognising him as a smart, independent man. Using his uniquely cheeky character, he taught us that we must never underestimate anyone.

Coraline is already teaching us all kinds of lessons and I can't wait to see her reaching her goals as she grows up and continuing to make an impact on the world.

Ellie

I decided to go for it and enter another set of blogging awards. This one was the UK-wide Bloody Awesome Parents (BAPS) SEND Blog Awards for parents and carers of children with additional needs. The deadline was mid-November.

Blogs had to be nominated by readers for the various categories in the awards, and then a panel of judges would draw up a shortlist of blogs for each category.

I asked readers of my blog if they might consider nominating *Coraline and Us* for the Wellbeing category, a new category in the awards. I loved what they said on the My Family Our Needs website, who run the annual awards:

> *Once upon a time, there was a group of parents. They weren't just any parents, they were parents who often:*
>
> *Had little or no sleep.*
>
> *Had to give up their jobs to attend appointments.*
>
> *Needed to learn a whole new language of acronyms, sign language or braille.*
>
> *Learnt how to stand up to big organisations.*
>
> *Became self-taught experts on the law, education, social care and health.*
>
> *These parents, are Bloody Awesome Parents.*

What struck me, when I read this list, was that I was now in a world I hadn't ever given any thought to; one of appointments and therapies.

Copious amounts of paperwork and becoming an expert on SEND (special educational needs and disabilities) regulations and the law was not yet something I was doing when Coraline was just over a year old. Her therapies had simply come to us on the NHS in her early years. This all changed in years to come when her Education, Health and Care Plan (EHCP) was first issued when she was almost four years old. An EHCP is a statement identifying needs and the additional support required to meet them, and it is reviewed annually. The legally binding "Section F" of Coraline's EHCP specified the hours of therapy to which she was entitled, and the provision of those hours was the responsibility of the local authority. It should have been straightforward. It was not; it was down to me to step up and become an expert on her rights to ensure she received the provision specified in her EHCP which ought legally to have been in place. It took hours of time, reaching out to helplines and friends who had trodden the path before me, and dedication on my part.

My dealings around Coraline's EHCP with the local authority actually did tip me into a feeling of a "fight" despite all I thought I knew. From the moment I entered the world of the EHCP, when she was about three and a half, until she was about six and a half (when I found a way to change my attitude), I lived in a state of stress. My life consisted of pushing, lists, guilt, overload, desperate attempts at challenging and asserting Coraline's rights and then feeling guilty. I didn't realise the stress I was living in for those three or so years. It would quickly lead me to emotional overwhelm and to sleepless nights, as the process was not straightforward.

The alternative would have been not to challenge for provision for Coraline and for her to slip through the cracks and not get the therapy provision I knew could help her and to which she was legally entitled. I know from friends whose children have EHCPs that's sometimes how it is. They have no more to give and have to step away from the stress of it for the sake of their own health. For me, I persisted but at the expense of myself, unaware of how much it was affecting me until I came to a point where I realised that I couldn't live in that state anymore.

I came to inhabit a new way of being after those three years of intensity. I found out that for me personally it didn't have to be a choice between challenging and not challenging. For me I was always going to challenge if I knew Coraline had legal rights. It was a choice about the spirit in which I challenged: I chose calm assertion and confidence which I could leave at the door and not have a sleepless night over. Things had to change because I couldn't keep living in the stressed state I was in and Coraline would have an EHCP for many years to come. I knew there was a different way. It just took me three years to get to it.

It was my coach Jo who helped me to find this new way. I changed my beliefs around speaking up to believing that I was capable of having tough conversations and that I was resilient, as opposed to shying away from them. I changed my beliefs around feeling that every email or form had to be done *immediately* to knowing that they could wait, and I could take my time over them in advance of their deadlines. If I sensed I was tipping into overwhelm I caught myself and did something physical, like a dance, to interrupt the pattern. I prioritised self-care and focused on bringing back joy and fun to my days, in addition to my admin, and this had a huge knock-on effect; my tired energy began to shift and I felt lighter. I set boundaries around my time and what I chose to do based on what was right for me, rather than on pleasing others. I discovered that the main thing was to speak up, and I couldn't control other people's reactions after that and wasn't responsible for them. And the big one, as I began to honour myself, I began to derive my validation internally, not externally.

Chapter 19:

Coraline's heart surgery

Thursday 1st November arrived, the day before Coraline's open-heart surgery. We had a day of pre-assessment for Coraline. I took a photo of the Evelina's values which were on a poster on the wall:

Put patients first: "what would I want for my family?"

Take pride in what we do: "am I doing my very best?"

Respect others: "what would it be like if I was in your shoes?"

Strive to be the best: "how could we do it better?"

Act with integrity: "am I doing the right thing?"

How privileged we were to be in a hospital like this, all provided for us on the NHS. I liked it that the values were also there as screen savers on computers. From time to time, I'd look up and see them scrolling across a computer screen in whichever room we were in for Coraline's pre-checks.

One of the elements of our pre-assessment day was a heart echo during which Kevin sang to Coraline to distract her. There is a famous jazz club in London called Ronnie Scott's and the lady doing the echo said, "Ooh, it's Daddy Scott's in here."

We were provided with accommodation next door to the hospital the night before Coraline's surgery; we planned to stay elsewhere in the hospital for the week afterwards. We all had an early night. It was still dark when we went to the cardiac ward the next morning and I sat with Coraline on the sofa in the parents' room waiting for them to tell us it was time to take her down to surgery.

We played with a shower sponge given to us by Teresa from Portage which was one of Coraline's favourite toys as she liked its texture. I looked up and a nurse was at the door: "It's time," she said.

The three of us headed down with the nurse in the hospital's huge lifts. We found ourselves in a room with Coraline's surgery team and the anaesthetist talked us through what was going to happen. Coraline sat on my lap as he anaesthetised her. Kevin and I made sure one of us was at Coraline's side at all times during our stay in hospital, apart from her operation itself. We knew we wanted to be right there before she went in and when she woke up. I kept talking to her as she was being anaesthetised, sat on my lap, and Kevin crouched down in front smiling at her. We explained to her what was happening and that we were with her, though she did not understand the language. "I don't know if I anaesthetised her or you hypnotised her," the anaesthetist said afterwards.

Of course we had apprehension, fear and racing minds, especially as we looked at our phones waiting for word from the team doing Coraline's surgery. But we talked to each other and decided the best use of our energy was to trust the team and be calm.

After five-and-a-half hours, the team called us to say that Coraline was out of surgery and that they felt it had gone well. Kevin and I looked at each other and smiled in gratitude to them and in relief. The surgeon told us it was an unusual scenario as Coraline's body had tried to repair itself, and tissue had formed itself around the lower hole in her heart. Before the operation they had thought her top hole had closed but when the surgeon came to operate, he found it was still there (her valve had been obscuring it). Having two holes in her heart and a leaky valve meant that her blood could flow in the wrong direction both through the holes and the leaky valve, and that oxygen-rich and oxygen-poor blood mixed together due to the holes.

He repaired her valve and both holes, so that the valve could now close tightly and do its job of keeping the blood flowing one way, instead of leaking backwards. Her heart could now pump more efficiently, the strain on it was reduced and it would improve oxygen delivery to her body, which was essential for her growth and development.

After Coraline's operation we had three nights on the Paediatric Intensive Care Unit (PICU) where one nurse looked after Coraline fully one-to-one for each 12-hour shift. Then the next nurse, solely dedicated to Coraline, was on for 12 hours. Either Kevin or I were always next to her bed too. There were four beds for children in the room, each one with their own assigned nurse. The nurses explained they normally had quilts made by volunteers for charities to give to families but that they were running low that year, so did not have them to give out to us. But we told them we were all good as we had the one that Val had made.

The hospital gave us a room in the hospital to sleep in one floor down, as the local Ronald McDonald House where most parents slept was full. Kevin and I took it in turns to use the room, whilst the other sat next to Coraline's bed on the PICU. Each time I walked down or up the stairs to or from our room I saw the hospital values painted on the wall. You can guess who did the night shifts (after sleeping a few hours in the early evening) because he is generally rather adaptable! Daddy Scott.

The PICU nurses thanked Kevin for staying up each night, whilst they took care of everything expertly, and they also made such cheerful comments about Coraline which made us happy. They were tremendous. Each one gave us such a high level of expert care.

I thought about how the NHS staff at the exceptional Evelina London Children's Hospital had made us feel during our stay. Respected and at ease by the surgeon; like we were in the hands of utter professionals, with discretion, empathy and efficiency and immeasurable warmth, by the nurses, cardiologists, paediatricians, doctors, ward clerks and all the other hospital staff. Everything was explained to us beautifully. Our surgeon approached our pre-admission chat with humour and quiet candour. Everyone followed suit afterwards. Coraline was in great hands. I had trusted in them which led to my sense of calm.

An amazing thing they did in the PICU was to give each child and their family a notebook to write in about what happened daily. Each time a nurse or doctor came to Coraline's bedside they also wrote in it. There was a sticker trolley to decorate the notebook, and the nurses took photos of Coraline and us, or whoever was visiting, which they printed out for us to stick in. We had two other visitors on the PICU as well as ourselves: Julian and Payne visited on separate occasions. They both wrote in her book and the nurses took photos. We were sat by Coraline's bedside a lot and it was great to write in it during those times.

I got to hold Coraline for the first time on the third day after her surgery, and they took a polaroid photo which we stuck in. The nurses explained that people had previously said they left the PICU and didn't remember what had happened there, and so they introduced the book.

I realised there is great depth to the simplicity of it too. A friend lent me a book called *The Whole-Brain Child* and at the time I was reading a chapter about integrating the left (logical) and right (emotional) sides of the brain for a child. There's one section called "Name it to Tame It: Telling Stories to Calm Big Emotions". After a difficult experience for a child, or something they are struggling to get past, the book explained that it's important to sit down with them and simply talk through what happened in order from start to finish, instead of saying, "It's OK, that's over now". By retelling it, the left and right side of the brain begin to engage together which starts to bring in logic (left side brain) to the powerful emotions (right side brain) which will have dominated the experience and perhaps set up emotional connections. The left side of the brain makes sense of what the right side is feeling, and the retelling helps that process happen. It even says that telling the story is important for babies as young as ten months old. The book talks about the power of journaling.

Years later, I had two heart procedures myself, for which it was necessary for me to be awake with mild sedation, which was something I never saw coming for me personally. I had Traumatic Incident Reduction therapy after them. Part of it was focused on me talking through each hospital experience from start to finish, again and again. The power of telling and retelling what had happened shifted something in my brain, and also energetically, to the point that I felt as though my system had decluttered and I was no longer living in a state of fear. My body and mind had been able to integrate the experience.

In the PICU we told Coraline step-by-step all that had just happened and why and explained where we were, even though she did not understand words. We will read her book together when she is old enough to understand it. I have re-read it myself recently: what a powerful thing it was to furnish families with. Coraline did not understand language nor, I think, did she understand she was going into hospital for an operation. We did what we could: one of us was always by her side and we talked her through what was happening.

A habit I have in my day-to-day life is to write a journal every morning. I sit down for ten or twenty minutes at the start of the day and write about what happened the day before. On occasions I write a list of ten things I am grateful for. I literally just write out what happened the day before, and actually I see how that can be helpful given what is explained in *The Whole-Brain Child*. Journaling is just something I instinctively love to begin my day with as it appeals to my love of writing. For my own two heart procedures I journaled every single day that I was in hospital about how I was feeling.

We are in touch with one of the nurses, Heather, who was in the PICU to this day; she was from America and now lives back there. She was a nurse to other patients, not Coraline, but we talked to her across the room. She came over to us as she has an uncle who has Down's syndrome.

We then moved from the PICU to the high-dependency bay on the cardiac ward where it was one nurse to three patients, and patients were in beds separated by curtains. The nurses there were also passionate and caring, and they made us smile a lot. The nurses and doctors adapted to us and moulded around us.

At this stage Kevin and I had to move from the room they had given us to sleep in, but the nurses allowed me to sleep in a ward which was not being used by night, whilst Kevin slept by Coraline's bedside as he was fine with the beeping of all the machines around.

Hamza. That's what we named a little lion which Coraline's Uncle Julian, Auntie Chris and cousins sweetly posted to us as a gift to open on the ward. They even sent it in the post directly to the ward. It was such a sweet, surprise idea that they had to do that. It was named after Coraline's neighbour on the ward, a two-week old baby. Just before our package arrived, Hamza's mother had told us about the origin of his name. She said they had learned he had a heart condition before he was born and that they knew he would need an operation soon after he was born, so they had named him Hamza which means strong, lionheart. We asked her what she thought about us naming Coraline's little lion Hamza and she liked the idea. Hamza had had his operation two days before Coraline. Coraline still has her little lion, Hamza.

We met so many skilled, kind professionals who infused us and Coraline with all their expertise and care. We remain in appreciation and gratitude for what they do impressively, daily, for so many. That's also what came out of our conversations with other parents in hospital.

I spoke to one in the parents' room on the day of our discharge whilst he was making a cup of tea kindly provided by the hospital. He said to me, "I now appreciate everything in life so much more, from the care we get, to making and having a cup of tea. I think that about sums it up."

Margaret and Dave came to visit us in hospital the day before Coraline was discharged. The next day, as we left, one of Coraline's nurses said, "She's too cute to discharge." Coraline had been calm during her time in hospital and, by the time we came home, was back to herself.

We were back at home just a week after Coraline's surgery.

It felt so cosy, quiet and comfortable to be in our little house. There were no words for how gorgeous it felt to be home. Or for how grateful we were to everyone at the hospital.

We knew that Coraline would have a six-week recovery period at home where we were advised to keep her well, so we didn't go to any classes and checked everyone we saw was well. We also had to pick her up in a "scoop fashion" rather than under her arms and had to avoid her well-used sling! Being asked to keep Coraline well was a familiar scenario to us, though it required some vigilance on our part.

"Steady." That was my plan for the wait during Coraline's operation, and for when we first saw her afterwards and for the days after in hospital. That's just how I was, to my surprise. The way she, and we, were looked after by the hospital staff supported it. Kev and I were a team, each balancing the other in our ways of being.

Contrary, intractable. That's how I began to feel the day after we got home. I hadn't even thought about this part. Perhaps Coraline felt more fragile or vulnerable to me after the operation than before somehow (though that is the opposite of reality, as the operation meant she could then "go get 'em"). The idea of keeping her well afterwards as she recovered, and picking her up in a special way, somehow led me to worry. More so than I had in the first nine months of her life when we were asked to keep her well (which entailed real supervision on our part). Kevin himself wasn't worried, he just felt she was fine.

Sophia came to visit and said, "Hold your hand against where you feel the worry in your body and feel it thoroughly, sit with it, until you reach a place of safety within it."

I did it. I fully felt my feelings and reached a different place inside them. Wow! I actually began to feel a sense of peace. By feeling into "worried", literally *feeling* worried, I felt a sense of steadiness begin to return, instead of being afraid of my feelings and trying to avoid them.

A couple of weeks after the operation we went for a follow-up cardiology appointment, and they said she was doing great so we could get out and about more. It felt so amazing to hear that.

A fortnight later, in early December, we were back for another check-up. Coraline's cardiologist said she was continuing to do very well. She said we could do whatever we pleased by the end of December.

"Really?" "We can go anywhere?" "We can do anything?"

I kept asking. Checking what I heard was correct. It all felt so free. We had asked them some months previously about some big travel plans we had, and they encouraged us in them. We had checked the timeframes with them around Coraline's operation.

First stop was going to be Australia in January 2019.

In mid-December it was our final cardiology check-up until February. All was looking really good, they said, and Coraline was fit to fly! We texted the family in our excitement.

Grandpa: "Wonderful news about Coraline. Good she can fly."

Coraline's Uncle Julian: "I can't believe she can fly! I have to see this!!"

Kevin: "Who needs to walk or crawl when you were born to fly?"

The night of that appointment Kevin lifted Coraline into bed and said to her: "You're the most beautiful girl I've ever looked at, or will ever look at."

It had been six weeks since Coraline's operation. Coraline had her first haircut courtesy of our friend Nadia who Kevin went to primary school with. She asked if she could be the first person to cut Coraline's hair. It was a gorgeous trim. And then the Christmas parties rolled around which the previous year we had been unable to attend due to not exposing Coraline to any potential illnesses. Kevin's mother had come to visit and she and I attended the Portage Christmas party together with Coraline, and I could show her the wider circle which was around us.

At the Home-Start Christmas party with Santa in mid-December, everyone was warm, friendly and fun. Coraline loved it and began swaying to the music in her pram as soon as we went in.

The day after the party we had our last Home-Start session

with Christine. Our time having Home-Start volunteers was coming to a close. Christine had been a dependable, encouraging presence for me, a woman of calmness, kindness and wisdom. I really enjoyed it each time she came to the house. It was time to end because we knew that the next year we would be able to take Coraline to groups and be more flexible, so we were fledged as it were.

We kept in touch with Christine afterwards, as she was so lovely. I made the decision to volunteer for Home-Start myself in the future, doing what Christine and Tracy had done for us. They had helped us to find our wings and I wanted to do the same for someone else! Christine herself would now volunteer with another family on the waiting list.

We gathered for a family Christmas at Julian's house near Winchester. Julian played the ukelele for Coraline whilst she sat in front of him and gazed up at him, her young cousins by her side. Kevin's mother then came to stay with us in late December as we built up to our big trip.

The time had come for us to get out there, not least to the other side of the world.

Chapter 20:

On our way

On 21st December 2018, when Coraline was a year and four months old, Kevin had had his last day in his job in the wholesale fish business supplying chefs in restaurants across London. He was taking the leap to start his own business making natural soap. Coraline had spent the past months eating the finest fish which he brought home and cooked beautifully. His employers were supportive of Kevin's move and had been so kind to us as a family. They recognised the energy and dedication he brought to his work and knew that his dream was to begin his own business. We are grateful for their belief in him and care for Coraline.

The plan was that whilst he set the business up over the next year, before launching it, he was going to take on sales consultancy roles alongside this. Declan, our friend and goals coach, had been encouraging him in preparing to take this step since the beginning of the year and now it was actually happening.

But before he commenced this new work-life, Kevin was going to take a break. We had taken out a loan and were all set to go on a six-week trip of a lifetime to Australia. For me, it was really important given that so much of my wider family lives there: aunts, uncles and cousins. And we had dear friends we wished to visit too. The prompt for our trip was an old friend's wedding scheduled for early January 2019.

I wrote another of my lists of what Coraline was up to the day before we flew off to Australia, which was also my mother's birthday.

30th December 2018: Things Coraline is up to at almost 17 months old

1. Swaying to music.
2. Sleeping through the night 7pm to 7am (since she was seven weeks old).
3. Sitting up straight, can move a bit towards toys, can get herself from lying down into sitting and vice versa in a wonderful manoeuvre.
4. Playing with her favourite toys: crocheted octopus, small giraffe, shower sponge, ball pit, beads (introduced by Portage recently and she loves them).
5. Drinking water through a straw and holding her own milk bottle, often one-handed (since she was 14 months old).
6. She is now allowed to get out, get ill and explore after her heart operation at 15 months old. She recovered so well afterwards and was back to herself within a week.
7. She is much better with loud laughter which used to startle her a couple of months ago.
8. She loves friends and family, and smiles when people come up to the pram and everyone loves her on our high street. She loves hanging out with our neighbours.
9. Delighting in her dad's cooking: skate curry, roasted peppers, octopus, salmon and more. She has liked everything we have given her so far.
10. Being amazing!

We set off for Australia on 31st December 2018 and transited in Kuala Lumpur, Malaysia. Coraline did us proud and slept in the bassinet for about eight hours, fished out only for turbulence when she needed a seatbelt, and at those times she slept on us. It was such a good move to have been able to book the bassinet seat. We were just on the right side of her still fitting into it. It was so exciting to spend New Year in the air! Given that I love the whole experience around flying on a plane.

My sense of wonder and excitement filled me during our transit in Kuala Lumpur, and when we set foot in Australia on 2nd January, I felt like my heart would burst with how good it felt to be there. We had done it!

On arrival we went straight to my Auntie Verna and Uncle Barry's house in the bayside suburbs of Melbourne. Their house feels so familiar to me as I have visited it over the years on childhood trips to Australia when we were lucky enough to go, and on various trips when I was older. I love it. In the first few days of the new year, I sat on their beautiful upstairs deck reflecting on what Coraline had taught me over the past 17 months.

I used to hold onto thoughts around how things must be very tightly, which felt so important. If these thoughts were a bound-up ball of wool, Coraline had tugged at it and the strands had unravelled. If they were a huge stone, she'd chiselled it away. If they were a ball, she'd chosen not to catch it when I threw it. If they were worth holding onto, I'd have held onto them more tightly. The thoughts? "What will people think?" "I must control this." "It must be this way."

As they fell away, acceptance in the everyday had begun its slow journey towards taking its place in ways so subtle, yet profound. I noticed how I was beginning to act differently in how I responded to a situation. The best way to put it is that my spirit had spread out.

Pippa had recently said to me, "You've changed – you used to hold onto everything so tightly and be so fixed. The change began with Kevin and was followed with Coraline."

The unravelling and the chiselling gently continued as Coraline and I brushed against each other each day. Like a butterfly's wing. A palimpsest.

I felt a new feeling and wrote it down: "Let go, let be, let love."

Our relatives showered Coraline with love and little boxes of toys to borrow.

Two years later my Auntie Verna passed away. This trip was the last time I saw this very important figure in my life. She loved Coraline and loved sitting with her during our visit. It does just show us to grab those moments in life, and not to spend precious time caught up in our heads, or time not being kind to ourselves. I loved her very much. She and Mum were devoted to each other and they had a weekly phone call on a Sunday from their opposite ends of the world. Their temperaments were different: Mum the introvert, Verna the extrovert.

For part of our visit, we spent three days on the Great Ocean Road and in Lorne marvelling at the scenery. This had been the planned destination for our friends' wedding, but they postponed it. Many of us gathered anyway. They married six months later instead.

Whilst Kevin, Coraline and I were out to a wonderful al fresco breakfast in Lorne, Susan – who had written me the guest blog – sent me an email. I read her message aloud to Kevin whilst we were sat at our table at a café across the road from Lorne Beach in the fabulous sun. Susan wrote:

> *I love the fact that Coraline is travelling the world. You post about it as if it's the easiest decision to take but I know it isn't. It's absolutely the right one – I'm so pleased. Once in one of my headships I took children on a roller coaster ride at Alton Towers. Some had Down's syndrome. Some people were furious with me because they said that those children would be frightened...my argument was that being frightened is a natural human reaction and right. We all feel it. To be disallowed to feel this emotion would be fundamentally wrong. To feel uncertain or out of place is OK if you are loved and within boundaries. How exciting that Coraline is being challenged and inspired! You are inspirational. Coraline is the luckiest of children to have you and Kevin.*

What she said always stuck with me. It is funny as her reply actually made me stop and think that our voyage wasn't just a matter of course. I replied to her at the time: "As you say, we feel like we can build a 'home' for Coraline wherever she is in terms of our constancy, our calmness, our happiness, and if we surround her with that, she is safe and can explore. Or maybe it's that we have a sense of her and what she will be OK with."

I understand Susan's words now; I didn't back then. As at that time it felt far easier to travel with Coraline than it is now. It would be much more of a consideration to take Coraline on a trip now that she is eight years old. She is much louder, more headstrong and she has more sensory challenges. There was a period of time when she was seven years old that every transition, even from room to room at home, unsettled her; for example, if she was in the living room and we said, "Coraline in five minutes, food," she would emit a piercing growl. This was the same for all transitions whether it was something she wanted to do or not. We always give her notice before a transition is coming, visually by holding up five fingers on our hand to signify "five minutes". On this trip when she was a baby she was obliging and even tempered.

In fact, the next time I went to Australia was six years later in January 2025 with Ed. We went without Kevin and Coraline. Kevin and I made this decision based on the level of care Coraline would need, and on what she would take in from the trip. We based this decision on our knowledge of her at this time and could not have pictured her doing the flight. But I bear in mind what Susan said to me. Don't be afraid of things, don't shy away from them or keep our world small. As always the right thing to do was to follow our instincts. I sincerely wished Kevin and Coraline could have come too but it just wasn't possible, and we visualise this being the case in the future.

Whilst in Lorne on this trip when Coraline was a baby, we picked up a sunscreen for her at a pharmacy. We thought we had chosen as natural a one as possible as that is Kevin's default, to examine all the ingredients and to choose organic and natural products. However, not long after applying it, half of Coraline's face turned bright red, as if there was one very clear central line down her face. We went straight back to the pharmacy to ask what to do. We wondered if it could be sunburn. But they felt it was an allergic reaction to the sunscreen.

This brought home again how sensitive Coraline's skin was to products. We often think back to this incident as more evidence of the reason Kevin has developed his range of handmade, natural and organic skincare. We took Coraline back to rest at our apartment and I felt anxious, hoping it was just a temporary reaction. I was sad that we couldn't be outside enjoying the sun and the wonder of Lorne, and I felt weighed down by worry and responsibility. My mind entered its loop: "Why is life so complicated for us?" Fortunately, all was well, and the redness receded as the day went on. And we got out and about again. And I got out of my head again. This tricky experience has led to Kevin looking to create his own organic, natural sunscreen in our business Coraline Skincare all these years later.

As well as my Auntie Verna, I spent time with my Uncle Piet and my Aunt Karen, my father's siblings, who were both in care homes. This was the last time I would see all of them, these treasured pillars of my life. We went on to stay with friends of my parents in Canberra and Chris and Debs made the journey to see us there with their daughter Elsden. They had made all the difference to us as our point of contact when Coraline was born, and it was so fun to see them all again now that Coraline was a year and a half old. Nowadays they have a son too.

On the trip Coraline was entirely herself in quieter moments, sometimes overwhelmed in company, sometimes the great entertainer clapping and waving in company, sometimes not keen to settle out in a café, sometimes beautifully settled. Grisly at others' houses! Happy at others' houses. Beautifully behaved on a plane and at other times really loud and unable to settle on a plane! Overarchingly it was a good age to travel with Coraline as she was easy going.

Then, as now, we didn't always get it right. A big thing I've always wanted to do for Coraline is to let her feel my calmness. I want her to feel safe, and cosy, when she sits on me. Nowadays when she's in a sensory spin, I sit peacefully with her hoping that can have some calming effect. We accept sometimes we don't have the answer! On our trip we slowed things down for her if we felt she was getting overstimulated, and we observed how she was doing.

When Coraline was overstimulated at this age it was an entirely different kettle of fish to now, when she is loud and cross. In years to come there was a period of a couple of years when she was between five and seven years old during which she pounded her head with her fist repeatedly over the course of a day, and resisted unfamiliar activities with prolonged, repeated growling. These were everyday things. Over the years, her sensory processing considerations were to become dramatically more pronounced. Kevin and I both found her hitting her head very difficult as we felt so sad seeing her do this, and we are grateful it is something she stopped doing at seven and a half years old.

On this trip, when Coraline was a year and a half old, we had the overriding sensation that it was good for her, and we were proud of her. Time with family and friends, parrots and trees, oceans, waving to people, eating seafood and the bright skies and the sun, she was absorbing it all around her. Her eating and sleeping at night in Australia were as lovely as ever. She had even settled into sleeping without waking within a day or two of arrival which was astonishing. Her daytime sleeping was erratic, just as in the UK.

"I am not you, and you are not me, and nor should we wish to be. But we can take things from each other." Kevin said to me when we had just a week left of our holiday. We were talking about me finding it hard to leave a place, a holiday, a moment. By this stage we were visiting Kevin's best man Chris, his wife Kaddi and their three children in Perth, where we had flown after Canberra.

Attachment to things and people and places: Kevin can go between things looking forward. I cling on. We stayed at Chris's mother's house in Perth, our final Australian destination. She kindly allowed us to stay there whilst she was away. It was just beautiful, with chairs on its front porch, and a swimming pool out the back, in the suburbs of Australian houses which I could look at all day long. Everything felt beautiful to me because it was different; the flora, fauna and birdsong outside the houses. Chris carried Coraline around in the pool and she did well.

Sitting out in the back garden one night I aired some thoughts I was having to Kevin, about how other babies Coraline's age were walking. This was something we sometimes mentioned in passing, just because it was good to not keep it in inside our heads. "Tortoise and hare," he said, gazing at the dazzling stars above us.

Another thing that I love which Kevin often says, when he's not saying "focus on what you do want, not what you don't want", is "we're a team" and he has shown me that as a team we can each do different things. For instance, out of preference he does most of the cooking, or the shopping, and I do most of the tidying and attend all the talks which might be of interest for parenting Coraline, and as a team we are navigating our journey in life. At different stages we are each taking charge of different things. And each of us in our family of three brings something valuable to the others.

A friend we met up with in Perth told us she was choosing to approach each thing that happened that coming year, whatever it may be, as an adventure. We'd approached every day with wonder in Australia. I decided I would try the "adventure" idea too when we got home.

Sophia said to me in one of my sessions with her years previously, "The magic happens when you're heartfelt living. Be grateful for, and relish, every moment. You create how you feel, and you can create thoughts of wonder at any time you choose. It's all about perception. You can think anything is exciting: a tree, a car journey, country roads. Let go of the thoughts that tell you it's not. Change your focus. Get into the flow of gratitude and creativity, otherwise you're still in the flow, just the wrong kind of flow. You're always going to find what you're looking for. If you look for great stuff, you'll find it."

In early February the sun set on our time in Australia. We had spent the whole of January there. How lucky we were. We flew to Kuala Lumpur for two nights. Coraline did well on the flight. She slept in the bassinet all the way there from Perth and on arrival we roamed the heady streets, with the ambience of Lunar New Year the next day. We had lots of admiring smiles for the backpack carrier in which Kevin carried Coraline. We had got it second-hand in Australia on Chris and Kaddi's recommendation. We took the metro out exploring and got caught in rain downpours and immersed ourselves in the beauty of botanical gardens.

Kevin had booked a hotel with jaw-dropping views and a swimming pool on the roof as he has an uncanny ability to find great places to stay. We brought Coraline into the pool together with us. At breakfast on our first morning, I saw two people stood next to each other for a moment who didn't know each other. One had a T-shirt saying, "Let be", the other a T-shirt saying "Unchanged". How funny the words I had written on my Auntie Verna's balcony on our arrival in Melbourne, "let be", were there on a person's T-shirt on our way home.

When we got on the plane again after our two days in Kuala Lumpur, Coraline slept for the first eight hours of the journey to London. So, we were big fans of the bassinet! And having baby crisps on hand for the flight and milk for take-off and landing. We even had time to watch the film *Bohemian Rhapsody*.

We learned that what we thought was packing lightly could be even lighter! Way, way lighter! OK, so it wasn't packing lightly in any way, shape or form. This is something we have not quite managed, even to this day! Chris suggested travelling without a pram even, as he said you can always borrow or arrange one when you get where you are going. We noticed a lot of the airports we saw in Australia had little prams around that you could use in there. The biggest thing about our trip was that we had gone for it both literally and figuratively speaking. We were thrilled with all it had brought us.

"Welcome Home" balloons bobbed around our front door, carefully put up by Margaret outside our house, on the day we got home. Margaret had been dreading our trip as she was going to miss Coraline so much, and here we were back again on the day Coraline turned 18 months old.

Coraline had done well at adjusting to the time difference after Australia and then Malaysia. She woke up once on her first night at home in the UK, then went back to sleep straight away, and slept through the night from then onwards.

It was funny setting foot outside into the cold each day, enjoying that new atmosphere. How appreciative I was that we had the time and the means to have gone to Australia. How I ached for the other side of the world and our family and friends there, but this was always the case for me and was heightened after a trip there.

But I was back home, and I would get back into our day-to-day gradually. This day-to-day had changed; around us was our new freedom after Coraline's surgery, there were all the classes we could go to, friends we could see and visits we could make. We decided we'd stay in Surrey a while and think about our move to Devon the following year.

Chapter 21:

Perspective

At the beginning of the year, whilst we were away in Australia, we had learned that we would begin receiving the middle rate of Disability Living Allowance (DLA). I had begun applying for it just after Coraline turned a year old which I was advised was the right time to do so by her preschool and the groups we belonged to.

The DLA form was a mighty one consisting of many pages. In total it had over 50 parts to complete. My initial application was rejected, and I submitted a detailed request for a reconsideration with help from local organisations who told me what to highlight the second time around. The help was excellent and meant we were then approved for it in January. It was not enough to simply state that my child had Down's syndrome and an associated global developmental delay, I needed to complete the entire form, and my responses were then assessed to determine whether the living allowance was warranted.

I now informally help other parents with advice on how to complete the form as I learned a lot from everyone who helped us. Receiving the middle rate DLA meant that we got a monthly payment from the government and that Coraline received 15 hours of free education a week from age two. Coraline received this a year earlier than children typically did, but the rules have changed since, I think. From the age of three I believe Coraline got 30 hours of free childcare per week.

Once we began to receive DLA, because I was not in employment, it meant that I was entitled to Carer's Allowance, which did not require much paperwork. I simply filled in a quick online form stating that Coraline received middle rate DLA and I was automatically allocated it. I received this as a weekly payment and still do today.

In terms of Coraline's developments, in March, we saw the cardiology team and they said Coraline was looking great, and we could now come back again in six months' time. We also spotted Coraline's first two teeth when she was 19 months old. She quietly had two top molars in place peeping through. It's so funny that they were there, and had been making their way through, unbeknownst to us.

On one of my daily walks with Coraline in the baby carrier I listened to a podcast which my phone fell upon. It was called *Oprah Winfrey: Your own truth,* an episode from her *Super Soul podcast.* In it she kept repeating, "Just be yourself". Oprah said that this was the best advice she'd ever been given. It reminded me that all Coraline was doing, and the stage she was uniquely at, was to be celebrated.

In April, Coraline gently began multi-room crawling when she was 20 months old. Before this she moved about in the room she was in. One evening, a month after she had begun to do this, I told Kevin a big realisation I had had that day at soft play.

> *There were loads of children Coraline's age shouting out, careering down slides and climbing into the ball pool. We met an 11-month-old baby who was zooming past crawling and pulling himself up on everything.*
>
> *I sat there on the floor silently with Coraline and I allowed myself to sit with where we were and to feel into what I was feeling. I felt the comparison I usually felt. What emotion was behind it? Fear. Fear of being different. What was behind this? Fear of standing out and being seen. What was behind this? Feeling unsafe at standing out. What was behind this? A feeling that life needed to be typical like that for us to be*

> *happy parenting, and that that kind of parenting would be a dreamland. We've never parented a typical child have we, so we can't comment of course.*
>
> *But is it not down to the same thing: being the parent your child needs, and loving your child?*

For many years Coraline did not show love or recognition back to us, but in time to come she began to once she turned five years old and then when she was almost six, her smiles and laughter increased. It was a sensational feeling, because we had waited so long. These were not huge demonstrations, and her eye contact was fleeting, but in the context of what we had known, they were significant. It had never occurred to me that my child might not show me any recognition, like when I came to pick her up from school or when I came into a room, but it was the case. Nowadays Coraline shows full recognition and broad smiles when she sees us. This has come about in the past couple of years.

In these years to come I read a book called *The Journey* by Brandon Bays which a friend recommended. On this occasion at soft play I had, in my own way, been doing a little of the process Brandon Bays describes in the book. Her process is around sitting with the emotion which has come up (which we would normally try to ignore or stuff down), then feeling into that emotion and going down the layers of feeling inside it until you reach a place of ultimate peace.

It is exactly what Sophia had suggested I do after Coraline's heart surgery; to feel into my worry and find a place of safety within it. Until I read Brandon Bays's book, I hadn't understood how feeling into an emotion could bring you into a place of safety as you work right through it. After reading *The Journey* I contacted a lovely practitioner of the methods described in it and actually did this process formally, going down through layers with her.

Still, that small sitting with my feeling of comparison and

identifying some of the layers to it, began to lead to a feeling of acceptance and love for what the children around us were up to that day, and an appreciation of what we were up to. I continued to tell Kevin:

What was remarkable about this was, it was as though we were glowing with who we were ourselves when we sat there at soft play. I had accepted the movement around us, which is unusual as usually I am there but so caught up in thoughts and mind loops of comparison. And I'd realised in a deep way how much I've grown through our experiences. I am slowly beginning to change because of Coraline, and I found I had come close to feeling a surprising inner stillness for a moment, but I think that only came when I really felt into the emotion, instead of getting into a debate around it or telling myself I shouldn't be feeling it.

The weirdest thing is I felt the richness of our life. I thought, wow, look how this past year and a half has formed us. I felt proud of Coraline, and a contentment at everything in her life so far, leading to that moment. Keeping her well for a year before her operation, her operation itself, Coraline's personality, all the people we have met, family, friends, our neighbours, our antenatal group, all Coraline's therapists and the groups we go to.

It has all shaped us to see the depth of life and to notice others and their lives with more of a keenness. I feel like all we have lived along the way has brought us here to this feeling of gratitude for the richness of who we are simply as we are and so, sat there in that soft play, I thought about who Coraline had made me. The children spinning around us, and us sat there, at the core.

I suppose what I am saying is I had a moment where I noticed what we have, and how deep what we have is. It felt to me as though our journey, and our speed, might be a bit different, but I felt a gratitude for it, and a knowing that it had actually allowed me to access this inner stillness.

Kevin listened. Kevin understood.

Now that Coraline is eight years old I inhabit this inner stillness concerning our lives more often than I do not inhabit it. Before this time, I had been more often out of it than in it. But how good it felt to put a foot in that day and begin my own "journey".

We kept up our adventures. We flew to Ireland again to spend time with Kevin's mum and Payne joined us too for a couple of days.

Back home, in May, I went to a day of talks at the Down's Syndrome Association headquarters organised by our local parent-run charity 21&Co. The talks were for parents of children with Down's syndrome and were on dentistry, wills and trusts, and vision. I learned so much, and there was a lot to take in. I learned that children with Down's syndrome have weaker tooth enamel. I learned about the importance of making a trust within a will for a child with additional needs, which was something that hadn't even occurred to me before (nor did Kevin or I even have a will, though we knew the importance of it).

The talk on vision was given by Dr Maggie Woodhouse OBE, Head of the Down's Syndrome Vision Research Unit at Cardiff University at the time, who had studied visual development in children with Down's syndrome since 1992. Her research has changed eye care practice across the UK and abroad. She highlighted how people with Down's syndrome tend to have an auditory processing weakness and a visual processing strength. They are visual learners. Therefore, if they have problems with their vision, it will affect them more.

She told us how the majority of children with Down's syndrome wearing glasses are long-sighted and only a handful are short-sighted. She even gave us some plastic glasses to put on to simulate how a child with Down's syndrome sees the world, which was a revelation. I had no idea that their baseline vision, irrespective of wearing glasses or not, was ever so slightly different to a typical person's. My view felt less defined. I realised when looking through the plastic glasses what a difference a larger font size made in a darker pen or pencil to how clearly I could read it. Through wearing these plastic glasses, Maggie helped us all to realise that children with Down's syndrome require larger print to read comfortably. Otherwise, they are working harder than any other child in school.

Maggie explained that we all need print 3–4 times bigger than our smallest limit of reading. For a typical child the smallest base font possible to read is size 4 so the print size needed to read comfortably is size 10-12 font. For a child with Down's syndrome, size 10–12 font is the tiniest size that they can read. So, if they are always looking at 10–12 font, it would be like a typical child always having to read font size 4 – in short, very tiring. Coraline ideally needs font size 20–25 as a minimum. Dark print is very important so that she can see it clearly.

I came home eagerly spilling all I'd learned to Kevin and delighted with what I now knew which could inform how we did things. I had pages of notes. The day after the talks I met Coraline's speech therapist. We went through a number of exercises that Kevin and I could do with Coraline. These entailed adding extra layers to things we did daily. The idea was to build learning into things like singing nursery rhymes or eating snacks. Coraline's speech therapist also suggested that I take photos of daily activities to have as a set of photos to show Coraline before we did them so she could see what we were about to do (e.g. go in the car) as Coraline did not yet understand language when I verbally said where we were going.

When Kevin came home from his consultancy work that evening, my eagerness had gently tipped into overwhelm at all there was to know, practise, consider and do. Vision is not just vision, dentistry is not just dentistry, speech is not just speech. And what did Kevin say:

It's good to express it. That's important. Let me help you. Let's work out what I can do. You don't have to do it all at once. Let's make a list. She's amazing. You're amazing. I love our life.

Kevin knows I love lists. He personally is not one for lists.

Coraline was wearing a T-shirt which she had received from Adeline and her children that day. On it, it said, "c'est par ici le bonheur". I guess that roughly translates as, "this way to happiness", or "happiness is here", or "this is happiness". Something like that! Coraline's T-shirt was covered with all sorts after the day, not from doing much as we moved around quite slowly but from food getting on it. I looked at how sweet she was in this T-shirt. I was grateful for her and for all we had in our lives, and appreciative of all the help we had too. Calmness lapped at the corners of my sea of overwhelm.

Gratitude and appreciation and being kind to myself and accepting whatever I'm feeling: "c'est par ici le bonheur."

A few months previously, I had heard that I was in the four finalist blogs in the Wellbeing category of the BAPS SEND Blog Awards 2019. I felt honoured, given the impressive line-up of judges who selected the final four from the original 15 nominees in this category (nominated by their readers). May was now upon us; the month that they were going to announce the winner at an Awards Ceremony.

It felt like the highest recognition that the judges listed my blog in the final four in my category, that they saw and appreciated all the values that were underpinning my writing. It boosted my faith in what I was doing. The winner was to be decided by votes from the public.

The BAPS SEND Awards night was in Coventry. Margaret and Dave kindly looked after Coraline overnight at their house which enabled Kevin to attend with me, both of us joined by Payne and Ed. I was so excited at meeting all the other bloggers in attendance.

Seated at our table, we clapped as each of the awards were called out. Before the winner of each category was announced they read a quote from someone who had nominated that person. When they began to read out the quote related to the winner of the Wellbeing category, I thought in slow-motion, "Hang on a minute, that sounds like me..." I could feel disbelief and excitement welling in my body.

> *They have shared their journey with their amazing daughter with us and helped everyone who has read it to understand and appreciate that children with Down's syndrome are first and foremost just children. Each child is special regardless of whether they have Down's syndrome or not. The love generated by the three of them radiates from each post and photograph and brightens up each and every day for me and all their followers.*

To my surprise my name was then called out. I had won the Wellbeing category! I was flabbergasted and delighted. It's funny that a ladybird had alighted on Kevin's hand at lunch that day on the way to the awards.

When I went up on stage to receive the award the host, Carrie Grant, asked me a couple of questions about the category, including: "Whose wellbeing are you writing about?"

I pondered for a moment and then said: "It's about all of our wellbeing. It's about the wellbeing Coraline brings to us. For me, wellbeing comes through being aware of our approach to life each day and realising how it creates our experience of life. It's all about our attitude."

That approach to life is all about perception, too, and knowing we can choose our perception. Or to put it another way, it is all about perspective. And fundamentally it is about self-care and self-love which are the cornerstone and springboard for choosing a different perspective.

For me, it's also about knowing that thoughts are just thoughts; they are not me. If I am in a loop of thoughts, I can just allow them and not enter into a dialogue with them. All these emotions that we try to push down, suppress and quash – why not just allow them out and not enter into a "I shouldn't feel that" dialogue? The thing is, if I am feeling something, I do feel it whether I try to suppress it or not. And if I suppress it, it's going to come out in a different way; my body might express it for me, or I may explode at a later date as I did not express my feelings at the time. So, it's better to let it out than suppress it. I know some days I might feel down but I know to just hang on in there and it will begin to shift the next day, or the day after.

All I ever need is to have my feelings listened to and validated. I began to realise over the years, in my internal dialogue, I was not doing that for myself. I wasn't listening to myself or validating myself; I was telling myself I shouldn't be feeling how I was feeling and berating myself.

It's also about language, and how this shapes your experience. If you listen to what you say, you see how it shapes your experience.

What shapes it all? Gratitude. It's a word I come back to a lot. That sets my mind up at the start and end of the day. And acceptance and allowing (unless it's something I want to get up and change). I once did a meditation where we were asked to focus on parts of the body that were struggling, ask them what they wanted to say, and then flood them with acceptance.

In years to come we had challenging moments every day when Coraline was seven years old; a world of sensory considerations which took a lot of learning about and patience as a parent. She emitted daily, frequent, loud frustrated growls that jolted my nervous system, and were about everyday transitions, or things like each time our car stopped at traffic lights as she did not like the feeling of the car stopping. The noise of her growls shot through my body each time she made them as they were so vehement. One time when she was particularly ill, she growled all day long, about every 30 seconds, as well as during the night whenever she woke up due to her illness. She had been shouting/growling to the point Kevin felt he needed to go next door to the neighbours of our semi-detached house the next morning to explain about all the noise.

When she was this age I had begun to feel tired as the months went on and wondered how I could manage with the constant piercing noise. Then I had a lightbulb moment and reminded myself that she no longer hit the side of her head with her fist when she was frustrated, something she had done repeatedly for the previous two years.

Saying "this is a phase" has become hugely useful to me. Right now, at eight years old, Coraline's loud shout/growl is much less noticeable across the day. She will make it a handful of times.

What if her growl is to be celebrated as it is her stepping into her own form of communication? Kevin and I did learn to allow the noise to wash over us when it came and not to attach any form of jolting or flinching to it. We realised it felt much better when we relaxed our systems around it. Alongside the challenges, is the great joy. These days that is in how she brings my hand to point at an animal in a book, how she bounces to music with such happiness, or her huge smile whenever she comes home from school now. She smiles widely whenever she sees us which we love every time. That smile that was there for a time in her first couple of years too but then disappeared for the next couple of years and has now come back resoundingly. So, who knows what happens with phases, whether they come and go fully, or come back again. Either way it is about being with what is.

At eight years old we can't do the coastal walks we long to do as her pram does not suit these tracks, or the visits to friends or outings in groups of friends as she often gets cross, and so on. And if we do try these things, we are trepidatious, and our nervous systems are steeled for them. Or we find an activity like going to see some sheep and pigs which we think she will like, but when we go she does not register, does not really look, and we feel deflated. But we don't know how that's going to be in the future, and we can focus on what she does like to do.

Back when Coraline was 21 months old, two things were beginning to mount up which did affect the wellbeing I was talking about in the BAPS Awards: To-Do lists and responding to emails! The difference after Coraline was born was that I had not been able to keep on top of them like I once did. The tasks

I had to do for work or administration in my personal life only used to stress me out sporadically before Coraline was born. At particularly busy work times I could usually, by sheer force of will and the hours that I put in, keep on top of them. I could work later, I could even go in on a Sunday to catch up for a few hours in a blissfully quiet office, and I would feel fabulously ordered after that (though on certain occasions I still fell apart over my list at work and how to manage it).

It was not about the To-Do lists themselves, it was about my attitude to them since I was looking at them as though I must do everything immediately, all at once. If I approached them with a state of overwhelm before I'd even begun, then that was what was going to come back at me. The "overloading" was in my mind and not the things on the To-Do list. It was time for a new way of thinking!

What had Sophia told me before around my moments of feeling overwhelmed? She said to pick someone super relaxed who I admired for how they got things done and then to copy them and imagine that I had stepped into their body and that that was now how I did things. She'd said:

> *Life will give you whatever you say. If you tell yourself, "I've loads of time, I can do this," your body has to feel calm. Every time you hit default overload you can say, "I am totally on top of all this, there's loads of time." Laugh at it, don't take it so seriously and look at it with a light heart and watch what changes!*

Chapter 22:

The beauty and the realism

I came across two situations which really symbolised our choice in the perspective we take on a situation. I had gone from being initially worked up about these situations, to suddenly feeling full of love for them. The two situations were:

1. Magpies outside our window, with a nest, chattering all day and waking me at 5am.
2. A little boy at soft play who was a bit boisterous with Coraline.

What changed? I heard more of the story.

Margaret and Dave told us the magpies had been there for decades. They said that they had their young every other year and that they were protective of them (hence noisy) for a short period of time as their young were growing.

That explained why we'd never heard them before, as we had moved there in August three years previously, which would have been after this early summer nesting period.

In my head I'd imagined that the birds were new, had just arrived, and would be noisy ever afterwards. Hearing this made me realise it was their home, and that they had been quiet for the first three years we'd been there, so I knew it was temporary. My whole outlook turned on its head and I felt a rush of appreciation to have them in the garden. It was their home! I began to love hearing them about and saw it as a lovely noise.

At soft play, the little boy's mum came over to me and said,

"I hope he's not too rough, we have recently adopted him, and he is just settling into things." My whole feelings became a rush of love.

I told Kevin about both things and said, "So because I heard more of the story, I feel totally different."

"That's brilliant, Liz. And you know what? You don't even need the story," said Kevin, "you can just choose to feel differently." Kev hadn't been bothered about the magpies, he'd embraced them.

Sophia used to say: "It's your choice if you let something affect your peace of mind. You've always got a choice. You could decide to just let go and you will have a shift in perception. A situation is just a situation, and it's you that makes it enjoyable or not. You tell yourself the story and you can choose to tell yourself a better story at any time. You can tell yourself a less scary story, that it's all going to be alright. The way we feel comes from a change in thinking."

Earlier in May I had documented what Coraline was up to:

6th May 2019: Things Coraline is up to at almost 21 months old

1. Love and fun with our wonderful neighbours Margaret and Dave. We feel lucky every day about this.
2. Going to a playgroup each day or seeing a friend. We go to a mix of typical playgroups, and playgroups for children with special educational needs (with amazing sensory rooms). Ideally, we do something in the morning so she can have a nap in the afternoon after lunch.
3. Sleeping through the night. She can settle wherever we take her. She doesn't generally fall asleep for her afternoon nap but it's good "rest" time we hear, and her paediatrician said it's OK if she doesn't, as she's sleeping 12 hours overnight.
4. Getting excited when Kevin gets home.

5. Loving food. She eats all sorts. She is sad when food ends. She can be quite loud about this. We do the Makaton sign "finished" to show her it's the end.
6. Laughing.
7. We've recently begun using flashcards for ten minutes a day at home through "Down Syndrome Education International". One set to encourage clear speech and one for vocabulary learning. This is because visual memory is stronger than verbal short-term memory for children with Down's syndrome. Coraline doesn't currently say any words.
8. Attempting to pull herself up to look at what's on the sofa.
9. Growing teeth (she has two upper molars, and two lower molars discovered last week). Teeth come later for children with Down's syndrome.
10. Crawling gradually across a room to reach a toy she would like.

I heard a lovely take on wellbeing at the start to a talk on Early Development at the Down's Syndrome Association which I attended in June 2019:

> *Being a member of a loving family beats anything you're going to learn today.*

The talk was all about how children with Down's syndrome learn, and language and communication. It was a real example of how delivery matters – the presenter was upbeat, clear and confident due to her years of experience, at the same time as being realistic. I came away feeling encouraged, informed and supported.

I learned something there which revolutionised how we communicated with Coraline. It was:

Copy Coraline's babbling, and actions, exactly, back to her.

It was as simple, and as profound, as that. If she said "gggggg"; I should reply "gggggg". If she said "babababa"; I should reply "babababa". I think they called this "Child led interaction". The idea was to mimic Coraline's sounds.

Since the talk, I began to copy what Coraline did in terms of her sounds. I had known this on some level before the talk, but previously Coraline might have said, "ggggg" to me and I would have replied, "yes, yes, yes, good chatting" but after the talk I began to reply saying exactly the same sound, "ggggg" back.

Coraline blossomed when I did this, which I do to this day, and her sounds are no longer single letters, more squawks. The lady giving the talk mentioned people who are naturals with children and said basically, the secret is that they copy the child's sounds and actions.

"Early intervention," I hadn't heard this term before we had Coraline. It's such a familiar term now. It was the basis of the developmental play we did with Coraline, and her therapies. Research has been done to show how children with Down's syndrome learn, so early intervention can focus on this way of learning early on. As they tend to have a strength in their visual short-term memory while their verbal short-term memory (i.e. learning from listening) tends to be less strong, the idea is to back things up visually. All Coraline's early intervention has been centred around this. Had we just tried to teach her through listening, the research suggested that her auditory processing loop would not have taken things in and really registered them.

Another factor to consider in terms of auditory learning for children with Down's syndrome is "glue ear". Coraline has had this occasionally during colds due to having smaller ear tubes which can block and take a while to clear. Glue ear is akin to listening as though you are underwater.

Coraline's speech therapist made her a key chain of large, laminated photos with a word written below each one in lower case. We would show her the one pertaining to what we were about to do (e.g. bath, walk, pram, car) so she knew what was coming rather than just telling her what we were going to do. We said the word out loud whilst we showed the card to her. The photos were all of us in our daily lives doing the activities to make them personal to her as opposed to generic images.

Just as Coraline's communication and engagement with what was around her developed gradually, so did her movement. We began to work on Coraline pulling herself up on things. Her physiotherapist suggested we put toys up on the sofa, so Coraline had to pull herself up onto her knees to see them, as it was all about motivation. She also recommended that Kevin or I sit with one leg out on the floor, and progress to two legs out together, with a toy on the other side so Coraline would need to climb over our legs to get to it. This would encourage Coraline to think about what she wanted to do and work out how to do it, building muscle strength and muscle memory for her.

Coraline's physiotherapist said it was important to build things up gradually as Coraline had a lot of flexibility in her joints, so her ankles and knees felt wobbly to her when she tried to pull herself up or stand. We also put cushions all over the floor and Coraline loved to move them about which was excellent since motivating Coraline to do what we wanted usually took a lot of time and encouragement. The pull, push and lifting of her arms worked her muscles too.

We saw great progress through our practice, with Coraline climbing right over our legs and pulling herself up a lot. She even began to crawl up a step on her own. Coraline was a speedy crawler and began kneeling up against things to look at them.

We also began working on how Coraline got down from – or out of – something backwards instead of forwards. We turned her round to show her that was how to do it, and then the plan was that the repetition would mean she would begin to remember that was the way to do it. Three months after we began work on Coraline pulling herself up against furniture kneeling, she started to pull herself up against things on straight legs!

At the end of May Kevin went away to Singapore and Hong Kong for ten days for his consultancy work that he did for a lovely family-run Spanish company.

The summer came and with it Kevin and Coraline's birthdays. The week before their birthdays Kevin had a work trip to Spain to see the Spanish family for whom he did the consultancy work. Coraline and I tagged along and amused ourselves whilst they had meetings during the day. They embraced us all into their lives. Coraline loved sitting at the quiet beach in the town where their business is based. I took her there and we sat on a mat. I couldn't go in the sea as I couldn't leave her for reasons of safety and understanding on her part, but we sat together on the gorgeous beach and absorbed the atmosphere. She would have resisted the sea if I had tried to take her in it.

Back home, a ladybird appeared for a third time on Kevin's birthday, the day before Coraline was two. The ladybird: symbolically a reminder to live your own truth with joy. It sat on the book Coraline was looking at when she and I were out and about with a friend and her son at Greenwich Maritime Museum. Kevin was at work.

On Coraline's second birthday the following day, Kevin said to her: "This time two years ago we didn't know what to expect, just that you'd be a lovely girl. And you are a lovely girl. More lovely than we could ever have imagined."

Kevin and I wrote down five things we wanted for Coraline's future on the occasion of her turning two years old. The top two are mine, and the bottom three are Kevin's:

1. That she loves herself
2. That she believes in herself
3. That she snowboards with Kevin
4. That we all go away for several months of the year snowboarding
5. That we watch loads of animation together.

My top two are the same for me today. The bottom three are the same for Kevin. She certainly embodies 1 and 2. We haven't done 3 and 4 yet but we will. We have done number 5, but it's only just begun to be what Kevin had in mind – Disney films and such. Coraline wasn't interested in them at all until Payne and Ed managed to get her to watch *The Lion King* when she was seven and a half. This then became her favourite film to watch on repeat every day whenever she had TV time. We've not yet watched any other Disney films, as she doesn't like them when we try. She likes short singing cartoons on YouTube. We have spent many years watching, and listening to, *In the Night Garden*.

In terms of Coraline's future, and whether we had any concerns around it when Coraline was two, we simply thought, "We are happy now, and our notion of the future is that it is also happy. And whatever happens along the way that's unexpected, we will handle it as it comes." That is also the same now that she is eight years old.

I took a walk with a friend who has a child with additional needs, and I told her: "I don't worry about Coraline's future. I don't worry about how it will be when she's at school or when she's an adult."

She replied, "Wow, I worry about that all the time. I wish I had that way of looking at it; that's amazing."

"Oh really? I hadn't considered it before. All I ask myself is, 'are we happy now?' then that's what I need to focus on, and be present in. I honestly don't worry about the future, as I cannot predict it. What I can do is trust in myself that whatever comes, I will have love around me, and Coraline will have love around her, from expected and unexpected quarters. For me, that's how I see the future."

I have another friend who has a child with a more serious condition, and for her, her child's condition means she does not think too far into the future, for that reason. She does not plan that year as she does not know what is going to happen for her child. So, her way of living is very much in the moment. It stems from a different reason, but it comes back to the same premise of living where you are at, and doing the best you can in that moment.

I definitely drop into worry around the everyday and I used

to permanently live in a space of worry about everything big or small that's just happened/is happening/is about to happen in the immediate future of the upcoming days and weeks. But these days, I am re-examining what the payoff is from this way of being. It returns as a default mode of being, and then I check myself and allow the thoughts, and remind myself I don't have to engage with them. However, a funny thing to me, given this default, is that I have never worried about the future as a general concept.

I wrote another update on what Coraline was doing:

15th August 2019: Things Coraline is up to aged two years and one week

1. Bashing toys together.
2. Really into her Iggle Piggle toy, pointing at books, crawling through tunnels in the park and at home
3. Crawling speedily and pulling herself up to things.
4. Growing two new bottom teeth which are just peeping through, to join her four molars.
5. About to begin two mornings at preschool up the road in September.
6. Going to Madrid for the wedding of a lovely couple in our amazing antenatal group.
7. Enjoying summer holidays, and little trips. Instilling a love of travel in her!
8. Adoring Mondays and Fridays with our neighbour Margaret! Getting excited as I hold her outside their front door.
9. Babbling – saying "dddd", "bbbb" and "gggg" sounds. She is just beginning to form her very first try at a Makaton sign – the sign for "Dad" (which I do each night when Kevin gets home). She points her two fingers together to have a go at it.

10. Sleeping well, and fine dining.

It was a busy summer. I can't believe all that we did. We took Coraline on the Eurostar to Amsterdam in Holland to stay with some dear Dutch relatives. We went as a group: Kevin, me, Coraline, my dad, Ed and Payne.

Later that August Kevin and I took Coraline to Madrid because she was still pretty content generally, so travel seemed fine. One half of a couple in our antenatal group was from there, and it was the destination for their simply stunning wedding. Together with some other members of our antenatal group, we attended their beautiful outdoor Saturday wedding day and the Sunday lunch paella after-party.

At the beginning of September Coraline, Kevin and I spent a week in Devon walking, swimming and seeing family and friends there. We went on breathtaking coastal walks and ventured into Cornwall. Kevin carried Coraline in the backpack on our walks along clifftops, gazing down at the sea. I cannot believe all we saw that summer.

We met a few people on our week away with whom we had conversations, short or long, which felt special. These people approached us. One evening, standing outdoors at a pub local to our accommodation in Newton Ferrers, gazing over the estuary, an outgoing middle-aged man approached us. He was with a group of jovial friends, and they had been smiling at us as we sat with Coraline. He told us that his son, who was not with him at the time, had additional needs. He talked about the pressure on his marriage due to all that they had to fight for and be vigilant about, the paperwork and the need to be on top of details. He said his marriage fell apart. He told us to keep on top of things and to keep strong. We had not yet entered the world of EHCPs. Nowadays I know how hard this process is and I have friends that are burnt out by challenging their local authority over their child's provision, just as this man described to us in the early evening light over the estuary. In times to come, I myself tipped into years of intensity around it, often angry, often stressed, and I credit Kevin's ability to move on from my moments of getting mad (often taken out on him) within hours, for our solid steadfast happiness together.

Another day we stopped for lunch in a pub next to a sweeping stretch of beach. A man appeared next to us at the table and knelt down to say hello to Coraline who was sat on her mat on the floor. Whilst looking at her, he said, "My brother has Down's syndrome and he's 50, and my son has Down's syndrome too, he's ten. It's an honour." He put his hand on my back and, like that, was gone, back to his table. That felt like a significant interaction, in its shortness and in the words he used. He was gone as quickly as he had come.

It's about all these different conversations, all these different sides to the same story and about balance.

That September we also went with Payne to Jersey for a long weekend to visit friends who lived there. We had fitted in so much that summer. We were assessing Coraline all the while, but she seemed content about where we went as she was with us. I marvelled at the expanses of sky and sea as we swam and stayed with our fun friends there.

A few sensory considerations had been appearing for Coraline. At a playgroup at home during the holidays a boy tapped Coraline just lightly and she burst into tears. At a different group, a baby brushed against Coraline and again she burst into tears. It happened a fair bit that Coraline dissolved around other children at groups.

It sounds like a small thing. It was a big thing.

So, when Kevin, Coraline, Payne and I arrived at our friends' house in Jersey, it was not unexpected that Coraline cried at their dog moving near her. She then cried near their one-year-old, and I began to wonder, "is this about sensory considerations, are we doing this right? Who can I ask about what this is? Coraline is starting preschool next week, how is she going to be with all the children there?"

I was telling myself a story and I was accelerating it in my head. I even felt tears come over me unannounced, which felt very unusual for me. A sadness, and a feeling that I didn't feel equipped to navigate it. I kept thinking, and overthinking, about this sensitivity.

"Is this sensory sensitivity? Will we learn what it is and what to do?"

On the last day of our long weekend in Jersey our friends held a get-together for us and their extended family in their garden. Coraline put her hand out to stroke their dog. She then sat in the ball pit with the two other toddlers at the party and was content. A few days had meant she'd got her sea legs and some familiarity with her surroundings. It just happened like that. We thought, "Wow, she did it!"

It sounds like a small thing. It was a big thing.

Payne had said all along, "It's a phase." It makes me smile recalling Payne saying that. She doesn't have children herself, but she knows many people who do and she always says to me, "It's a phase," when I tell her something Coraline is doing. And, I'd say, she's been right every time. There had been the phase where Coraline couldn't stand Payne laughing as the noise was too much for her system, but she was now OK with it.

There is a pertinent message contained in Deepak Chopra's *21-Day Meditation Challenge*: that it doesn't have to be good; you just have to know it will pass. That life is made up of the good days and the bad days. And that the phrase equally applies to the good times; so remember to cherish them too.

It was lucky we packed in enough travel to last a lifetime that summer as it turned out Jersey would be the last time I would board a plane or go to a different country until almost three years later. Six months after this long weekend in Jersey, in March 2020, COVID-19 arrived in the world.

As Coraline has got older we have travelled less together with her as her sensory aversions have deepened, and we cannot simply carry her about in the sling if we want to do a long walk. She does not do long walks as she does not have the strength and does not readily "walk on demand" (instead she sits down and refuses to move). So, we have a pram supplied by the NHS for children up to 50kg, but it is best on smooth pavements with its small rattling wheels.

In September 2019, aged two years and one month old, Coraline began at a local mainstream preschool which was a 15-minute walk from our house. Coraline went for two half mornings a week until that Christmas and three half mornings from January 2020 onwards, then built up slowly to doing a full week. When she came out after her first day, they said to us, "She has been very vocal, and no tears!" The second half morning went really well, and the next, and the next.

Coraline also began classes with the local charity PSDS, which is dedicated to "providing support for individuals with Down's syndrome and their families", at a group called Digbies (Developing individual growth by imaginative play, education and speech).

Digbies was recommended to me so highly by many parents at Get on Down's. Coraline and I had begun going to the Get on Down's weekly coffee, cake and play sessions that year after we got back from Australia. I even managed to drive the 50 minutes to Digbies because of what everyone was telling me was worth it at the other end.

Our Digbies group was infused with fun and we are friends to this day with our group leaders, other families and their children from our group, as well as many of the volunteers and a trustee.

Long before we began attending groups, I had watched a video of Pablo Piñeda, the Spanish writer and actor with Down's syndrome, that 21&Co put up on their Facebook page. I had always remembered this video and it is the spirit with which we attended the clubs. I noted down the translation under the video, though I may not have got it word-for-word:

> *My message to parents of children with Down's syndrome is at the same time easy and very difficult. Think of them as your child, not as someone with a disability. A child that you have to educate, not as a person with a disability that you have to take care of. It's very different.*

Pablo hails from Malaga in Spain, a fact I learnt from a taxi driver when I went there on a short holiday with Pippa a few years ago. Our taxi driver happened to have a daughter with Down's syndrome a few years older than Coraline.

Whilst I receive Carer's Allowance from the government, I have never described myself as Coraline's carer, just her mum. We do care for her throughout the day, of course, and at age eight Coraline requires our full support with all her personal care needs, like getting dressed (she cannot yet do this herself), lifting her into and out of the bath, changing her nappy and so on. We are also vigilant about Coraline's safety and wellbeing in assessing the environment around her, and being with her continually, as she does not have an awareness of safety, such as around roads or doors, or whether something is too hot to touch.

It was rather a special occasion when Coraline was photographed at the end of September by the fashion and celebrity photographer Nicky Johnston. The photos were going to appear in the Christmas issue of *Prima* magazine in a feature about four different mums and their children and their stories. The press officer at the Down's Syndrome Association recommended us for the piece as she knew me from my blog writing. Nicky and the *Prima* team were great, and the team chose Coraline and me gorgeous outfits to wear. *Prima* magazine is full of real and uplifting personal stories. Now ours was going to be amongst them. I looked at Coraline in her dress sat on the floor for the photos and how adorable she looked, with such pride.

Chapter 23:

Thinking outside the box

I had thought motherhood would be about love, and it was. In another way, however, there was a whole other level to this. I was discovering far more about love than I had expected I might. About unconditional love for myself, our lives and for Coraline.

Day-to-day parenting was different from what I had expected. Well, in fact, it was the same, but with extras: going to talks pertaining to children with Down's syndrome, reading books on learning about development, doing exercises set by Coraline's therapists, using flashcards, being much more aware of health, going to appointments, working developmental play into playtime, learning about language and communication, learning Makaton sign language, joining local groups specific to Down's syndrome, and being exposed to knowledge from local professionals in areas I had not even thought about before.

I appreciate that everyone has their own set of extras in parenting. Today we have extras in addition to this list. Handling sensory behaviours, navigating Coraline's very strong reactions to changes in routine, and so on. Today I feel we can do less on a weekend than we did when she was younger.

I was learning about myself, about attitude, and about love. I was learning what life was about through parenting my child with Down's syndrome. This I didn't expect!

My thoughts left unchecked, the potent world of high-level comparison which was always at the fringes of our days, could creep further in. It nudged me as I looked through the parents' WhatsApp group messages or at the emails that preschool sent out when Coraline was two years old. The emails popped in weekly: "Practise dressing up with your child this weekend", or "Look at the different coloured doors on your walks", or "Talk about the leaves on the trees". Simple, fun, activities and emails to which I would not have given a second thought ordinarily and which I would have done happily with my child.

With each email that came, I thought, "Ah no, Coraline is not at this level yet. We cannot do this. She doesn't have comprehension of this." I remember my niece's sheer joy at wearing princess dresses at around age two or three. Today, at eight years old, Coraline is not aware of what Disney movies are or of princesses or dressing up, though she does watch *The Lion King* on repeat. These concepts do not yet register with her. Nor does an understanding of language around doors on houses or leaves on trees.

But I didn't leave my thoughts unchecked around the emails. Whereas I used to control my world to achieve the peace and stability I was after, I now knew I couldn't control the world around me, only my reaction. I knew I had a choice with those emails. I could either experience them as hammering the feeling of disquiet home every time I read one, as I imagined what it might be like to be able to do this or that with my child instead of our rather repetitive routine-based existence where we went for walks with her in the pram and looked at books at home because she did not engage with anything else, or I could look at what we *were* doing rather than what we were *not* doing. I could choose to see equal value in that. I could choose to think, "OK what does life boil down to? Being in the moment, experiencing the wonder around us in our own way. Are we each doing this? Yes. Well, OK then."

I could see the value in our own existence, and I could do something for myself too. I began my training to become a Home-Start volunteer. That autumn I did eight sessions of training. I met a fantastic group of people on the training which was brilliantly run.

For Down Syndrome Awareness Month in October, I shared on my blog the insights of two teachers I knew from eTwinning who taught in the field of special educational needs and disabilities (SEND). I asked them to write about a topic of their choosing to do with their teaching and I have included excerpts from both their pieces here. Ruth, who taught pupils with a wide range of additional learning needs at a special school in South Wales, wrote me a piece entitled "Thinking outside the box":

> I feel so privileged to have been given the opportunity to work with pupils with additional learning needs.
>
> Individualising and differentiating work became my aim. Why couldn't everybody have a chance at success?
>
> My pupils have taught me to be passionate about what I teach – to teach outside the box. They have taught me that there is no single route to success. They have taught me that just because I plan a lesson doesn't mean it will actually succeed – there is far more to consider. For some of my pupils, the fact that they have got to school at all that day is a miracle and well worth celebrating. Others just need that extra bit of nurturing to have more confidence in their own ability.
>
> Liz – you are such an inspiration to us all. Just as Coraline is lucky to have you, you are so lucky to have her in your life. Things happen for a reason and your little family is proof of that. You are all made for each other like a little jigsaw puzzle. I am proud to know you!

Sharon, a Special Needs teacher with a post graduate degree in Special Needs Teaching with additional pathway of teaching the profoundly and multiply disabled, wrote me a piece on "Seeing the ability":

> Liz and I met while travelling to Sweden as part of a British Council eTwinning professional development workshop in 2015.
>
> The moment I met Liz I just knew we would get on. She is fun, caring, beautiful both inside and out and, from

memory, a little, not shy, but reserved in her ability? I feel I remember a little self-doubt.

I felt a rush of emotion following the news that Coraline had Down's syndrome. I too have a daughter with a disability and remember so well those first overwhelming days in hospital following the birth. The news that hits you in the chest, the confusion, the enormity of it all. Liz's post made my memories come flooding back.

Then I sat and thought about what my aunt had told me when my daughter was born. "It's a gift". I shared this with Liz.

Knowing that she would be receiving lots of messages I wrote just once I think, stating that Coraline was a blessing, she would bring a new way of thinking and a new world would open to all of them.

And mostly not to see the disability but trust in the ability.

I assured her (as no one had assured or reassured me) that Coraline would thrive and grow and be a little girl just like all others, there would be challenges, but most of all, she was exactly what Liz and Kevin were expecting. A baby for now, a child as she grows, and an adult when older.

When I worked at "Action for Children" at a respite centre in the Forest of Dean, Gloucestershire, the young people who came to stay had a variety of diagnoses that made them all unique. I have many cherished memories of this time.

One specific memory was after taking a nonverbal, highly autistic young man to the cinema, an experience he thoroughly enjoyed. We met with his parents and told them about our cinema trip. His mum was shocked. I could have broken down in tears there and then! I spent much time encouraging them to engage with the outside world as a family. To my great pleasure, a year or two later, this family, who had restricted their world, took their son on holiday on

> an aeroplane. I was overjoyed to say the least.
>
> The students taught me so much, mostly that nothing is a barrier. Give them a challenge they accept it and try, mostly achieving. They also taught me to trust in their abilities, let them have a go and do not smother. Patience is something else I learnt, don't rush, just let things flow. There is always a way to find a way.
>
> To Coraline I would just say, enjoy being YOU all through your life.
>
> I could write on and on about taking opportunities, not putting barriers up etc. etc., but actually all I want to say is Coraline enjoy being YOU.

As Sharon says, Coraline did bring me a new way of thinking. A big thing Coraline had taught me was to widen my whole field of vision. See everyone! One thing I began to do, which Coraline changed in me, was to just go up and say "Hi" to anyone! That's what we, as a family, would say too; if you see us at a party, come over and say "Hello". I sometimes notice at gatherings that people won't go up to Coraline as they don't instinctively know what to do, or feel like she's in her own world, but I would say, in the case of us:

> *Just go up to her, interact with her by sitting quietly near her, and that will be amazing for her, you and us as her parents.*

I know for every child that's individual, so I personally ask the parent/carer first if it's OK or if their child does not like unfamiliar people in their space. Another thing I have realised is that I love it when people talk directly to Coraline, even if she doesn't respond. Kevin and I have learned through Coraline to do this with other people's children. To think about whether they need their personal space or, if not, to be present and get down on their level and talk to them.

At Coraline's cardiology check-up that month they said she was doing great, and our next appointment would now be in a year. That was amazing after having monthly appointments, then three monthly, then the last one six months before this one.

I began to see that within all the vigilance we had been living with, self-care was 100% so important for Kevin and me. I think it's the key for us all, whoever we are. Self-care made me feel good and then I brought that energy to whatever I was doing. But knowing it and doing it were two different things. Now that Coraline is eight I am unequivocal about it. It is a fundamental in my days and weeks. When Coraline was two I was more sporadic about it as I had not yet fully realised it was the cornerstone to everything.

There are so many things I love for self-care: laughter, fun, going out with friends and family, travel, nature, walking, wild swimming, tenpin bowling, reading, watching TV series, seeing the beauty in small things, writing letters and cards to people and sticking stickers into them, and going for tiny jogs. My favourite place to be is by the sea, as there's something about its majesty that instantly shifts how I feel.

What stopped me back when Coraline was two years old was feeling like I did not have the time to make these things happen. The tiredness was bubbling but I was ploughing on. Nowadays I know that ten minutes of self-care counts and makes a difference, such as ten minutes meditating or ten minutes spent looking around my garden, which is something my coach Jo pointed out to me when Coraline was seven years old. I did, of course, have time due to Margaret who loved to have Coraline, although I didn't allow myself to use it for self-care which was what Margaret could see was more important than all my admin but I could not. I also spent the time that Coraline was with Margaret feeling guilty that I should have been looking after her, instead of truly appreciating the once-in-a-lifetime relationship that Margaret and Coraline had, and Dave's devotion to them both during Coraline's time at their house. I certainly did, however, appreciate relaxation more now that we had Coraline, as I didn't take having time for myself for granted. In years to come Coraline went on to stay at Margaret and Dave's house for a week at a time, or longer, and Kevin and I still used the time to catch up on work and such. But in recent years we learned to use the time to go on holiday and to know that Coraline was having the time of her life at their house too. We truly could not believe how fortunate we were to live next door to them. They not only offered us the opportunity to go away, but whilst we were away Margaret sent texts at the end of each day full of love and photographs of what Coraline was doing. Dave was just lovely with Coraline, engaging in her activities with her, and so kind.

One thing Kevin and I did do was to go out once a week each with friends. I caught up with different friends each time and planned my nights out in advance. I used to take the train into central London which took about half an hour. I loved going out for dinner and drinks! Kevin and I also factored in going out together, though that was less often, but important. We were lucky too that we also had a lot of time for self-care in the evenings, as Coraline was in bed by 7pm each night and went to sleep quickly. I loved this time for watching TV and then reading before bed. I do not take this for granted, or the fact that we could get up well-rested the next day.

Self-care for me was present in talking to Kev, family and friends if anything was on my mind to do with Coraline, e.g. about medical appointments or about anything else, since as soon as I shared it, it felt like it was that bit better and I could begin to form ways to approach it. There were practical considerations too in terms of self-care. As Coraline was not yet walking, I carried her between rooms if I needed to, or out to the car, so it was a lot of lifting! Self-care in terms of that would have been to make sure I bent my knees when I picked her up. Yet, I didn't really do this, in the flurry of the moment. And I went on lifting her for many years to come. I think that typifies self-care, you can get into or out of the habit. And these days it's factored into my days as the most important element, as everything else revolves around it. As I say, it doesn't need to be hours. A mindful walk along the street observing nature for ten minutes is enough.

Chapter 24:

Presence

25th October 2019: Things Coraline is up to aged two and two months

1. Pulling herself up straight legged against things. In the past couple of days this has changed immensely! She pulls herself up to look in the fridge, on the sofa and so on. It's how quickly she can do it though, in a fluid motion, compared to when she first began tentatively a month ago.

2. When we do flashcards where I say letters to her (we do ten minutes every day) she now attempts to sound some of the letters with me. Just ever so slightly, for a handful of them, but it feels huge! When we began them (gosh maybe a year ago?) she wasn't at all and hasn't until the past couple of months.

3. Coraline goes to Digbies on a Monday which we began in September. I am proud of myself for driving 50 mins to get there (20 mins is my comfort zone!). We are doing numbers 1–6 and colours red, blue, yellow, green with repetition. We practise at home and do the Makaton sign language for the colours. She doesn't say or recognise them yet but repetition is key.

4. 4. On TV she likes *Bing*. And she still likes *In the Night Garden*. She sits and sways up and down to them!

5. We've been resting a spoon on her tray when she eats with her hands. Her paediatrician said to leave it there. She's just beginning to pick it up and bang it. Good progress!

6. Loving preschool on Tuesday and Thursday mornings. Doing painting for the first time.

7. Time with an amazing childminder and other children on Wednesday mornings whilst I am doing eight weeks training to become a Home-Start volunteer.

8. Hanging out with our neighbour Margaret on a Friday (and before and after Digbies on a Monday).

9. Laughing a lot with her dad.

10. In the space of September to November she will have seen her aunt and uncle, Grandpa, her aunt, uncle and cousins, Nana and Grandma. We all live in different places!

Coraline was quite calm generally and we took her on weekends away where she was content. We went to visit good friends in Leeds. We went to the café and shop 21 Co. which is part of Leeds-based parent-led charity Sunshine & Smiles and is run for, and by, people with Down's syndrome. I loved the words on the pictures they had on their walls ("Dream Big", "Stay Curious"), the beautiful ambience and the room to roam amongst books and toys that they had there which were great for Coraline.

That same weekend at a pub in Leeds a large group of us had lunch together. A man walked past our table, gestured to Coraline and smiled: "She's beautiful."

Then a woman came up to our table: "My friend said be discreet and have a look at that girl loving her food and covered in ketchup* as we go past." I love that she told us this. The woman then also said, "She's beautiful." (*It was in fact a purple carrot Coraline was eating of all things. I didn't know purple carrots existed.)

I hadn't even realised they'd noticed us. That weekend I recognised how strongly all these collective incidences of smiles and comments all added together around us.

Across Coraline's life, in a café, in the supermarket or on the bus, people have come up and simply said to us that Coraline is beautiful.

Coraline was very present in the moment wherever we were. She did not know necessarily where we were going next, or what we were going to be doing, though we tried to show her with pictures. At the time Kevin was listening to Eckhart Tolle audiobooks about this.

I had understood being present in the moment when Coraline and I were in a train carriage going to my mum's that November-time. I was not present in the moment in our carriage, and had constant thoughts going round my head:

> *I should have realised there was an earlier connecting train, then I wouldn't have kept Coraline cold on the platform for half an hour. That train had actually pulled in whilst we were stood there. How come I didn't even look or realise that was a train we could have caught? Why didn't I check the screen to see? She could have had lunch in the waiting room at our next stop, instead of me feeding her here on the train due to our tight connection time for our next connection now. It's hard feeding her here as there are so many people around. I wonder if the other train had less people. Can I carry all our stuff, will we make our next connection...*

All going around in my head. My organisational, detailed, overthinking way of being now exacerbated into a realm of hypervigilance parenting Coraline. This had quietly arisen as a tight cocoon around me of considerations about her health and developmental delay, e.g. always watching her as she did not have a concept of safety.

Then I thought, whilst holding her tray of food in front of her, "What if I just accept we are on this train? We caught this train. This one. This is where we are right now in this moment." I looked out the window and around our carriage. I felt an ease and peace from any thoughts. I just felt lightness with where we were as I was present with it not wondering what might have been.

That lightness, to me, showed me why there's so much talk about being present in the moment. I think it's tied to acceptance.

We visited my mother again at Christmas with Kevin's mum, Payne and Ed and we all stayed in a little cottage near her house. I did not know it at the time, but this was going to be our last Christmas with my mother. Coraline had spent Christmas with her grandmother every year since she was born.

Funnily enough, my mum was also a big fan of Eckhart Tolle and used to listen to his CDs on her little CD player; never one to have got a proper mobile phone or a computer. Though she was famed for her fast typing and shorthand, Mum was a great appreciator of the value of just being and not doing. Of stillness. That was how she lived.

Often people ask me how Coraline feels about Christmas. It was Coraline's third Christmas, and she was two years and four months old. Coraline did not have an awareness of what Christmas was, nor does she now that she is eight years old. Or of what presents are. She does not yet open them or recognise that they are there. She, and we, enjoy the fact she is surrounded by family and friends.

We took Coraline to two Christmas parties on the same day one Saturday in mid-December; Portage, followed by PSDS. It reminded us what amazing people we were surrounded by, and the effort they put in to host the parties. I enjoyed being able to go. I had the usual feelings about Coraline not really interacting. But I was grateful for the atmosphere around us, and the fact we could attend compared to Coraline's first Christmas when she could not go to any of the parties because she couldn't get ill before her heart operation. So, when we could just go along with abandon it made us really appreciate it.

Coraline was also in her first Christmas performance at her preschool. It was a ten-minute song; Coraline did not sing. She was in a surprise outfit provided by preschool, with a tinsel halo which she wouldn't wear. She sat and rang a bell with hand over hand assistance to do so from one of the staff and broke into bouts of clapping when the mood took her. We felt proud to be attending her first show, lined up on gym benches with all the other parents, guardians and carers.

We wanted Coraline to have a sibling. I had discovered I was pregnant in the last months of 2019. We were so happy. We had waited to try until after Coraline's heart surgery and our trip to Australia. All the family were so happy for us that Christmas and encouraged me to rest while everyone looked after Coraline.

We had a lovely family Christmas that year and Julian and his family joined us for a visit after Christmas. On New Year's Eve we had a great moment (well Kevin did, as I was in the other room): Coraline climbed onto our sofa unaided for the first time at 28 months old.

As 2020 began, Coraline enjoyed hanging out with family, cousins and friends, and amazing Margaret and Dave next door; all of this connection was so important for her. She liked hitting a little xylophone, crawling through tunnels, listening to Kevin's singing, throwing things around out of boxes and swaying to the radio. We often spent weekends walking in the countryside and, as Coraline was not yet walking, we would pop her in a beautiful turquoise Toddler Tula Carrier or in the fancy Deuter Kid Carrier Backpack (a padded backpack with a seat in it) which Kev was great at carrying her in.

We were met with interest, love and fun when we were out and about. We had to bring lots of toys, books and Coraline's ubiquitous rice cakes to keep her occupied if ever we went out at mealtimes. We developed a taste for going out to breakfast. Coraline was going to preschool three mornings a week and I drove her to her speech and physio groups in addition to this. We had a good routine going on.

At this age Coraline had a centredness and a joy about her which I fully appreciated. The activity she and I did together which I enjoyed the most was bouncing or swaying on the bed to music on the radio. I felt the beauty of her in these moments. She possessed a loveliness and that was her essence.

She developed a love for flicking through photo albums (and

ripping the pages). They also provided great physio when we put them on the sofa as we were working on Coraline standing for longer periods of time against things. She had begun to stand up against me ever so briefly too. Coraline's communication was also a joy. She did not have words, but I loved seeing new developments all the time which felt so interactive. I remarked upon the fact that that February I had seen her wave "bye" when she heard the word and I had also seen her do the Makaton sign for "more" when she heard it spoken. This was totally new in terms of her understanding and responding to a word.

I went in for my 12-week scan in January 2020. Kevin and Coraline were with me. We felt excited in the waiting room. It happened to be Susana who was doing it and we were happy to see her again. She admired Coraline for a while and then began the scan. Then her words came, "I'm not seeing what I am supposed to be seeing." She paused the scan, looked at me and said, "I'm so sorry Liz, I don't have good news".

I learned that I had had a "missed miscarriage" which is not a term I had heard of. I appreciate that Susana told me the news quickly instead of prolonging breaking it to me. I felt my whole being sink. I left that hospital waiting room very differently emotionally to how I had entered it. I always dreamed of having a second child, but it never happened for us.

In due course we tried again but I had another miscarriage the following year at six weeks. I allow this feeling to consume me at times. The wondering over it. We tried, yet I often wonder if I did enough. We tried naturally and I visited one IVF clinic who said they could not help me any more than us trying naturally. Should I have tried another IVF clinic for a second opinion? Was I too hung up about my age (which I certainly was: we began trying for a second child when I was 43, and I had my miscarriages when I was 44 and 45 years old)? But really, do I have control over how things turned out? Or over the fact Kevin and I met later in life? Our hope is to foster or adopt a child in the future. When I learned I had had the missed miscarriage, Coraline was almost two and a half years old. I kept on with my daily life, though I felt sad.

One evening some weeks later, I spoke at a community fundraising event called "Sutton Soup" to a crowd of over 200 people about the volunteering I was now doing for Home-Start after my training the previous autumn. I had done four home visits myself as a volunteer. I told the mum I volunteered with that I used to look forward to my Home-Start volunteer's visits each week and, after a couple of sessions, she said, "You know, I think I am going to be like you were and look forward to your visits."

I was a little nervous but not overly so and I was keen to speak at this event. I really wanted to convey my message about all I had gained from Home-Start and the reason I decided to then become a volunteer myself.

Pam from Playwise who was there, said to me before I went up to speak, "Oh I am sure this is a walk in the park for you." I didn't tell her at the time but wanted to explain just how out of my comfort zone this once would have been for me.

I used to hate reading aloud in class throughout my entire school career and used to "go red" (as they say) whenever I was asked to speak. It was similar when I did my A levels and at university, or really in any group setting or at a dinner party, unless I felt really comfortable. Later on in employment at training days, when each of us had to introduce ourselves, my heart thudded as it came to my turn.

When I began my career at the British Council, I was lucky that my manager Christa on the Language Assistants team cared and believed I could get past this fear. She suggested I go on a public speaking course, which I did, and then ensured I did not one, but multiple talks for the programme.

Oh, the ordeal of the first talk, and the build-up in my mind before and during! I couldn't believe she wanted me to do it again. But I did the next talk too, and the one after that, and I slowly got better and better the more I did it. What I realised in the talks was that, if I was really passionate about the subject, and could tell personal stories related to it, then it brought it alive for me and my audience. I had to believe in what I was presenting, and in myself.

Fast forward to today and I am totally fine getting up in front of people, whatever the group size. I have Christa to thank for getting me to this point.

One of the volunteers I had trained with for Home-Start even said to me, "You were so good, Liz, and your passion really came across. You could be a public speaker." I felt ten feet tall with her compliment.

That night, Get on Down's won the funding available out of four pitches from different organisations. Coraline and I were now regularly attending the Get on Down's weekly coffee, cake and chat catch-ups each Wednesday morning. It is the powerful simplicity of this idea which makes it so amazing: expertise shared between generations of parents, and children and adults with Down's syndrome, important incidental chats, support, guest speakers and laughs. It's still running today! Get on Down's was begun by Lu, one sparkling woman with a vision, and it had been running for six years at the time she received this funding. She has two sons, one with Down's syndrome.

Parents I met at Get on Down's had recommended a charity called Small Steps in Richmond, South West London which was a 30-minute drive away from our house. They ran group sessions for children with disabilities each week, free of charge, using the principles of conductive education to help each child reach their next developmental steps and actual physical steps. Coraline began going that January. There were about six children in Coraline's group, and she changed group a couple of times, so we met lots of different children with a range of conditions and reasons for coming, along with their parents. As Coraline was working that much harder with her mobility (due to lower muscle tone), Small Steps proved to be a game changer with its backdrop of routine, familiarity and repetition. We kept going week after week and, over the year to come, we saw Coraline's resistance to the activities change. In time to come, a year and a half later, she actually took steps across the room using a walking frame that they had there, which they then lent to her pre-school for her to use there.

Chapter 25:

Following our dreams

On 17th February 2020, Kevin launched Coraleen Skincare (as he spelt it at the time to signify the way we pronounce her name – we have now changed the business name to Coraline Skincare to avoid confusion): handmade, natural, organic, vegan soap, made by him in a stable in Berkshire in the UK. He had had a long conversation with our goals coach Declan around it, around fear. Declan had encouraged him to go for his dream and Kevin had been building up to this launch over the past year.

The soaps are calming for people with dry and sensitive skin. Our friend Kaddi created the colourful and beautiful packaging artwork for them. Kevin did his consultancy work at the same time as building the business but knew that one day he would go all-in full-time on the business. Whilst Kevin had launched the business, it soon became clear that it was a partnership as I was involved in each decision we made and a lot of the day-to-day running of it. We had our very own website.

I was proud of him. Kevin was inspired by Coraline to set it up (and hence named it after her), because of how much he cared what ingredients were in the products we used for her. Each bar of soap came with a little picture of Coraline inside. This is still the case for all our soaps today.

Given the rollercoaster ride it is to run your own business, and the fact that Kevin would be taking risks (not something I normally ever did in my life), the goals coaching we were doing was invaluable. Declan had begun working in partnership with another goals coach called Christa who was based in the USA.

I loved the group calls with Christa that I attended. Christa helped me to rewire my approach to keep everything "just so" by having a new phrase: "I am safe, I have safety inside me." The lightbulb moment for me was to see that my wish to control everything was around feeling safe, and to move on from this and discover that safety was a feeling I could bring to myself. Christa told me to visualise that I had a safety backpack on, and I could wear that anywhere.

I also delighted in drawing us up a "team charter" for our business, something I had learned about on a training course at the British Council. It included our goals, mission statement and values.

I found out that for the second year in a row I was a finalist in the Wellbeing category of the BAPS SEND Blogging Awards. I was thrilled to have been shortlisted by the judges along with three other blogs from the original 11 nominees in my category. The winner was to be announced at an awards ceremony in May. What was interesting was that as I had continued to write my blog, mothers of children with sensory processing disorder, undiagnosed chromosomal conditions and mothers of typical children all wrote to me to say the impact my posts had had on them in terms of reframing their experiences.

March 2020 began just as the other months of the year had begun, with our routine of Coraline going into preschool. Her favourite song was *Wind the Bobbin Up* – something that was completely new to me! We heard it at playgroups and Margaret sang it to her a lot with the actions. I loved that Coraline had just started doing the actions to it herself over the previous couple of weeks. It was the first song she was doing all the actions to. She had delighted her Nana with this when she had been over for one of her regular visits the month before.

It felt like a real stage of flashes of communication and actions with Coraline. She adored music, and this was evident throughout our day. At preschool they were doing "Now" and "Next" boards with Coraline to show her what they were currently doing and what was coming next. Though she did not show outward signs of understanding them, she may have deep down, and it was so important to show her visually.

Some March events arrived that we had come to know – World Book Day, Down Syndrome Awareness Week and World Down Syndrome Day.

I asked readers of my blog to complete the sentence, "Reading *Coraline and Us...*" so I could post one or two during Down Syndrome Awareness Week. Doreen, a Scottish eTwinning Ambassador, said:

> *Reading* Coraline and Us *has made me realise joy is found everywhere and that celebrating the positive and our differences brings so much joy to so many diverse people. Your blog has been poignant, heart wrenching but so, so happy and has brought understanding to so many people – many may not have met the amazing wee lass Coraline or her stupendous parents but all three have warmed their hearts through the blog. Thank you for sharing, and continuing to share your journey – I feel honoured to be able to follow it.*

I had asked Coraline's preschool if they could do a day where the children wore odd socks for Down Syndrome Awareness (traditionally done on World Down Syndrome Day which was on a Saturday that year). Her preschool went one step further and asked the children to wear odd socks every day of Down Syndrome Awareness Week and that "show and tell" each day that week was the children's socks. Wow!

And there it was. The moment things changed in 2020. Coraline could not attend preschool that week due to guidelines around children with a fever, which she had had on Sunday 15th March, and which meant we needed to be in self-isolation for the next 14 days. We were going to miss out on what was happening in preschool, with everyone in their odd socks each day. I felt sad about that. Less than one week later, from Friday 20th March, her preschool closed entirely for the national lockdown. Her classes and therapies were cancelled for all who attended them.

On World Down Syndrome Day 2020, we simply wore our

odd socks at home. What kept coming back to me during that very first week of enforced self-isolation was that we had the power to choose our response. That came back to me time and again over the months that were to follow.

Chapter 26:

The world shuts down

By the end of March 2020, the best "stay at home" tips we had received were some texts from Hannah to our group of mums who we usually went to Digbies with each week. Hannah delivered some of the sessions at Digbies and had two children at the time (now three) and one of them has Down's syndrome:

> *Give yourselves time to adjust to all this and suddenly being your child's teacher. Our children learn through play and repetition. You are teaching them all day without realising it. We will all have different ways of teaching our children, as our home lives are all different, as are our children. Over this time never beat yourself up thinking you haven't done enough. You really have. Stay as positive and happy as you can and do something each day for yourself as it's important to have a break too.*

And then a later text:

> *It's just an idea but if you are doing the washing take your little one with you to help. Count as you put it in together. Name the people's clothes going in and sign the names. Also you can say daddy's trousers are big. Coraline's are small etc. You can use colours as well for the clothes and you can do "same" and "different" for the socks. All in all, a lesson done, and washing complete, win win.*

I just loved the washing tip, as after beginning each week with a proper routine of activities we would do with Coraline, we quickly morphed to a relaxed approach of play and fun, with some learning on the side. Coraline loved moving washing about into little piles at the time so I could comment on it as Hannah suggested. As Coraline did not have language, this kind of describing time felt so important. I loved Hannah's whole ethos.

And there were The Body Coach Joe Wicks's early morning *PE with Joe* workouts which he put on for the nation each day as we all locked down. By the end of March, I had done six days in a row of his workout live each morning on YouTube at 9am. I loved it so much. I had never really done workouts but loved this and it became a lockdown habit. It was so fun, and I felt great afterwards. Joe's enthusiasm was a real joy to us first thing in the morning. Kevin and I would both do the workout together.

At first Coraline was a bit disoriented by what was going on and was climbing on us when we were doing the workout. But as the days went on, she knew exactly what was happening and examined the TV, then just went and sat down and looked at her books. For me that was such a lovely show of understanding from her, it really struck me. It was during lockdown that we began TV for Coraline. Until then she had watched no TV at all and when she was about two and a half, she began to watch about an hour a day. That is our loose notion these days too, that she watches an hour or so a day, and she loves to watch musical cartoons.

One of my favourite things I saw on the news was from an astronaut who said his tip for lockdown was to have a hobby, and that that's what he told his whole crew to do as an astronaut. And also, to plan the time for the day with little goals!

In terms of Coraline's response to being at home, she seemed to be herself looking at her books and musical books, with the usual ups and downs. She was enjoying more of Kevin's singing, certainly. It felt odd that we could not explain to her what was happening, or why her days were different, as she didn't have the receptive language for that.

I wondered what she felt about it. But she seemed accepting

and was developing in her interaction – getting us to point to things in her books by taking our hand in hers, showing us she wanted *Wind the Bobbin Up* by doing the first action of it, and bringing us her empty crisp packet as if to say, "fix this being empty." All of these were new things which we loved seeing. We were lucky that she continued to sleep through the night.

What kept me going during that time was *PE with Joe*, lists of what I was grateful for, Kevin and I sharing parenting Coraline across the day, connecting with friends online, kindness and thinking of others, continuing to work towards our goals and taking it easy on ourselves for Coraline's "schedule".

Coraline was making some animal sounds when she saw them in books ("pig" and "cow"). She was really having a go at signing, e.g. she could do "monkey" and "teddy" when she saw them in books. She tried the sign for "kite" when she saw it in a book and "egg".

Every time she did a sign I just thought, "Wow, this is amazing!" as she was reconnecting signs we'd done on other days and remembering them herself when she saw a picture.

Coraline also handed us objects if she wanted help, or a book if she wanted us to read it to her. I would sign "Thank you" when she handed it to me and she would sign "Thank you" back. All new stuff!

She began to match a collection of small farm animal pieces to flashcards with their photo on. She was making some new sounds to flashcards like "p" and "f". And if we were counting, she held up all her fingers as she knew we would hold up fingers when we were counting. And of course there was the word "cat". It was her first and only word to date and she said it when she saw a cat in a book. She now doesn't say any words.

We had been repeating flashcards and signs for months, or rather years, and we had begun to see the first shoots of her using it. For us it felt like communication had taken off. This interaction was a real joy as it was on a completely new level. Over the years to come, she stopped doing many of these things, but it does not mean to say they are not still in her head.

Kevin said at the time, "She's become so much more engaged

and expressive in all ways, including shouting."

As our days were spent at home, we devoted a lot of time to reading her books. We had been lucky that many friends and family had given Coraline books after she was born or for presents. I used to put a little label on the back of each book to say who gave it to Coraline and when (e.g. Christmas), so we thought of the people who had given her the book when we read it. At this age Coraline loved to simply leaf through books. We didn't read all the words. I would often point to what was on each page and say the word for it. She loved to simply turn the pages and look at what was on them. In fact, what we do today is the same.

At 33 months old, Coraline crawled up all our stairs and held a spoon to feed herself. Both firsts, both on the same day. She usually ate with her hands, or we would feed her with a spoon, though there was always a second spoon on the tray there for her to try. What is funny is that since Coraline held the spoon to feed herself that day, she did not do it again until about two years later. We had no idea that would be the case. We thought that was it!

We were fortunate during lockdown because Coraline was quiet and malleable and was content with books, walks and being at home. She did not have the sensory behaviours which developed in later years where she was hitting her head repeatedly or biting hard objects. She had a sense of calm in her body back then. We really did not appreciate what a gift this was at the time of lockdown.

I have kept shoeboxes for each year since August 2017, the summer Coraline was born. I put in little treasured items, postcards from friends, cards we have all received or news clippings from that year. In 2017's box there are all the amazing cards we received when Coraline was born and our engagement cards full of love. In 2018 we have wedding congratulations cards.

To add to 2020's shoebox I handwrote a letter to Coraline to tell her about this time, and how it had all unfolded from the date we began staying at home. It was to tell her what we, as her parents, had learned about ourselves from it, and how she, herself, had delighted us with her engagement and development at this moment in time.

Towards the end of May, after nine and a half weeks in lockdown, I had found that I was noticing things more.

When I took Coraline for a walk I looked out for the flowers, and the blossom, and I stood close and marvelled at their colour and design. They brought me wonder as I looked at them. There was no "elsewhere" to be at that moment, and there had been no "elsewhere" to be in the weeks before that moment, so my attentions had, little by little, come to what was around us, almost to a communion with it. I found a real fulfilment in it.

When I lay under the tree in our garden, I noticed its leaves and I found real joy too there in listening to the leaves in the breeze, in staring at them and in the feel of the sun around. We were so lucky to have had our garden.

By this time, I could now run for a steady beat on my Couch to 5k for 25 minutes. I looked at the people as I ran, at the trees, at the horses and grass in the fields near our house.

For me, this was a time of slowing down. I used to feel that if Coraline had preschool in the morning and we had a free afternoon, that I needed to do something with her – go to soft play, head out somewhere, even though she herself didn't really engage. The biggest gift of this time was to know now that, after a morning of preschool, if she didn't have a physio or speech group we could, quite simply, hang out at home and bring things back to simplicity.

This time had given me permission, and also the insight, to do that. We had done over nine weeks at home, and she was happy. Therefore, in future we could do, and embrace, an afternoon of just being, feeling the rejuvenation of the time and the greater importance of that to her, rather than going anywhere. From then onwards I knew that it would be a choice to do that instead; lockdown time had taught me to notice the beauty of quiet time, the necessity of it, the connectedness of it.

I feel I was looking at our days in an upside down way before, thinking I had to keep her having fun or "doing". But during that period in 2020 I realised she needed that quiet time, we all do.

Yet somehow, as the world opened up in time to come, I let busyness and "doing" return to the fore, until health issues that I experienced myself between 2023 and 2024 brought me back again to the immense importance of slowing down, noticing and appreciating again. I am so pleased I returned to this realisation.

A friend wrote to me about a photo of Coraline, "It's like her gorgeous soul jumps through the image."

Coraline's essence at two years and 10 months old:

Sincere

Developing so well

Endearing

Pure love

Pure contentment (unless not content for concrete reasons, e.g. food ending/in the pram/hair washing/teething)

Sweetness

In the moment

Trusting

Loveliness

Loving

Radiant

Joyful

Beautiful

Adorable

Lockdown had brought us back to the essence of simply "being".

Chapter 27:

Purpose

I lost count of the number of times I would call my mother (who lived two and a half hours away from us by car) whilst taking Coraline for a walk in the pram or the sling during her early years and during lockdown. One June day I went for a walk on my own in my favourite park near our house. It's a park full of American-style weatherboard houses that looks immaculate, and that I adored. I knew the results of some tests my mum had had would be coming through. I was expecting Julian to call as Mum had asked him to call us all whatever the results turned out to be. Julian rang: Mum had been diagnosed with end-stage pancreatic cancer, and she had a few months to live. The park span before me. I sank to my knees and thought, "I can't believe this."

I thought about Mum a lot. She lived alone in Suffolk, and had had back pain for a while, and difficulty walking very far, but we didn't know why. Then all of a sudden, she had this diagnosis and prognosis. Everything in my spirit told me that I wanted her to come and live with us.

My instinct was to be by her side. To stay with her at her house in Suffolk. This is what my two brothers and I did from the moment we heard the news. We took it in turns to go to be with her.

Kevin and I made a plan to move to a larger rental house within Worcester Park so that she could come and live with us. I wouldn't have dared move during COVID times myself, but it was Kevin's firm decision-making and belief that we could which meant that we began looking. Each time I spoke to Mum on the phone she was buoyed up by this idea and I reported back on potential rental houses we were going to view or had viewed. We put our idea of moving to Devon on hold again.

To keep my mind busy, I narrowed down the professional goals I had set with Declan and Chrisa of writing guest blog posts, writing a column, writing a book and hosting a podcast, to my key goal of writing my book, which was what I decided to work on first.

Declan and Christa told me it would happen in "divine timing" as it were. It turned out 2025 was the year for me to publish it. But this timing probably just meant I had more to learn before I put it out into the world.

A big thing Declan and Christa taught me is that the way you feel creates your experience. The order, as they told me, is: "beliefs, thoughts, feelings, actions". Your thoughts arise from your perception of a situation and it's true that a group of people can all experience the same situation yet perceive it differently. And your thoughts create how you feel.

"I don't know why but I'm just not making the time to sit down and write my book, Declan. I am prevaricating and do everything but write it," I told him on a phone call.

"I think your feelings are causing your resistance to taking action. I've seen you doing a lot of overthinking; stuck in thoughts, and not realising you have a choice about them. And also entering into a dialogue with your thoughts. So, you are taking 'actions', i.e. the action of sitting down to write your book, but you have not actually changed your beliefs – and therefore your thoughts and feelings – around this goal. That's why you're procrastinating. Firstly, tell me what your belief is around this goal."

"Well, I think my belief is, 'who would want to read it?' and that people are going to say, 'look at her preaching, what does she know, she's got no idea, she's got it easy'".

"So that's your belief. What thoughts is that leading to?"

"That I can't possibly do this, this feels separate from who I am. I don't actually believe I can do it. And I don't really believe anyone will want to read it, or they will criticise what I've written."

"How do those thoughts make you feel?"

"That it's hard and I don't feel confident doing it."

"And so your action is you don't properly sit down to do it. If you choose a different belief about writing your book, this will lead to better-feeling thoughts and feelings and to you taking action confidently. You can allow all your thoughts and choose which ones to entertain. The real way to have different thoughts though is to change your core belief about what you're doing."

"Yes, I get it. I do get it that basically the start of the whole thoughts, feelings, actions chain is beliefs?"

"Yes!"

One way to shift my belief was some work I did with Christa. We actually approached it from the end result that I wanted. I spent three minutes visualising a scenario where I had written and published my book and it was on my bookshelf. From that space I could believe in the merit of what I was doing and that I absolutely had something to share. I thought of my book as already written and tapped into the emotions I had around that: proud, centred, excited, thrilled, radiant. I realised how happy I felt within myself when I visualised my book as written.

I wrote those emotions on a Post-it note and stuck it on my wall. Christa said I should inhabit those emotions daily. By picturing my book as already written, and a success, I could change my belief.

Christa asked me, "If you knew this was the end result, how would you approach your goal now?"

"I would keep going with persistence with the mindset of believing it's going to happen," I replied.

This exercise helped me to choose a new belief which, for want of a better word, I really did believe:

> Belief (I am worthy of doing this. My book will mean something to people.)
>
> Thoughts (I can't wait to get started on this. I feel confident I have something to say. I can do this, I can picture it.)

Feeling (This is exciting, this feels great, it is fun to do this.)

Actions (Sitting down to write and it flows, feels effortless and is fun.)

As Declan said to me, "Beliefs shape your thoughts, thoughts inform how you feel. Your thoughts make it feel hard when in fact it isn't; it's just whatever your mindset tells you it is. Feeling is the secret and it leads to the actions you take."

I defined my wider purpose during my work with Christa around my book too: to inspire new parents of children with Down's syndrome, and to spread a general message of love. Our lives had angled in a new direction, opened through Coraline. She had given both Kevin and me our purpose. My work at the British Council before Coraline was born was about broadening horizons and shifting perspectives. I felt that what I learned there was all around me when I wrote my blog and began writing this book. I was lucky to have this background to draw on. Nowadays I think, some people will criticise my book, and that is OK. I am writing it for those for whom it will mean something.

The timing of Kevin's launch of Coraline Skincare meant that he learned and grew so much and had no choice but to do so. When he couldn't go to all the farmers' markets he had planned to attend, but which were now cancelled, Kevin, in a mask and gloves, dropped 500 sample packs of his soaps into local letter boxes. We then built up lots of new local customers with whom we loved to have doorstep chats when rules allowed us to deliver their orders at a distance.

Whilst I was away staying with Mum in Suffolk one week, Kevin found a potential house for us that could work. I came home, saw it, and we signed everything so that we would move a few weeks later.

We had been looking whilst Mum was still at her home, with the idea she could just transfer to us, but then she got admitted to hospital in Suffolk and never returned to her own house. My brothers and I stayed at the house in turns and visited her in hospital.

Coraline didn't return to preschool that term. Instead, we decided not to send Coraline back and so she stayed in a bubble seeing our neighbours, which we had begun to do again in late May. Had Coraline gone back, we would not have been able to do that, as it would have exposed our neighbours if Coraline had seen them after going to school. That July, one of Coraline's friends at preschool was telling her mum what she'd done there and then said, "Coraline isn't there now, just her raincoat." Her mum, who we met at the two NHS antenatal sessions we went to, let me know. I thought that was so poignant and sweet.

In mid-July 2020 we moved to the new house, a 25-minute walk away from our old one.

During our time living at our old house we had got engaged, Coraline had been born, and we had got married. Not to mention the serendipity of living next door to Margaret and Dave and Coraline's relationship with them. I really did not want to leave being right next door to them. All these moments and more had happened at our little cottage, like setting off on our big trip to Australia on New Year's Eve 2018. Moments, moments. Sitting in the garden with Coraline by the passion flowers. Listening to Margaret singing to Coraline in the garden next door, saying "Hi" to Margaret and Dave over the fence, a conversation I had with a builder coming to do some work in the bathroom at the house one time. He told me that one of his best friends has Down's syndrome, and I loved that, the simple way he said it. My dad coming and helping us get the garden looking good after we'd moved in. All these moments.

Kevin and I had lived there, in our first house together, for four years, and for three of those years with Coraline too. Every day I said to myself, "Wow, I love this house!" I loved walking up its path. I loved the relationship we had with our landlords, too, who were so lovely and used to live there before renting it to us.

I knew that I found change hard, and Christa and Declan were thoughtful around helping me to step into this house move. I loved what a member of my coaching group said to me: "There will be hidden benefits you haven't even thought about and, yes, it will be different, but look on those differences as positive."

Meanwhile Mum went from the hospital in Suffolk to a hospice near our house in Surrey. This location choice was so that my brothers and I could all drive to visit her each day as it was nearer to us all. Kevin and I felt sad that the idea of her living with us might not happen after all, in the house we had moved to with extra space for that very reason, but at least she was nearby.

One positive was that in the new house Coraline had her own room. When Coraline was almost three years old she began taking a protocol of Targeted Nutritional Intervention (TNI) Nutrivene supplements which we ordered from America. We learned about them from a number of other parents we knew with children with Down's syndrome. They are specifically formulated for the biochemistry of children with Down's syndrome. Some parents have not heard of (or do not believe in) them, but we decided to do this for Coraline after reading all the literature around them.

For Kevin's and Coraline's birthdays in 2020, we had quiet days. We spent time in the garden at our new house and admired Coraline's birthday gifts from friends and family. Margaret and Dave joined us for some of the day on Coraline's birthday as did my two brothers, in between our visits to Mum at the nearby hospice.

Then something happened that we hadn't contemplated as a possibility; Mum rallied a little once at the hospice, and they suggested she could be discharged to come and live with us. There was a special service that was provided during COVID times for us to receive a hospital bed at our house and paid-for carers to come and look after Mum at home instead of her being in the hospice. This service would be provided with the knowledge that she would need to go back into the hospice at some point when we could not provide the care she needed. A week or so later my mother came to live with us.

In the end she was with us for five and a half weeks at our new house, where she had her own room. She arrived by ambulance and I accompanied her in it from the hospice, as she was too ill by then to travel in a car. I had been excited for her arrival, to look out at the little green parakeets flying around which you could see in the garden of our new house. I thought that she would love looking at them from her bed. I didn't realise that she would not really see or register them. She was no longer in a place to be able to do that. The ambulance crew lifted her up the stairs.

This time that she stayed with us makes a huge difference to me in how I look back on things, in terms of surrounding my mum with care and love. Oh, I missed our first house very, very much, but I could see that it was so important that we were able to have Mum live with us.

I asked my mum what the time of being ill had taught her and she said: "Appreciate each day (e.g. when you see people walking down the street), appreciate strength and muscles to do things and appreciate people."

She liked it when I sat with her and read to her. I read from Anita Moorjani's book *Dying to be Me*, as I wanted her to know what Anita Moorjani had seen in her near-death experience. Mum was more interested in me reading the passages to her around how Anita felt having cancer (though a different type to my mum's) and how Anita felt physically from it, which she describes in the book. Mum felt less alone when I read to her about the similar sensations Anita Moorjani had felt. Mum herself was no longer reading.

It is my favourite book of life messages, and I return to it time and again. I took from the book the fact that when you're in resistance with life it's tricky. After her near-death experience, Anita lives life differently. She ends up pleasing far more people when she's simply being herself and not trying to please them, than when she was actually contorting herself and trying to please them in her old way of living. She conveyed that the breakdown in her life before was due to comparisons outwards and you can only focus on yourself and your happiness.

I led my life for years governed by the phrase, "What will people think?" Coupled with this, I always tried to blend in. Kevin starting a business pushed me above the parapet, as it were, and out of my comfort zone, and has continued to do so ever since! But I have my own safety backpack.

Over the years when I have had to be assertive with the local authority on Coraline's behalf, I have morphed from living in anguish at what they think of me to now calmly sending my emails but not spending time wondering about this. Funnily enough, if you asked me what I would say to Coraline about worrying what others think, I would tell her, "What is important is what you think, and the rest will fall into place."

As I moved away from needing the approval of others, and in years to come saying "No" more often to things I didn't want to do, I felt more centred and liberated. I realised the world doesn't fall apart and people even respect me for saying "No". It is simply taking a moment to recognise when I am looking to something outside of me to make me feel a certain way, but the feeling of wholeness comes instead from within.

The other thing is, whenever people ask me for advice, I tell them to trust their own instinct on what to do because what might be right for someone else, might not be right for them. So doing everything to please others actually doesn't work anyway because you can't please all of them all the time, so the belief, "I'll be happy if I make everyone else happy," isn't really achievable.

I often read to Mum, and pairs of carers came three times a day and then one carer would stay overnight at our house. The day carers were part of the NHS package, and the night carers were through MacMillan Cancer Support. One thing my mother said to me during those weeks at our house was, "For a long time I have not felt so at home, such as I do here." I loved the way she shaped this sentence, conveying her literary sensibilities. That sentence meant everything to me. Our conversations did too. I could see how utterly, straightforwardly she loved me during these weeks at our house.

At the time I was a member of a blogging group of parents with children with Down's syndrome and additional needs. Within our group we all volunteered ideas of questions that would serve as writing prompts. Then, each week, we took one question and every one of us in our group answered it on social media and we tagged each other. I loved the questions as they spurred me to write about things I might not have otherwise. I equally loved the sense of community and seeing what everyone else responded.

A Monday blogging question in September 2020 was: "As Coraline's parents, what can you do to help her have the most inclusive social life possible? What would you ask or want to tell other parents?" I wrote:

> I think as her parents we can keep doing what we've always done, and do it with Coraline too! Kevin will answer, "snowboarding" to this. We keep our spirit wide and bright. If our spirit and intention is an inclusive social life, then that's what it will be.
>
> …Difference is to be celebrated, to be welcomed, and enriches us all…
>
> My old life coach Sophia used to say to me, "Know your value". As her parents, the best we can do is know our value and let our light shine, and encourage Coraline to know her value and let her light shine. The rest will follow.

Nowadays I would add to this:

> Thank you to all the parents and carers who have invited Coraline to parties and playdates. Even if we don't come or, if we do, even if we don't stay long, it means a lot.

That's what I'd want to tell other parents; that we have to think about where we go and what we do as Coraline does not like non-routine activities or new places and social occasions can overwhelm her and her sensory reactions can be pronounced. But I think invitations are lovely and I am learning to be honest in my replies about what Coraline will and won't tolerate and to explain why we have loved being invited but may not attend because the experience might simply be too difficult for us at the stage we are at. Or that ten minutes' attendance is a success in our book.

I know for me personally I tend to feel quite hypervigilant when we go to parties or events as Coraline can become quite dysregulated as the setting is not routine for her. I have seen, on occasion, in a playground that for some children with additional needs they might not understand about personal space of other children or about waiting or sharing, and their parent – my friend – will be hot on their tail. Pre-empting, preventing, 24/7. A constant hypervigilance. I know children with additional needs who might be reaching for everything, or eating anything and everything off the floor and their parent is always checking and watching. And I suppose I would say that from my personal experience of parenting a child with additional needs, there are some behaviours that are simply beyond any parent's capabilities – point-blank refusal of certain things, and so on. Before I had Coraline I would have said, "Oh, I could have said 'No' to my child, that wouldn't happen with my child." But I categorically don't think that now. I can tell when it is sensory, as if a child's system is wired differently, and then I just "get it". I really, really get it. And I think that is what I would like to say in this book; that some things are beyond what we can regulate as parents and that we are doing our best. But this is all for another book and comes much later in our story. I do believe there's a fine line between hypervigilance and anxiety, intensity and burnout. I feel they are all interwoven.

Another Monday blogging question in late September 2020: "If you could take Coraline's special educational needs away, would you?" Here's what I wrote:

> Of course as a parent you think about these things. But I've realised there's a different way to look at this, and it's a beautiful understanding to have come to. That understanding is: I actually don't think this is up to me.
>
> I have been reading an amazing book recently by Anita Moorjani called Dying to be Me. She writes about her near-death experience after having cancer where she goes to a place of pure unconditional love beyond anything she's ever known. She says that this is the place we have all come from and are going to. Her message is that we are all created by pure love as beings of unconditional love, and it is our role to love ourselves fully.

> She says the message from this place is that we all have a purpose and to all be who we are and know our greatness. I am paraphrasing, but this is what I have taken from the book.
>
> Here's a quote from the book on the message she received from her near-death experience: "Every aspect of you is perfect. There's nothing to let go, nothing to forgive, nothing to attain. You already are everything you need to be." She later explains that the most important lesson was to love herself unconditionally and live fearlessly as her true self.
>
> So, what is up to me is to know Coraline is an expression of unconditional love, as we all are. What is up to me is to love her unconditionally, and for her to be exactly who she is, as for each of us.

This is what I had wanted to convey to Mum when I read this book to her.

When we reached September 2020, Coraline had been out of school for six months and had not had her therapies for that time, either. When we had the opportunity to send her back, with full precautions from the school, we felt that that was in her best interests. Those weekends with her seeing our neighbours across the summer were idyllic for us all.

Mum loved Coraline very much and Coraline and I used to sit with her in her room at our house. Mum did not move from her hospital bed for the entirety of her stay with us.

I wrote down the top ten things Coraline was up to that September. She was not yet walking or talking (apart from the word "aat" for "cat"):

1. Coraline loves to hand us the TV remote control. She also hands it to us again if what's on isn't to her taste. I love this communication beyond words!
2. Homemade flashcards: photos of everything around our house, with words underneath and laminated.

3. Flashcards of letter sounds and matching flashcard activities.
4. Reading books to her and her pointing at pictures in them.
5. Singing nursery rhymes and doing Makaton signs to them.
6. I've been thinking about potty training and when to start, feeling bad we haven't, and had a fascinating chat with Coraline's new occupational therapist who said that perhaps to think of it around age four when Coraline shows an awareness. She said that Coraline has lax ligaments and muscles, which are lax on the inside too, so it will take longer for her to become aware that she needs to go.
7. Encouraging Coraline to use a spoon for eating which she doesn't (she picked one up a couple of months ago and we thought, "ooh that's it!" and she's not done it since!). I told the occupational therapist that Coraline puts a lot of food in her mouth at once. I found her reply fascinating: the muscles are lax so she puts more food in to feel the sensation that it's in her mouth.
8. Finding motivating scenarios to encourage Coraline to stand up, as shown to us by her physiotherapist. We are practising trunk rotation by putting a toy a bit behind her, as she needs rotation for walking. We have other fascinating exercises to do too. Because her joints are hypermobile, she is not keen to stand and it's a case of building strength and it all happening when she's ready.
9. Return to preschool – stimulation and socialisation.
10. Taking care around sensory factors, e.g. brushing her hair, touching her face, etc.

I said to my mother: "I think Coraline's bored."

"I don't think she's bored; I think you're bored."

"I feel like maybe she needs different books with musical buttons."

"I think she likes the buttons in the books she has. You know the main thing she likes is to be with you."

Mum was bringing life back to *being* not *doing*.

We made the decision for Coraline to return to preschool carefully around Mum too, and making sure that Mum was not exposed to anything. I think maybe we did not bring Coraline into her room so much after that, but I cannot fully remember.

My mum went back into the hospice in mid-September on my brother Ed's birthday as she needed a greater level of care than we could provide at home. Julian, Ed and I visited her in the hospice. Due to COVID rules, only two of us were allowed in each day for a separate visit for an hour at a time, and we had to wear a mask. We each drove from our respective houses. She died at the end of September 2020, four days after my birthday. Right around this time, on one of my visits, I saw a small white feather on the floor in her room. Ever since, whenever I see white feathers on the ground, they make me think of Mum and I tell myself they are a sign from her. I take them to mean a positive reinforcement of whatever way I am taking at the time whenever I see one.

We had a small, socially distanced funeral for her in her town in Suffolk that October. Julian spoke eloquently and authentically about her and who she truly was. We recorded the service for our relatives, especially those in Australia, and her dear sister Verna who was the mainstay of Mum's life.

For me, when my mum passed away, I had reached a place where I understood who she was as a person and what had shaped her mindset in life.

Chapter 28:

Belief

At the end of October, Kevin and I had breakfast out together for the first time in eight months. We spoke of Mum all the time. Our house felt strange without Mum there. It is hard to adapt to life again when a person is no longer there. The world was going on around me. Things were slowly opening up. As things opened up, Coraline got the usual colds and one longer virus – so far all she had had were colds in her life and this one virus.

The BAPS SEND Blog Awards 2020 were delayed and then transferred online and in early November I opened a beautiful box they sent me containing a little champagne flute and other things to have a party with at home when the results were announced.

Watching live on YouTube in our house, I caught my breath as the screen flashed up with *Coraline and Us* – my blog – as the winner of the Wellbeing category. I couldn't believe it!

They read out this quote from one of the people who had nominated me:

> *Liz is the best mum to Coraline and, amongst all that she does to ensure that Coraline thrives and flourishes, Liz makes the time to celebrate, share and enlighten people with all that she's learned in her life and all that she learns from her days with Coraline. I believe that her writing is honest and uplifting to all that read it and it can help others to see the beauty in life.*

This was the second year in a row I had won this category, which felt huge in terms of really cementing my purpose in writing the blog. I also celebrated all the other nominees, finalists and winners too with Kevin at home, and was either already following them all on social media or began doing so.

That same night after winning the award, I received these words from Helen, a mum who began reading my blog shortly after her second daughter was born, who has Down's syndrome. They made my day:

> *Liz, I know I've said it before, but your writing was life-changing for us, and I'm sure many others. Thank you, and this award couldn't have gone to a more fantastic person and family. My memories of holding my little girl in hospital after she was born and reading your blog about Coraline, are ones I'll never forget. I knew then everything would be okay.*

Coraline spent her first year at preschool in Surrey without a 1-1 but the school worked hard to secure funding for her to have one from that Autumn term onwards. Coraline's 1-1, Aruni, was already a member of the preschool staff, so she knew Coraline already. When she began, she said she'd noticed Coraline loved cats in books, then opened her apron pocket to reveal a small plastic cat. She said she was going to keep it in there all day, "just because Coraline loves it."

In December 2020, Coraline liked pressing buttons in books which produce music, and leafing through books. She looked through the books whilst we prepared breakfast each morning.

During these lockdown days I started to think, "Hmm, she just likes pressing buttons in books, she's not interested in the rest of her toys and she definitely doesn't like to sit to do set activities from her therapists."

It made me feel guilty, like I should be doing more, especially if we were not doing the flashcards and activities as it was easier to let them slip.

Then, lo and behold, I was delivering some soaps locally and I had a doorstep conversation with a woman who told me she had taught children with special educational needs for years. It was the first time I had met her, but I thought, why not ask her a question. "Do you mind if I ask your opinion? I don't think Coraline is interested in toys, and I am not really sure why. We have blocks for building, little hoops on a post, a shapes basket, puzzles, rolling a ball back and forth, and so on; she's not interested."

"It sounds like the toys are too advanced for where Coraline is at, especially in terms of dexterity. Also, I tell you what, a parent doing an activity doesn't cut it! If she's around other children, she will be motivated to copy them. What does Coraline like?"

"Well, anything to do with music. She loves nursery rhymes, a little keyboard, a little xylophone, a tambourine, a snail with musical buttons."

"I suggest you go with what she likes. Make fun games with the things she likes and centre play and learning around this."

It's all about how you look at it.

Kevin and I decided that we would spend 15 minutes together daily with Coraline to make it fun doing the activities and flashcards set by her Digbies class and her speech therapist. We would build that habit of sitting for them, which she got out of when we stopped going to the classes during lockdown. We persisted with that, and she responded really well to the routine of it.

For the rest; acceptance, trust, love and joy in play.

We realised she was going to flourish by doing what she loved, as she was motivated by it. Dancing to her own tune.

In mid-December, we were able to go for a haircut and Coraline got her first bob cut by Nadia at her home salon. Also in December, Coraline had her annual cardiology check-up at the Evelina. They said everything looked good, which was fabulous news.

Christmas 2020 approached, the first without Mum which felt sad. We arranged our plans around London's "Tier 4" needs. We decided to have a little Christmas at home with Coraline's Uncle Ed. It was the first time we had been at home for Christmas in years. We decided to savour it and to toast lots of people. But in fact, what happened, was that Ed did indeed come for Christmas as part of our bubble, but we gave him COVID. We had no idea that we had it when he arrived but the moment he arrived to spend Christmas with us, he said astutely, "I don't think you guys can smell anything? Here, smell this orange."

"I can't smell it," I replied.

"Then you need to go to the COVID test centre."

We did, on Christmas Eve. We received our results by text on Christmas Day. We had COVID and sadly, of course, that meant our one Christmas guest got it too. Coraline probably had it as well but was absolutely fine.

Kevin loved to say to Coraline back then, and still does now, "You rule the roost, Mini." And I must say there were lots of presents under the tree from family and friends and they were mainly for one person. That's the same every year.

2020 was a year that led us to appreciate both the big and the small. That's the phrase that kept coming back to me. It was the year my mother died so that led to heartache and some big reflections. 2020 had also been the first year of the pandemic, and the year of shielding. Having worked with Christa and Declan for the vast majority of that year towards achieving my goals, I felt I had learned a lot, and that I had begun to come into myself. That was the secret. That is what I feel parenting Coraline had taught me. I had realised the key to liberty was in loving her for exactly who she is and celebrating her for exactly who she is; and I knew then that that was the key for me too.

I had a remarkable session with Christa at the end of December, where she asked me and another lady on the call to write down what our feelings were as we looked back on our past year. For me, I actually realised the key was the feelings. I wrote mine down in the form of gratitudes:

> I am grateful for connecting essence to essence with my mother from June to September 2020.
>
> I am grateful for coming to sit with, and know, my own essence.

I am grateful to my body and to be really connected to it.

I chose to extrapolate what Christa had told me to do for my goal of writing my book, to my other goals. I wrote down the emotions I had around Coraline continuing to develop at her own pace and me just going with that:

Excited

Proud

Happy

Lighter

Opened up

I realised I could choose to feel those feelings right now. If I ignored the peripheral chat in my head of guilt at not doing enough, I could choose to feel those emotions right then and there. In fact, I did feel them right then.

What I was hopefully encouraging Coraline to do, to be herself, is what I was taught in 2020. My mother told me that year how much she valued me simply for being me, and I had never realised this before. I wrote to myself:

Follow your instincts. Tap into them. Turn the tap on. Believe. Unfurl. Shine.

The thing that keeps coming back to me is that when you are truly yourself, and truly connected to the essence of yourself, you feel purity and joy and you give that out into the world. So, the secret was letting go of all the mind's chatter and coming home to myself.

Then, as Christa said, "If superficial thoughts return, create space for a moment of stillness and let your soul talk to you in that moment. Let it be your guide."

Chapter 29:

Love

2021 began. Coraline started the New Year bouncing up and down and pressing buttons for music in her musical books. She went back to preschool in early January.

We had a blogging question in my group that January: "How do you think that people close to you (family, friends, neighbours, etc.) see Coraline?"

I answered: "They love her. They think she's pretty cool." Here is what they said when I asked them the question:

> Grandpa: I love the way Coraline is just so naturally herself and contented.
>
> Uncle Ed: A source of warm love who echoes back my own cheeky playful side (like how she bounces up and down with joy watching TV, or just dismissively sweeps all her books and toys off the sofa when she's had enough of them).
>
> Nana in Ireland: She brings joy.
>
> Auntie Roxy: I see Coraline as a happy, sweet little girl who is learning every day.
>
> Coraline's Uncle Julian: She's a very sweet presence who you want to cuddle but can't because of COVID restrictions and because of *In the Night Garden* on TV being better.
>
> Coraline's cousins: She is energetic, brave, happy, a really good cousin and really cute.

> Coraline's godmother Payne: She's my best pal and her husband's daughter. My goddaughter. So is everything they are to me.
>
> My mum, Coraline's Grandma, told me last summer that when she thought about Coraline she thought of prettiness and of a real presence. She called her "a little movie star". She was a big fan of Coraline and loved her dearly.
>
> Coraline's family in Australia, Ireland, America and Holland and all our friends are also taken with her and love hearing about her.
>
> We also know what our old neighbour Margaret and her husband Dave think of Coraline: they think she's simply the best.

Margaret has always been 100% focused on Coraline. Whenever Coraline stayed at their house I loved how Margaret said, and still does, "Coraline's bedtime is my worst time of the day," so deeply does she enjoy their time together.

Margaret is a beacon to me of constant love, adoration and positivity about whatever Coraline is doing and who Coraline is. She has all sorts of practical knowledge about babies and children having two sons and two lovely grandchildren of her own, but she only offers it when asked. She celebrates Coraline and then celebrates her some more. Margaret tells us that it's her privilege to have Coraline as she and Coraline feel happy together. She offered to have Coraline round regularly without us asking. During the lockdown times, Margaret texted us old photos of Coraline and said, "remember these ones?" We knew that as soon as lockdown allowed, we would start their visits up again, as at that time in accordance with the current rules they were not seeing each other.

I had been writing a few monthly pieces for the website of the charity Wouldn't Change A Thing, further to my winning the BAPS Awards. I wrote another one as lockdown continued:

4th February 2021: How we have grown this month – A matter of the little things

I was listening to a podcast interview recently with Nims Purja, a Nepalese mountaineer, who set and accomplished amazing goals. He climbed 14 mountains in a significantly quicker time than has ever been done before. I wanted to share with you what he said that struck me.

He said the little things matter. He said that what's really important is to do the basics in life in a great way. He talked about having a razor-sharp focus. He also mentioned that he began climbing at age 29, so it's never too late to start something new; what matters is self-belief.

Earlier this week Kevin realised that Coraline, our three-and-a-half-year-old daughter, was actually matching the animal sound buttons in her musical books (the ones down the side with a small picture of an animal on each one) with the larger pictures of the animals on the pages when she flipped them. She was matching! She was doing this. We hadn't shown her this. She'd worked it out. We were amazed. We were thrilled. I was beaming! It felt monumental. I had never seen her do anything like this before. I felt so proud of her and so excited.

That "wow" feeling is still with me today. Can you believe we hadn't noticed this before? She'd probably been doing this a while. We just thought she was pressing buttons randomly. When he realised, Kevin said, "look this is what you notice when you're present in what you're doing."

My feeling of jubilation brings home the fact that the little things matter. When thinking about this achievement of Coraline's, I realised that I fully notice the little things in life so much more these days, and I rejoice in them. For that presence and awareness, I thank Coraline. I think that is something current times have taught us too. We begin to focus on where we are and as we go on a walk, for example, we notice all the little things around us such as the design and

> beauty of flowers, or seeing shoots grow, and we feel grateful for each small thing, because we are seeing it and appreciating it. This morning, wheeling Coraline to preschool, I marvelled at the frost patterns on the parked cars.
>
> Thinking about this I realised what a gift Coraline has given us. When you notice the little things, you become more present in your experience in life. I realised how much joy I get from the little things now, because I see them. Coraline, and 2020, have taught me to open my eyes.

I came back to the notion "this too shall pass" and I knew that in a wider context someday the lockdown would pass. And on a smaller level, we were experiencing "this too shall pass" moments with Coraline all the time. In February she wore her hat all the way on the walk in the pram to preschool in the morning. A month before she wasn't tolerating it and would pull it off as soon as it was on. Again, a little thing, but a big thing for us!

I remember the day of the hat, and we had put some huge gloves on her. Kevin and I had both gone for the ten-minute walk to preschool with her in the pram. Kevin took a picture of Coraline in her hat and me crouched down next to her and he said, "She looks like you. You just need some over-sized gloves now." I'd had the same thought too when I'd seen her in the hat that morning. It felt like looking at myself. Kevin often says he sees himself in her too. I was very excited that we had some snow falling in the days previously. It was a beautifully bright day.

We approached mid-February, and our small business of handmade organic soap was one year old. I saw each day how Kevin loved running the business, and the love he had for organic and natural ingredients, and for our customers. We felt grateful for all the support we had from family, friends and customers and for their belief in Kevin's vision and dream.

Later that month, when Kevin went to pick up Coraline from preschool one day, her 1-1 told him that Coraline had gone and sat down and picked up a paintbrush herself. This too was huge.

A couple of days later I went to collect Coraline, and her 1-1, Aruni, told me that Coraline had done two paintings herself. We had the conversations outside in the socially distanced queue of parents when they brought the children out.

"Oh, my goodness," I said. "Coraline doesn't draw or paint at home. We try it sat at her little table."

"Oh yes, we have observed that Coraline doesn't paint sat at a table. We put the paper up on the wall and Coraline sits on a chair at the wall and paints that way," Aruni told me. "You have to watch out as the brush goes flying when Coraline is done."

"Oh yes, I can imagine, as with most things!"

It's a funny thing as it seems to be a characteristic of a few of the children with Down's syndrome who we know; simply throwing things when they are finished with them. If Coraline is drinking from her closed cup with a straw in the pram, when she's finished, she just throws it on the floor. She still drinks from the same type of cup today, as she does not yet drink from an open cup, and still throws it to the floor when she's finished. We have tried modelling behaviour where you don't throw things but haven't got there yet.

Kev began developing new products for Coraline Skincare (facial oils, a body oil, balms and a cleanser) to complement the range of soaps. We were also meeting regularly with a marketing firm to draft up our Coraline Skincare Vision, Mission and Purpose. We re-designed our branding, logo and packaging artwork with them, and completed a whole website rebuild and so on. It was intense work but amazing what we came up with and it is what we have today in the business. I was directly involved in this and giving a lot of time to it, as was my brother Ed with his insightful mind. This was the first time I began to feel the pressures of running our own business coinciding with a time of considerable paperwork for Coraline.

At the time, we were applying to request a needs assessment (via her preschool) with a view to Coraline getting an EHCP (Education, Health and Care Plan). We were taking her to appointments to feed into this: an eye test, audiology appointment and a paediatrician appointment. We had just been granted mobility allowance which we applied for as she was not yet walking. She was also fitted by orthotics for some "Piedro" boots to give firm support to her wobbly ankles, and in early 2021 she began wearing these at preschool each day after we dropped her off in the pram. She wears a pair today too. I was loving work with my goals coaches and was writing this book.

Whilst we were waiting for NHS occupational therapy to begin for Coraline, Vaida, a friend of mine who was a mum of one of the children at Coraline's preschool, raved about a private occupational therapist, Shelley, who her son was seeing. Shelley offered a free 20-minute introductory chat on her website.

I booked my introductory chat with Shelley in April and she answered every question that had been puzzling me for ages. I could see how specialised her knowledge was as she had also worked in neurology and neurosurgery. Her specialty was neurodevelopmental and reflex integration. Shelley chatted to me about neurodevelopment which I found eye opening, and how some of the early stages would have remained immature when Coraline was born as a result of her having Down's syndrome. For example, some reflexes develop *in utero* and are practised there so when a child is born these are active, and this may not have happened for Coraline. When she spoke about reflexes, they were not just the ones we are used to talking about; there were reflexes with names I'd never heard of: spinal gallant, tonic labyrinthine reflex (TLR) and asymmetrical tonic neck reflex (ATNR).

I actually had my call to Shelley outdoors in a car sales carpark in central London where we were choosing a new car. We'd long had a little second-hand Yaris which my dad had given to us, but a lady had recently pulled out into me after I had barely left our house and wrote off our car. Coraline was in the back seat, but no one was hurt as we were fortunately going slowly. We were covered by insurance and the lady accepted liability. We had to get a new car, and the one we chose was an automatic which was wonderful. We have it to this day and love it.

Kevin was watching Coraline whilst I took the call. I think I felt I could do it from there as it was just 20 minutes, but I had no idea how much information there would be. I was crouched down outside making notes on a piece of paper on my knee, so invaluable were the insights Shelley was giving me. I had my list with me.

"OK, so can I ask you all my questions? They are things I just haven't understood to date, and we can't really get an answer to them."

"Of course."

"Coraline doesn't like having her face and head touched or her hair brushed, but she likes us stroking her foot or hand, so I don't really understand this."

"Oh, yes, it's a completely different neural system. The body has long nerves from the cortex, down the spine into the body. Whereas for the face and head the cranial nerves go straight to the brain stem, and for Coraline this is too much sensory input. The process to help with this is desensitisation using touch, just a light hold with light pressure. I can give you exercises to do for 5–10 minutes a day to help with this."

"Oh wow, that's fascinating. I see, thank you. Oh my gosh, that explains it! Can I ask you another one?"

"Yes sure."

"So Coraline doesn't like playgrounds or going on swings, or a roundabout, and we don't understand why she doesn't want to go on anything. And we keep trying to introduce her to things and she doesn't want to go on them. She hates swings!"

"This is to do with her vestibular system (balance). Coraline doesn't have a grasp on where her body is in space due to her lower muscle tone as the feedback she receives through her body is less. But we can do exercises to help here too. Counter to the vestibular system is proprioception (awareness of body in space) and so by doing some joint compression and squeezing exercises Coraline will become more aware of her body and will be less frightened of those kinds of movements."

We have been working with Shelley, seeing her every two months and doing the exercises she sets in between, ever since. We say the same thing after every call with her: "Wow!" Kevin and I both attend each appointment with Shelley, as we value her expertise so much.

Coraline went for her first appointment with Shelley in person at her *Hemispheres* clinic in Surrey not too long after our first call. Shelley set us 5–10 minutes of exercises to do each weekday with Coraline before our next appointment in two months' time. We continued the appointments face-to-face and knew that we could switch them online if we did indeed move to Devon which had now come to the fore again to us as a plan to move there later that year. I have lost count of the number of people we have recommended to see Shelley with their child. Shelley's advent in our lives has been life-changing for us and for Coraline's progress.

That February, I answered a Monday blogging question: "What are three truths about living with a person with special educational needs that you wish everyone knew?" Kevin and I both answered this:

Kevin:

It's a journey where you learn to be patient. When milestones come, you celebrate them joyously and purely.

Coraline is a child first and foremost, like every other child. She has likes and dislikes, happiness and sadness (and everything in between) – she knows how to behave to get what she wants. If she doesn't want to do something, she won't do it.

It is up to us, as parents of a child with additional needs, to create an attitude and expectation of things going well (good advice for every single person anywhere). It doesn't mean that it always does go well, nor that you cannot be disappointed or sad when challenges and unexpected setbacks do come your way, it is more the realisation of just accepting and acknowledging that challenges come for everyone, and knowing that dwelling on them doesn't change them, or make you feel better. Then you are able to keep moving forward, even if these setbacks sometimes slow you. You will soon be on the up once again.

Me:

I will answer this giving the example of Coraline's annual optometrist appointment which we had today.

That as her parents, we are just parents like any other.

That we have quite a few appointments; either therapies or medical. You adapt to how it is, as with everything in life. Today it was optometry. We had been to the community paediatrician for our annual check-up last week and she used the terms "sensory defensiveness" and "sensory seeking" which, even with all my considerable reading, are not terms I had heard before. But they made sense to me in relation to how Coraline does not tolerate certain things, most notably medical appointments if professionals come into her space. Today I knew at her eye test at the hospital that I had to try to keep Coraline occupied as we waited and try to keep her settled during the appointment. I knew they might tell me things that I would need to absorb afterwards.

Today's news was that she almost certainly does need glasses. We were not able to get the measurements for the glasses today as it would have meant putting drops into her eyes to paralyse her focusing muscles (three sets of drops, which sting), and I had heard at a talk that there was another way which did not require the use of drops. At the talk by Maggie Woodhouse, a specialist in vision in children with Down's syndrome, she had also let us know these drops were contraindicated for children with Down's syndrome. As her parent, I made this decision. I knew that I could not explain to Coraline what was about to happen as she would not have understood me, and I did not want to distress her with these drops until I had checked whether she absolutely had to have them.

As a parent you are aware (in your research, of giving your consent, of the medical professionals doing their utmost for Coraline, of behaviour management and feeling vigilant, and of your own emotions).

That our child brings us joy, just like any other child.

As it happened, I emailed Maggie's clinic to ask if the hospital could have done it without the drops. I couldn't believe she replied to me personally. She said you have to be trained to do it without and why didn't we come and see her? Wow, just like that we got to go and see this lady whose specialist knowledge had astounded me at the talk. What is more, she said that coming to see her would be on the NHS. We have been to see her ever since. At our appointment which we had a couple of months later, Maggie said that Coraline did not currently need spectacles but, in common with all children with Down's syndrome, her vision was poorer than that of a typical child and she would need modification of her learning materials, such as a larger baseline font, to accommodate that. All in all, this was pretty huge; to have seen such an expert, to have avoided the drops and to have found out Coraline actually did not need glasses after all. This was lucky as it would have been a long road for Coraline to tolerate wearing them with her sensitivity to anything around her face.

As a parent I was beginning to feel confident to make the decision that felt right to me. I know many parents who go to eye appointments where they use the drops for their child with Down's syndrome as there is no other alternative nearby, or they have many other things to think about and this is one thing too many, or they may not have known there is a different way to do the appointment. As for everything, it is all personal choice. And for me, the moral of this story, was that I was beginning to use my voice and stand up for what mattered to me personally as regards my child.

The global theme of World Down Syndrome Day that March was "connect". We had found our way to different professionals who had guided us since Coraline was born: now we had met Maggie and Shelley who also became key figures for us and enhanced our world. We gravitated to where it was comfortable for us to sit in terms of how many face-to-face and online groups we were part of which specifically pertained to Down's syndrome. What resonated for us was that the local groups we had found were just right for us and I did not really join many online groups.

I found it interesting talking to friends who had children with undiagnosed conditions as they said that we were fortunate Coraline had a diagnosis and that we also had a community of other families with children with Down's syndrome to sit amongst. That was not something I had considered properly until they told me.

Coraline's preschool did odd socks again that year, and I felt quite emotional as one of her classmates scooted past us on the walk into school with one long pink sock and one long blue sock on, and then in the queue to go in I spied all the kids' odd socks. Coraline's 1-1, Aruni, also greeted her at the door wearing her odd socks. Every year I have felt this same emotion when I see people sporting their odd socks. The mother of one of Coraline's classmates explained to me that her son would not be wearing odd socks as it would have been far too stressful for him to do so. We too were always learning. We simply hadn't thought about that, and we do now.

As World Down Syndrome Day approached in March 2021, I reflected on what it meant to me to parent Coraline. A line from *Hamlet*, which I studied at A level, came to mind:

> *There are more things in heaven and earth, Horatio, than are dreamt of in your philosophy (Hamlet, Act 1, Scene 5)*

I was aware that my life parenting Coraline was making me aware of many things which I had never even contemplated before.

Since Coraline was born, my ship had changed course. The wind in its sails was a bit different. The horizons I was seeing had expanded. What I had begun to be was "open to possibility". I didn't know what was ahead over the coming years, but I knew this.

I suppose this whole book is my answer to the blogging question asking what truths I wish everyone knew about what living with Coraline has brought to us. Deep love has come to the fore for my child and for myself.

I received a message from my friend Jacqui two years after we first spoke following the birth of her son. He has an, as yet, undiagnosed condition. He does not have Down's syndrome, though the emotions she was feeling when we first spoke were akin to those I felt after Coraline was born. She wrote this to me after he was two years old:

> *Just wanting to say what a full circle I've been on. I remember contacting you in my early days and you were simply amazing. You changed my life and I'll be forever grateful. Quite honestly your patience and resilience is beyond words. If only I can pay that forward one day.*

Her words spurred me on to keep writing this book. They reminded me that all of us, even as one person, can make a difference. It is the ripple effect. Coraline, as one person, has made a difference in my life.

Chapter 30:

Congratulations!

Whenever new parents contact me, either a bit before, or just after, their baby is born who has Down's syndrome, I feel like it is my deepest purpose to have the privilege of talking with them.

So I consider it a privilege to make this final chapter about the top ten things I wish to impart.

I am going to write this chapter directly to you, the prospective, or new, parent of a child with Down's syndrome.

1. Congratulations!
2. Feel exactly what you are feeling. Whatever you are feeling; love, not love, happiness, confusion, overwhelm, numbness, shock, comparison or resistance to the new reality is OK. Feel it and keep feeling it. Let it come. It is natural to feel that way. This, quite simply, is the biggest thing I can say. It's OK to feel however you feel. If you do feel overwhelmed, it's a case of one foot in front of the other and go through the motions. You can be aware of whether or not you feel love for your child. If you are not there yet, that's fine too, just put one foot in front of the other. That point will come. Just know that your child, by simply being your child, is going to show you all that.

   I wouldn't change how I felt after Coraline was born, and I had many, many tears. I had to feel that way because my whole understanding of life up until the point of Coraline's birth meant that it was only natural that I felt that way. In my case, I had a default setting of trying to control situations and would often manage to do so, though it was exhausting. I was not fond of change and, again, could often engineer situations so I didn't have to face that. I had a notion of how things should be, and my world was rocked when we heard that Coraline had Down's syndrome as it triggered every vulnerability I had in terms of control and the fact I liked to blend in and be the same as everyone else. I loved planning and hated spontaneity or the unexpected. Note this was all about me! I really was only thinking about myself and what it meant for me and my experience in life – but that's OK too. I have realised that the answer I was looking for was not to be found on a head level; it was to be found through the act of living life and what began to happen to me on a heart level. And that you can't put a timeframe on this. You just keep living your life, keep living from the heart, and all of a sudden one day, you will realise that you are grounded in your own experience of life, and comparison will have subsided like the tide pulling away.

Of course, at the beginning you have to adjust because you had one expectation, but your reality is another, and you have not yet let go of the expectation that you had. And the unknown always takes time to become the known. I felt I had so much to find out and understand so I could then gain my footing. Of course reframing comes, all in its own time. The big thing is to be kind to yourself. Kind, kind, kind. You could try a little shift in expectation and say to yourself, "my expectation is to put one foot in front of the other and to feel whatever I feel too," and to try that as a simple shift in your expectation of yourself.

3. You just need to know your baby. Fear for the future may come up, in all sorts of imagined scenarios. Just feel

it as it too is a natural response as, after all, you had a whole other future mapped out. But how can we know what the future holds for any of us? For me I go back to the midwife who told us that in our first days, all we had to do was to know our baby.

Life does not always follow our carefully laid plans. We can't possibly know what the future is going to be, but we can know ourselves and we can trust ourselves. Though you may not know what the future brings, you know yourself and the approach you can bring to anything. So, in addition to all the other thoughts, just allowing that notion in. I don't think about the future myself with any fear. Now, I say to myself, let me just be in a moment, or a situation, without judging it. Who am I to know the bigger picture of it?

I'd say to you, of course there are unknowns and challenges, and that's OK. And my even saying that goes to show how changed as a person I am thanks to Coraline!

4. Your experience is unique to you and your child.

5. Follow your instincts. If you want to talk to people, talk. If you want to read, read. If you want to shut down for a while, shut down. For me, talking and others listening to me was huge. I believe the act of retelling what has happened is powerful in itself, simply describing from start to finish what has happened, and how it happened. I found that through the retelling, and being heard, I began to find small insights which occurred to me as I was speaking, and the act of telling the whole story has quite a powerful effect in your mind processing it.

6. Coraline has taught me to be myself. If you are focusing on everything that your child isn't doing, or won't be doing in a typical timeframe, then you have hit upon a huge one: comparison. If your child does something they enjoy, or you do something you enjoy, focus on

that too, as well as what you feel isn't happening. Notice the feelings each thought pattern produces. We get what we focus on. The beauty is in being with your child, just as they are.

7. You will be surrounded by support and connections will go deep. A prospective parent who knew her baby was going to have Down's syndrome told me when we spoke that she did not show vulnerability in her life. I said that her baby soon to be arriving was the very definition of vulnerability and that she would be connected to the world and to everyone around her, in a deep way. I feel a connectedness every day. So many friends have shared deep life experiences with me, and people in the street have done the same.

8. You don't need to know the how. The people will appear that you need and you can trust your child and trust yourself.

9. If you are looking for a phrase to help you trust in life, one will come, and it will be individual to you. For me, when I was comparing, Kevin often used to say, "but that's not our journey". Somehow that never worked for me and never quelled that voice in my head. Then a phrase came to me. "This path has chosen me." In fact, it's a phrase pertaining to my dad's life that he told me came to him in a dream when Coraline was four years old. That's when I found my phrase. The phrase that brings me trust in life. It's pretty miraculous that Coraline made it here. She beat all the odds and got here. I do feel personally that there is something beyond us which has designed life for us as a family as it has and you will have your own beliefs in this respect. And I am pretty sure that the reason is to lead Kevin and me to come to know unconditional love for both Coraline and ourselves, to know ourselves better, to feel more connected to others, and to discover our purpose in life.

Without this experience, I would not have come close to knowing unconditional love. Nor would I have met all the people who have come into my life whose profound knowledge and life experience has shaped my thinking. And, boy, am I lucky to know and love Coraline.

Kevin and I have reached our true potential through Coraline; me in starting my blog and writing my book, and Kevin in beginning our organic skincare business named after her. I know that the eyes with which I see the world too have changed for the better and, again, this is through Coraline. I don't judge so much, I don't leap to conclusions, and I have come to know compassion and pure love.

10. Lastly, put yourself in the picture. Keep a piece of "you". If you lose confidence, if you become exhausted, if you feel challenged, it's all OK. Look for the support around you, find it, let it in. And let this push you towards self-care and self-love. If I could say one thing, it is to care for yourself. I honestly believe having Coraline has led me to love myself, care for myself and value myself as I realised that I had nothing to give if I did not come from this standpoint. It is the key. It is allowed!

    People love to help, so ask them. I say it like it's easy. In more recent years with all the challenging of the authorities I began to do, I was too tired to ask for help or to get more support in place. I didn't know where to begin. It was easier just to carry on as we were. So I understand that. But then I reached a place where I needed to. Open up. Know you can go out, you can do things, you can still be you! And if you feel you can't, that's OK too. You are doing brilliantly. We are all doing our best.

So, if you and I were to meet, what would I say to you?

I would say, "Congratulations, your baby is beautiful."

I would listen.

I would adapt to you.

I would smile.

I would say, "Read my book, I wrote it for you."

And all of what I say to you, you can sift through it, see how it sits with you, and find a place for it. Hopefully in your heart.

Afterword:

Self-publishing my book

I decided not to do an "Acknowledgements" page most notably because I do not know where to begin or end with them.

"Knowing you Arriens, you're so lovely you'd want to thank the people who made the ink that goes on the page," said Payne when I presented her with my dilemma. Payne and I always call each other by our surnames.

"That's exactly it," I let out a loud laugh, "So, what do you think about a page about how I came to self-publishing it instead?'"

"Yes, you know at the end of a David Attenborough documentary when they have the bit at the end about how they made it, I love that bit!" Payne replied enthusiastically.

That settled it.

How did my book come about? Well, it's been eight years in the making as I always knew I'd write one, as far back as the week after Coraline was born! I've drawn on the blog I began writing a few days after her birth in 2017.

I set writing my book as a clear goal with my goals coaches Christa and Declan in 2020; they lit the flame of belief in me and held me accountable at the start of sitting down to my book writing in earnest that year.

In 2021, my book was well on the way, and I approached a dozen agents who I had researched. I chose those who specialised in the following types of books: memoirs, books around wellbeing, female voices, inspiring stories and books that make a difference, first-time authors or books around special educational needs. I carefully put my letter and book proposal together using the framework suggested by the Hay House Writer's Community which I had joined. I commissioned a book editor and former literary agent on Reedsy to read over my cover letter and proposal, and she gave me tips to enhance them, which I implemented.

Many of the agents did not reply, which I know is the norm, and I also know that it is customary to approach far more agents than I did, and to keep going. Of those who did reply the message was that it was not appropriate for their current list or that they did not see the market for it.

I went on a six-week Curtis Brown Creative "Writing a Memoir" course in 2021 which Ed recommended, just one of his many highly helpful suggestions to me along the way. I am grateful for what I learned from my tutor, the editors who gave feedback on my and the other participants' work as part of the course, and to my fellow course participants for encouraging me.

In the back of my mind, I knew that self-publishing was the way I was going to go, but for years my book took a backseat as we built our business and I navigated Coraline's paperwork and our challenges to the authorities over the provision of her therapies. All that time I missed my book writing. It was what truly spoke to my soul.

My coach Jo, who I began to see in 2024, carried me on at the end of my journey writing this book across that year and 2025. She helped me to put my book first and to value it highly as it was what I truly loved to do. Through my work with her I prioritised my book writing and began each day with it before moving on to anything else I had to do, instead of leaving it to the end of the day and never getting to it. She helped me to see the importance of my book, to truly believe in myself and to keep writing daily.

In 2025 I approached two local contacts in the town where I live, Marcus and Ned, about helping me to self-publish my book. I told them I had about 300,000 words of material and they said that was rather a lot for one book! For a while I looked at that as a problem and wondered what on earth was I going to do. Then, with a remark from Kevin, I began to see it as a good thing; I simply had enough content for three books. This, in itself, is a brilliant example of choosing your perspective.

Thank you:

To Coraline, for being yourself.

To Kevin and all our family and friends, for continually encouraging me in my writing and celebrating what I've been doing every step of the way.

To Kevin's mum, for first telling me my writing was good and that I should share it as a book which sparked the idea, for telling everyone you meet about Coraline and for being my unofficial book promoter in Ireland.

To my goals coaches, Christa, Declan and Jo, for holding me accountable during the process of writing this book.

To my proofreader, Marcus. I felt like we were on the same page from day one.

To my editors, Dad and Ed, what a privilege it has been. I cannot thank you both enough for your loving and insightful suggested cuts.

To Louise, for your beautiful back cover watercolour illustration.

To Ned, for bringing my book cover and layout to life, and for your expertise and experience in the world of publishing.

To Sarah, for your indexing work.

To our Coraline Skincare team past and present, our customers, and the community of Topsham, for your interest and enthusiasm around my book.

Some of the beautiful comments I received from friends encouraging me to write more widely in Coraline's first two months.

> *"I have so loved reading your posts and have been so moved by them all. You should make them public to inspire others in your situation. Please keep writing – it's inspirational."* Sarah

> *"I've always thought you'd make a terrific writer. Ever since I met you I thought you had a way with words. Maybe there'll be a book one day."* Stephen

> *"Liz. You must consider writing this as a book."* Drew

Author's Note

My aim is for this book to be the first of a trilogy:

> Book 1: *Everybody Wants a Dance with Coraline*: Stepping into love with my daughter with Down's syndrome
>
> Book 2: (Title to be confirmed). Stepping out of intensity and into balance with my daughter with Down's syndrome
>
> Book 3: (Title to be confirmed). Practical tips for SEND paperwork, appointments and therapies with my daughter with Down's syndrome

To receive updates on when Books 2 and 3 will be published, please check www.dancewithcoraline.com.

Book 2

I cover our move from Surrey to Devon and how Coraline's sensory considerations intensified as she grew older from age four to eight. I convey the slow, relentless increase in paperwork and challenging of the authorities to get provision for her that took over my life. I saw similar feelings of stress from challenging the local authority, over provision which legally should have been in place, echoed around me in friends with children with additional needs. I recount how I learned and grew when faced with my own unexpected heart condition and my associated hospital visits and stays.

I share how I was not aware of the state of intensity that I had slipped into, and how I began to realise this and the steps I took to change. At the core of this shift was prioritising my own self-care.

Book 3

A practical book which might be of interest if you have a child with Down's syndrome. I address the problems I encountered in completing paperwork and securing provision for Coraline. I present my solutions, from my perspective as a parent of a child with additional needs. The areas I cover are not exhaustive but are a stepping stone. These include what I have learned about:

Physiotherapy, speech and occupational therapy, optometry and dentistry (insights from experts)

Expressing breastmilk when Coraline could not latch on

Coraline's rights in the EHCP process, who to ask for help, writing a strong EHCP and ensuring the local authority honours it

Filling in the Disability Living Allowance form

Managing my emotions

My mindset around paperwork

Challenging the local authority calmly and sleeping soundly at night

I want to share what I have learned, as it is only because others shared what they knew with me, that I managed to both get support in place and to become calm and balanced whilst doing so.

Bibliography

Angelou, Maya, *Wouldn't Take Nothing for My Journey Now.* Virago.

Barks, Coleman with Moyne, John (translations by), *"The Guest House". The Essential Rumi.* HarperOne.

Bays, Brandon, *The Journey.* HarperElement.

Beck, Martha, *Expecting Adam: A True Story of Birth, Transformation and Unconditional Love.* Piatkus.

Byrne, Rhonda, *The Magic.* Simon & Schuster UK.

Celebrate T21 (produced by), *Wouldn't Change A Thing.* Wouldn't Change A Thing.

Dispenza, Joe, *Becoming Supernatural: How Common People Are Doing the Uncommon.* Hay House UK.

Enoch, Nicola (compiled and created by) PADS, *#NobodyToldMe: The truth about Down syndrome.* Positive about Down syndrome.

Gibran, Khalil, *The Prophet.* Macmillan Collector's Library.

Isaacson, Rupert, *The Horse Boy.* Penguin.

Jeffers, Susan, *Feel the Fear and Do It Anyway.* Vermilion.

Katie, Byron, *Loving What Is: Four Questions That Can Change Your Life.* Rider.

Moorjani, Anita, *Dying to be Me: My Journey from Cancer, to Near Death, to True Healing.* Hay House UK.

Pritchett, Price, *You²*. Pritchett & Associates.

Seuss, Dr., *Oh, The Places You'll Go!* HarperCollins Children's Books.

Shakespeare, William, *Hamlet*. Penguin Classics.

Siegel, Daniel J. and Bryson, Tina Payne, *The Whole-Brain Child*. Robinson.

Singer, Michael A., *The Surrender Experiment: My Journey into Life's Perfection*. Yellow Kite.

Skallerup, Susan J. (ed.), *Babies with Down Syndrome: A New Parents' Guide*. Woodbine House.

Snoijink, Eva, *Down's Upside: A Positive View of Down's Syndrome*. Lannoo.

Spock, Benjamin, *Baby and Childcare,* Simon & Schuster UK.

White, Caroline, *The Label: A story for families*. Ivy Press.

Williamson, Marianne, "*Our Deepest Fear*". *A Return to Love: Reflections on the Principles of A Course in Miracles,* Harper Thorsons.

Wordsworth, William, "*Surprised by Joy - impatient as the Wind*". *William Wordsworth: Selected Poems*. Penguin Classics.

Audio/Films/Podcasts/Quotes/Song/Video

Chopra, Deepak, *21-Day Meditation Challenge* (guided meditation programme). Chopra Center.

David Holmes: The Boy Who Lived. HBO Documentary Films.

Dispenza, Joe, *Widely attributed quote.*

Hicks, Esther/ Hicks, Abraham, *General idea from an audio clip or podcast.*

Howes, Lewis, *General idea from an audio or video clip.*

Karate Kid, *Mr Miyagi reference.* Columbia Pictures.

King Jr., Martin Luther, *Widely attributed quote.*

Kings of Leon, *Comeback Story, Mechanical Bull.* RCA Records.

Mathews, Mark, *Lewis Howes School of Greatness podcast, Episode 515: "Face Your Biggest Fears and Bounce Back with Pro Surfer Mark Mathews".*

Piñeda, Pablo, *Public video interview.*

Purja, Nims, *Jake Humphrey and Damian Hughes High Performance Podcast, Episode 32: "Nims Purja: Make Your Dreams a Reality".*

Robbins, Tony, *Public Video.*

Roosevelt, Theodore, *Widely attributed quote.*

Winfrey, Oprah, "*Oprah Winfrey: Your Own Truth,*" *Oprah's Super Soul podcast,* recorded live at UCLA's Royce Hall.

My coaches

Davis, Sophia, *www.sophiadavis.co.uk*
Molter, Christa, Coaching services not available at this time.
O'Donoghue, Declan, *www.declanodonoghue.com*
Sims, Jo, *www.joannesimswellbeing.com*

Permissions have been sought for all quoted sources wherever required. Every effort has been made to ensure the accuracy of these credits, and any errors will be corrected in future editions.

Thanks to Coleman Barks and HarperCollins for the use of *The Guest House* by Jalaluddin Rumi © Barks, Coleman with Moyne, John (translations by), *The Essential Rumi.* HarperOne, 1995. Non-exclusive in the English language throughout the world.

Index

About the Author:

Liz lives in the estuary town of Topsham, Devon, in the UK with her husband Kevin and daughter Coraline. They run their multi-award-winning business, Coraline Skincare, from their shop on the town's high street – a business inspired by Coraline.

At the time of publication, Coraline was eight years old.

Liz's blog, *Coraline and Us*, won the Wellbeing category in the BAPS SEND Blogging Awards in both 2019 and 2020, and was a finalist in the Fresh Voice category of the Brilliance in Blogging (BiB) Awards in 2018. Her writing has been featured by *the Down's Syndrome Association,* the charity *Wouldn't Change a Thing* and *Sutton & Epsom NCT magazine* amongst others.

www.dancewithcoraline.com

Instagram: @coraline_and_us

Facebook: Coraline and Us